The Measurement
of Economic Growth

DAN USHER

The Measurement
of Economic Growth

New York · Columbia University Press · 1980

Library of Congress Cataloging in Publication Data

Usher, Dan, 1934–
  The measurement of economic growth.

  1. Economic development. 2. Canada—Economic
conditions—1918–   I. Title.
HD82.U84   330′.01′8   79–14908
ISBN 0–231–04904–8

PRINTED IN GREAT BRITAIN

To my parents

Abe Usher
Rose Leventhal Usher

Contents

Acknowledgements

This book could not have been written without the assistance over the years of students in the Economics Department of Queen's University. I gratefully acknowledge the painstaking work of data collection and computer programming of David Anderson, Claude Baillergeon, Torben Drews, Paul Hobson, Victoria Kierzkowski, Robert Lippens, Anahit Mamourian, Philip Near, Alastair Robertson, Philip Smith, Arthur Stewart, Joanne Stewart, and of Ruth Simonton of Statistics Canada and John Weymark at the University of British Columbia.

This work was financed by grants of the Canada Council, including a Killam Award which freed me from teaching duties for a year and a half. I spent two summers at Statistics Canada studying the national accounts and working on the estimates of real consumption for quantity data and on the imputation for life expectancy. At Statistics Canada, Hans Adler, Joel Diena, and Dev Khosla were particularly helpful in supplying me with data and in teaching me about some of the intricacies of national accounting. A first draft of the book was written while I was a visitor at the Economics Department of the University of British Columbia. Thanks are due to Milton Moore, Head of the Economics Department and to the Faculty of the Economics Department for making my visit a pleasant one. This revised version has had the benefit of comments by my colleagues, Rolf Dumke, Steve Kaliski, Neil Swan, and Malcolm Urquhart. The final version of this book was completed while I was a Visiting Fellow in the Domestic Studies Program at the Hoover Institution on War, Revolution, and Peace. I am grateful to the Hoover Institution for the opportunity it provided and the financial assistance in preparing the manuscript.

Parts of the book, slightly modified, have appeared as articles: 'An Imputation to the Measure of Economic Growth for Changes in Life Expectancy' and 'Is Growth Obsolete?: Comment' in M. Moss (ed.), *The Measurement of Economic and Social Performance*, Studies in Income and Wealth, No. 38, National Bureau of Economic Research, 1973; 'The Suitability of the Divisia Index for the Measurement of Economic Aggregates', *The Review of Income and Wealth*, 1974, pp. 273–88; 'The Measurement of Real Income', *The Review of Income and*

Wealth, 1976, pp. 305–29; 'Measuring Real Consumption from Quantity Data, Canada, 1935–1968', in N. Terleckyj (ed.), *Household Production and Consumption*, Studies in Income and Wealth, No. 40, National Bureau of Economic Research, 1976. An early draft of the book appeared as Queen's Discussion Paper No. 131.

1

Introduction

What is economic growth? As a statistic, it is the rate of growth of real income per head where real income is a number compiled from a great mass of primary data in accordance with more or less well-specified rules. But the rate of economic growth is not just a statistic. It is a statistic interpreted in a certain way. To economists, journalists, historians, politicians and the general public, the rate of economic growth is a summary measure of all favourable developments in the economy. We are pleased when economic growth occurs and displeased when it does not. The presence or absence of growth is looked upon as an indicator of the success or failure of economic policy. Periods in history with high rates of economic growth are in some sense 'good' periods, and periods with low rates of growth are 'bad' ones.

This book is a comprehensive study of the concept and measurement of economic growth with emphasis on the problem of how to design a statistic to conform as closely as the data allow to the usage of the term in economic history and economic policy. It is an attempt to specify which aspects of life are accounted for in measures of real income and economic growth, to identify the 'ideal' measure of economic growth in terms of which we assess the presence of growth as good and its absence unfortunate, and to design alternative statistics conforming more closely than the usual statistics to usage of the term in formal economic analysis or in common speech. The book is primarily theoretical and as such applicable to any time or place, but the theory is illustrated with Canadian data for the years 1926–74.

The major premise of the book is that statistics of economic growth may be interpreted and proposals for improvement may be judged appropriate or otherwise by means of an analogy between a country and a person: economic growth to a country is like a raise in salary to an individual. Consider, for instance, the rate of economic growth in Canada from 1926 to 1974. The usual measure of economic growth is the rate of appreciation of gross national expenditure per head; the rate turned out to be 2.45% per annum over the whole period, and the average family income in 1974 was $14,800. A number growing at 2.45% for 48 years is at the end of the period about $3\frac{1}{4}$ times what it was at the beginning. So if income had been growing at 2.45% since 1926, and if we can translate statistics of national income into statistics of family income, we can say the improvement is comparable to what I would experience if my family income in 1974 increased from $4566 to $14,800.

The detail of the translation from national to family income is always open to question. Gross national expenditure may not be the right income concept. Perhaps a net figure would be better. Perhaps some imputations are warranted. Perhaps we know that our income concept is less than ideal but use it anyway because we do not have the means to improve it or because the corrections require so much statistical guesswork that the resulting numbers would lose all claim to accuracy. But we take it as a premise that the identification of average income in 1926 with a family income of $4566 in 1974 is right or can be made approximately right by appropriate changes in our measures.

For without such a translation, measures of real income and economic growth are mere numbers with no apparent effect upon our lives and no status as indicators of progress toward goals that people might want the economy to achieve. Without the possibility of such a translation, the measurement of economic growth is nonsense. Why, after all, would we want to measure economic growth, why is public policy directed to the promotion of economic growth, why do economic historians and specialists in economic development search for the explanation of economic growth, if we are not better off after economic growth than we were before? Furthermore, economic growth is not exclusively qualitative. It is not like a chess game that you win or lose, or like a tennis game where the values of the points are entirely conventional. The number 2.45% is expected to tell us something about the circumstances of people in 1926. The figure of $4566 as the income of a family in 1974 as well off as the average family in 1926 may not be quite right, but it has got to be close to the true figure unless the growth rate of 2.45% is itself in error. If we are told for instance that: (a) the average family in 1926 was as well off as a family with $13,320 in 1974 ($\frac{9}{10}$ of average income); and (b) the rate of economic growth is still 2.45%, our reaction would be that these facts cannot both be true. Economic growth and growth of family income may not be identical, but they are similar and connected. Whatever it is we mean by income is inconsistent with an average growth rate of 2.45% over 48 years having so little impact on our daily lives. The fuss over growth would not be worth it. A measure of economic growth that registered 2.45% per year in these circumstances could only be conveying misinformation for it would fail to signify what economic growth is commonly understood to mean.

But as soon as we accept the principle that economic growth of a country can be translated into comparisons among people or families at different periods of time, and as soon as we accept this translation as a criterion for the design or interpretation of statistics of real income and economic growth, we are at once confronted with a wide range of problems of application of the criterion to the detail of the economy. We have to take account of the *difference in relative prices* between 1926 and 1974. Rail transport was comparatively cheap in 1926, road transport was comparatively dear, and the uses of these modes of transport varied accordingly. Any attempt at connecting average income in 1926 to income in 1974 must make allowance for the substitutions among goods that this and other differences in relative prices would entail. We have to take account of *changes in the nature of goods and services*. Food, clothing, housing, medicine, education—all commodities have changed over the years and some attempt has to be made, explicitly or implicitly, to link up new and old varieties of goods if expenditure patterns in 1926 and 1974 are to be compared at all. We must decide what to do about the switch from fresh to frozen food, the change in styles of clothing, differences in the construction and heating of houses, differences in medical practice, and so on. We have to take account of the *introduction of totally new products*. The television set, the hi-fi set, the mini-computer, and, for all practical purposes, the telephone and air travel made their appearance in consumption between 1926 and 1974. If average income in 1926 is to be identified with a particular income in 1974, the cost to a man in 1926 of not being able to purchase these items has somehow to be measured. The problem is particularly acute in the comparison of investment because the capital goods in many industries have changed beyond recognition. We have to take account of *changes in the environment*. The average family in 1974 is better off if the air is cleaner, the water purer, the hours of work shorter, the length of life longer, and if there is greater access to nature than was the case in 1926; and vice versa, if the balance of advantages goes the other way. This too needs to be thrown into the balance as average income in 1926 is translated into an income in 1974, or income needs to be carefully defined so we know what it contains and what it does not. We have to take account of the *peculiar character of investment*. A family saves, but does not normally identify its saving with the acquisition of particular capital goods. Real gross national expenditure includes a measure of gross capital formation in real terms. The translation of economic growth into a statement about family income must include a translation of real gross capital formation into some equivalent of personal saving. The issue becomes very complex when we allow for the enormous changes over time in the nature of capital goods, for changes in the relative price of capital goods and consumption goods, and for the impact of differences in productivity change among capital goods on the structure of relative prices of final goods and services. We have to allow for *changes in the size of the public sector*. Tax rates are higher in 1974 than in 1926 but public services are greater too. The measure of economic growth should include all final goods and services, as would people or families comparing incomes between two periods of time. And we should at least recognize that economic growth is a comparison of *circumstances of groups of people* whose welfare may only be measured on a common scale by some prior assumption of comparability among them. This is not just a matter of averaging incomes. We must average tastes as well if we are to account for changes over time in relative prices, types of goods consumed or other factors considered in this paragraph. Some of the problems on this list are dealt with automatically in the procedures by which real income is measured in the official national accounts, others can be dealt with by changes in statistical procedures, and still others are for all practical purposes beyond our control so all we can do is to recognize the limitations of the statistics we compile. Each of these problems has been discussed extensively in the literature of national accounting and index numbers. Alternative rules of measurement have been proposed and their numerical implications investigated, as we shall see when we come to study these problems in detail.

Within the general theme of measuring real income and economic growth, the book has a threefold purpose: to bring together a number of studies I have undertaken over the years on various aspects of the subject; to develop a connected and unified account of how to measure economic growth starting from first principles and extending to detailed problems in organizing data to measure what we understand economic growth to be; and to put forward a particular point of view as to what economic growth is and how it comes about. I hope these purposes are complementary. The special studies should illustrate the general principles, the general principles should justify the procedures adopted in the special studies, and the book as a whole should entice the reader to see the process of economic growth as I do.

The design of the book is that the first half is a systematic account of the theory of the measurement of economic growth and the second half is a series of special studies on particular aspects of the problem based, with one or two exceptions, on Canadian data for the years 1926 to 1974. However, some empirical work is included as illustrative material in the first part, and the emphasis in the second is on methods of revising measures of real income and economic growth rather than on the Canadian economy *per se*. The book should be within the grasp of someone who has completed a good undergraduate course on microeconomics and who understands the rudiments of the differential calculus, or who can read the easier half of the articles in journals like the *Economic Journal* and the *American Economic Review*. I use no linear algebra or formal statistical inference.

Part I is a study of how to measure real income to record the progress of an economy over a long period of time. We begin in Chapter 2 with an examination of the concept of real consumption, building on the analogy between the economic growth of a country and a raise in salary to a person. The definition of real consumption is in accordance with what is known in the literature as the economic theory of index numbers. This is fundamental, and everything else in the book depends upon it. In the next two chapters, we try to extend the concept of real consumption from a model with a representative consumer to a model in which the existence of many consumers is taken into account, and we consider the alternative, which we reject as unsuitable for our purposes, of defining real consumption to reflect the productivity of the economy as distinct from the welfare of consumers. There is then a long and somewhat difficult chapter on the concept of real investment, followed by shorter chapters on depreciation, imputations, the specification of commodities, and index numbers.

The emphasis throughout is on how to construct the best statistics for the purpose at hand, even if that means departing from established conventions in the official national accounts. Take as given our general conception of economic growth, but suppose we had no statistics at all and that virtually any primary data we might imagine are collectable as long as they represent the answers to unambiguous questions we might pose. Our problem is to decide what questions to pose, to whom, and how to process the data we acquire to reflect economic growth as we understand the term. This exercise can be valuable in two respects: It identifies ideal statistics that may serve as a standard for evaluating proposed reforms to statistical conventions and as a framework for understanding the strengths, weaknesses and implications of the statistics we have when, for want of data or because the available data are unreliable, we must make do with statistics that differ in some respects from the ideal. It also enables us to design new time series based on statistical conventions different from those now in force. There is room in a study such as this to experiment with alternative statistical conventions in ways that would be inappropriate for a government agency responsible to the legislature for the accuracy and reliability of its numbers. Our purpose in measuring real income differs to some extent from that in the official national accounts where conventions are often a compromise among several objectives – short and medium term forecasting of the economy, and budgeting for the public sector, in addition to recording the progress of the economy over a long period of time. Since our concern is with the last of these objectives exclusively, it sometimes happens that the best statistics from our point of view are quite unsuitable for the other purposes of the national accounts. Conflict among objectives arises particularly over imputations; we shall have occasion to extend the scope of real income to incorporate additional information about the welfare of the average person, though the resulting statistics are probably less useful for forecasting or budgeting. And it is arguable that our preferred interpretations of investment and depreciation, to be discussed in Chapter 5, make more sense for measuring growth than for other purposes of the national accounts.

Part II consists of four separate applications of the theory. These are studies of how to measure real consumption from quantity data rather than by deflating values by price indexes, of the imputation to the measure of economic growth for changes in life expectancy, of the role of technical change as a prerequisite to economic growth, and of alternative measures of economic growth in Canada. The special studies in Part II are brought together here, not just to have them in one place but to show how they relate to one another and where they fit in the general scheme of the measurement of economic growth. For instance, the procedure for imputing for changes in life expectancy only makes sense if the reader accepts the distinction, set out in an early chapter, between imputation for goods and services and imputation for changes in the environment, and if the reader is prepared to define investment in a certain way. And these interpretations of imputation and investment in real terms both depend in turn on the definition of real consumption set out in Chapter 2. It is because the special studies draw heavily on the first principles of growth measurement that it is useful to embed the studies in a more general and systematic treatise as is contained in the first half of the book.

The subject matter of this book is distinct from standard textbooks on the national accounting, from descriptions of sources and methods in the national accounts and from studies of index numbers, though it is related in a general way to all three. It is distinct from texts on national accounting in what it includes and in what it omits. There is more theorizing and more formal economic analysis than one would expect to find in a textbook on national accounting because our purpose is to specify what we mean by economic growth and to design statistics accordingly. On the other hand, we shall have nothing to say about input–output tables, flow of funds data, wealth estimates or even the income and product accounts, for we are concerned exclusively with the expenditure side of the national accounts. We shall, of course, have something to say about the primary data, especially in Chapter 8 where we deal with the discrepancy between the concept of commodities in economic theory and the time series data at our disposal, but we do not discuss the sources of data—tax statistics, consumer expenditure surveys, surveys of manufacturers, and so on—from which the national accounts are compiled. The division of labour between this book and studies of sources and methods in the national accounts is that we are not so much concerned to describe in detail how the accounts are compiled as to explain why they are what they are and to consider how they might be altered to make the numbers correspond more closely to the outcome of the conceptual experiment, alluded to at the beginning of this chapter and discussed in detail in Chapter 2, where average incomes at different times are connected to incomes of different people in a given base year. The book is closer to index number theory. In particular, we accept and develop the basic insight of the theory of index numbers, that the object in processing time series of quantities and prices into a measure of real income is to reflect the value of a utility function presumed to be generating the observed data. The book differs from standard treatments of index number theory in that the emphasis is entirely on quantity indexes (real income is quantity index) rather than on price indexes, and in extending the basic ideas to topics that studies of index number theory tend to ignore such as the concept of investment, the theory of imputations, and the choice between deflation and revaluation in converting values to real terms.

The subject of the book is in one respect rather unusual. We are accustomed to drawing a firm line between theory and data. In the standard description of scientific method (in economics texts at least), we invent theories out of our heads and test them with data, where the data are thought of as entirely external to the theory—as facts beyond the range of our influence. In this book, on the other hand, we theorize about the data. No question here of testing theory with facts, but rather of using theory as a guide to constructing the facts. The measure of economic growth—the 2.45% mentioned at the beginning of this chapter—is based on facts in the sense that it is constructed out of large amounts of primary data, but it is also based on theory, for we would have no inkling of what data to collect or of what to do with the data if economic theory did not serve as a guide at each stage of the construction of the statistics.

One special feature of what might be called 'the theory of measurement' is worth emphasizing here. A statistic is at once a word with a meaning in common speech and a number constructed in accordance with a given set of rules. The rules are, of course, designed to capture the meaning of the word as closely as possible, but the correspondence between meaning and numbers is always less than perfect, though the discrepancy may be small. The discrepancy is at a minimum for a simple statistic like the price of a can of peas where the correct number is the amount of money that changes hands when the can of peas is bought. The discrepancy may be considerable in the measurement of real income because there is, as it were, a wide gap between the primary data and the final number—a gap that can only be crossed by the extensive use of economic and statistical theory and by the cooperative effort of literally thousands of people—and because the meaning of real income in common speech is not precise enough to serve as a guide to the statistician in all of the decisions that have to be made in choosing and manipulating the data. It is for this reason that the terms real consumption and real income are best defined within the context of a complete model of the economy, where the relations among price, quantity, and income in real terms are well specified.

Two models have a central and indispensable role to play in designing measures of economic growth. For defining real consumption, we draw upon the standard model of the utility-maximizing consumer. Real consumption itself is treated as an indicator of utility expressed in dollars worth in some chosen base year, as we have already done implicitly when we postulated an average family in 1926 to be as well off as a family with $4566 in 1974. The numerical measure of utility—for that is what we are claiming real consumption to be—is sometimes said to be an illegitimate construct because of the ordinal character of utility. We claim that there is no conflict when the concept of ordinality is properly understood. For defining real income inclusive of consumption and investment, we appeal to a simple one-sector growth model such as might be found in the first chapter of any book on growth theory or intertemporal economics. The model consists mainly of a production function in which a supposedly homogeneous stuff called income is produced with labour and capital, and an accounting identity expressing income as the sum of consumption and the increase in capital over the year. We claim that there is an intimate connection between the model and the concept of real income, so much so that statements about real income will typically involve the application of the model to the problem at hand. The model becomes central to the analysis of the concept of investment in Chapter 5 where the essence of the problem is how best to impose the model on a world that is very much more complex than the model allows.

The study of how to measure economic growth cannot but influence one's views of what economic growth is and how it comes about. I would be inclined to place considerably more emphasis on the role of technical change in economic growth than is customary among national accountants and economists. I argue in the course of the book that: (a) technical change is a substantial component of economic growth as we would like to measure it; a major part of the improvement in welfare over time originates, not in the mere replication of goods and services, but in the improvement of goods and in the appearance of entirely new types of goods unavailable in the initial year of the time series; and (b) technical change in the means of production is a prerequisite to the enjoyment of ány economic growth at all.

The share of quality change in the growth of real consumption in Canada is estimated in Chapter 10 by comparing the rate of change of consumption per head as measured in the Canadian national accounts with that in a comparable series from which quality change is systematically excluded. This latter series is an estimate of real consumption from 1935 to 1974 (data for the years 1926 to 1935 were insufficient) in which quantities are weighted by prices in a chosen base year. The result, subject to many qualifications to be discussed when the time comes, is that of the 3% increase in real consumption per head per year recorded in the national accounts from 1935 to 1974, about 2% can be accounted for as changes in quantities of goods consumed—greater use of automobiles, consumption of meat, fruit and vegetables rather than cereals, much larger consumption of alcohol and tobacco, and so on—leaving a residual of 1% to be attributed to unidentifiable quality change, part of which may represent improvement in goods that could have been effected in 1935 if people had wanted to buy the higher quality goods, but part of which (for instance, improved safety of automobiles) must be due to technical change that took place after 1935.

The benefit from the introduction of wholly new products is more difficult to assess and there is reason to believe that it is less than adequately accounted for in the measures of real income and economic growth in the official national accounts. Though the increase in quantities of the kinds of goods already available in 1926 has been substantial, I cannot help feeling that the greater part of the improvement in standards of living—if we could only measure it—from 1926 to 1974 is attributable to the introduction since that time of television, hi-fi sets, convenient travel by air, electrification, and provision of telephone services in areas of the country not covered in 1926, and above all to improvements in medical care that have lengthened our lives and added immeasurably to our comfort. The attempt in Chapter 11 to impute for changes in life expectancy adds about half of 1% to the rate of economic growth from 1926 to 1974. That is not a small imputation, but I suspect that the true figure is larger still, for I believe that the average person would sacrifice an amount of income considerably in excess of what can be accounted for by a growth rate of half of 1% since 1926 to avoid returning to mortality rates and standards of medical care of that time. The source of the difficulty in accounting for new products is that the greater part of their benefits accrue as economic surplus which tends, as will be explained in Chapter 8, to escape measurement altogether. One of the principal advantages of defining real income in the first instance as an indicator of the welfare of the average person rather than as the outcome of a particular computational procedure is that we have a criterion for assessing bias in the computational procedure we ultimately adopt, even if we can only estimate the direction and not the magnitude of the bias.

The other facet of technical change is as a prerequisite to economic growth. Many studies have attempted to apportion observed economic growth between what can be explained by augmentation of factors of production and a residual that has to be explained by technical change. I take an extreme position on this issue. I argue in Chapter 12 that if income is defined as it should be for the measurement of economic growth, there can be no sustained economic growth at all without technical change—that, with some minor exceptions and subject to certain qualifications, the rate of economic growth and the rate of technical change must be one and the same. This is not as bold an assertion as it may seem at first, for technical change is being defined comprehensively to include the invention of new processes, adoption of technology from abroad, improvements in economic organization, or anything whatsoever that may be interpreted as shifting the production function. To say that technical change is the source of economic growth is really to rule out an explanation rather than to provide one, for technical change is a cover phrase for all alternatives to capital formation within a fixed technology. What determines technical change is another question altogether. We are not ruling out the possibility that high investment is a requirement for growth because it is the channel through which technical change is transmitted. We are only asserting that investment alone cannot sustain economic growth unless it is the source of improvement of the technology of the economy.

The downgrading of investment as a source of economic growth suggests in its turn that economic growth may best be looked upon as the outcome of a war between technical change and population growth, with saving and investment having a very small role to play, except possibly as a purveyor of technical change. Without technical change, population growth would rapidly impoverish a country; without population growth and with a modest rate of net saving, normal technical change can be relied upon to raise the standard of living indefinitely. If this is a sensible way to view the course of economic growth, then it is at least arguable that the introduction of national accounting categories into the study of economic history and economic development, with the inevitable emphasis on saving and capital formation and the tendency to underemphasize science, economic organization, new products and processes, and other aspects of economic life that have no independent place in the accounting categories, has on balance distorted our perception of economic history and misdirected policy to promote economic growth.

The rate of economic growth itself depends very much on how one chooses to define real income—what is included and what is not. There is no obviously best definition. Thus, to end the book, I present a collection of growth rates under alternative definitions of income. Starting with the common definition of income as real gross national expenditure per head—the definition that gave rise to the 2.45% in the opening paragraphs of this chapter—I introduce various combinations of imputations and changes in the concept of income that will have been discussed individually throughout the book to yield growth rates for the years 1926 to 1974 varying from about 2% to 4%, implying that a return from economic conditions in 1974 to economic conditions in 1926 would be like a reduction in salary from $14,800 to somewhere between $5650 and $2170 depending on which aspects of the economy are taken into account.

NOTES FOR FURTHER READING

The notes on literature at the end of each chapter in Part 1 of this book do not constitute a comprehensive or even adequate bibliography of index numbers or national accounting. They are intended to help the reader to get into some of the literature on the topics discussed.

There are many introductions to national accounting. Among these are J. W. Kendrick, *Economic Accounts and their Users*, McGraw-Hill Book Company, 1972; and R. Stone, *National Income and Expenditure*, Bowes and Bowes, 1961. Though not really elementary and now somewhat out of date, P. Studenski's *The Income of Nations*, New York University Press, 1958, is particularly recommended for its discussion of the concepts of the national accounts and for its account of the different views of economists and national accountants as to how income ought to be measured. National accountants tend to communicate with one another in *The Review of Income and Wealth*, published quarterly, and in the series *Studies in Income and Wealth*, published under the auspices of the National Bureau of Economic Research and appearing irregularly about once or twice a year.

In most countries, the construction of the official national accounts is described in a volume of sources and methods. The Canadian sources and methods volume is the third in a three volume series entitled *National Income and Expenditure Accounts*, Statistics Canada, No. 13-531, No. 13-533 and No. 13-549E, 1976, in which the first two volumes contain the complete national accounts from 1926 to 1974, the period covered by this book.

2

Consumption: The Welfare of the Representative Consumer

We begin our study of economic growth with a very simple case. The economy consists of only one person, called the representative consumer, whose well-being may be described by an ordinary utility function entirely dependent on the quantities consumed of a finite set of consumption goods, and who obtains different amounts of consumption goods each year. This case will serve as a foundation for the rest of the book. Only when we understand this case thoroughly can we go on to treat the more difficult and more realistic cases where, for instance, part of income is invested, the nature of goods is changing over time, a distinction must be made between goods and aspects of the environment, or the interactions among consumers are taken into account. At the end of this chapter we review the assumptions we are making as an introduction to subsequent chapters where these assumptions are successively relaxed.

A. THREE EQUIVALENT WAYS OF DEFINING REAL INCOME IN CIRCUMSTANCES WHERE INCOME CONSISTS ENTIRELY OF CONSUMPTION GOODS

Suppose we are measuring the rate of economic growth between two dates, say 1926 and 1974, which are, in fact, the beginning and the end of the time series we shall use in our empirical work. The assumptions we are making circumscribe rather drastically the kinds of changes we are allowed to observe between any pair of years. The commodities have to be the same. Only the quantities may differ. Thus if the representative consumer consumes one pound of bread and one pound of cheese per day in 1926, we might suppose that he consumes 1.4 pounds of bread and 1.7 pounds of cheese in 1974 and we can allow the relative price of bread and cheese to change, but we cannot allow him to begin consuming fish. The question at hand is what number we ought to attach to the overall change in quantities consumed from 1926 to 1974.

To deal with this question we must endow the representative consumer with a modicum of characteristics: not too much, for that would complicate the problem, but just enough to make economic growth a meaningful notion. Following well-worn grooves in the analysis of this problem, we endow the representative consumer with a utility function defined over the types of goods available in the economy.

What in this simple case do we mean by the rate of economic growth? I suggest that the rate of economic growth between any two dates, 1926 and 1974 in this instance, is the number we get in the following conceptual experiment: choose a set of prices, one for each good. Typically, these would be the actual prices in some particular year which we call the base year, but they could equally well be arbitrarily chosen prices that do not correspond to any year at all. For convenience, let the base year be 1961. Then ask the representative consumer to say how much money he would need in the base year, 1961, to be as well off as he would be with the bundle of goods consumed in 1926. To answer this question, the representative consumer makes the same kind of comparison among bundles of goods that we require him to make in the conceptual experiment by which indifference curves are derived in the theory of demand. He has to compare the utility of the bundle of goods consumed in 1926 with the utilities of all possible bundles of goods that might be purchased with any given amount of money in 1961. The answer to the question is a sum of money required in 1961 to purchase a bundle of goods that yields the same utility as the bundle of goods consumed in 1926. This sum of money is real income (or real consumption, for we have excluded investment by definition) in 1926 with respect to 1961 as the base year. Next ask the representative consumer how much money he would need in 1961 to be as well off as he would be with the bundle of goods consumed in 1974. The answer to this question is real consumption in 1974 with respect to 1961 as the base year. The rate of economic growth between 1926 and 1974, with respect to 1961 as the base year, is simply that rate which brings real consumption in 1926 up to real consumption in 1974 in the course of 48 years.

This experiment can be depicted in three ways, on what might be called an income thermometer, on an indifference curve diagram, and as a property of the indirect utility function. We shall consider these in turn.

The income thermometer is illustrated in Figure 2.1. The units on the thermometer are dollars in the base year rather than temperature (in this case, 1961 dollars) and values of real income in all other years are connected to 1961 dollars by the conceptual experiment just described. Thus the identification of the year 1926 with $1000 means that the representative consumer would be as well off in 1961 with an income of $1000 as he would be with the bundle of goods consumed in 1926. The actual income in 1926 might have been less than $1000 because prices

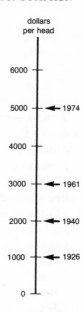

Figure 2.1 The income thermometer

were generally lower in 1926 than in 1961, and the value at 1961 prices
of the bundle of goods consumed in 1926 need not equal $1000 (in fact,
it would normally be somewhat in excess of $1000) because relative
prices have changed. The figure of $1000 is the sum of money which
would leave the representative consumer indifferent between living in
1961 at that income and living in 1926 with the actual quantities of
goods consumed at that time. Similarly, real consumption per head in
1940 is shown to be $2000, real consumption per head in 1961 is shown
to be $3000 and real consumption per head in 1974 is shown to be
$5000. The rate of economic growth between 1926 and 1974 is,
therefore, 3.35%, because that is the solution for r in the equation
$r = (1/48)\ln(5000/1000)$. The incomes on the left-hand side of the scale
can be interpreted as personal incomes in 1961. The income of $5000
per head is that of a comparatively rich man; the income of $1000 per
head is that of a comparatively poor man. Thus, to measure real income
per head as we are doing is to draw a comparison among comparisons.
To say that the rate of economic growth from 1926 to 1974 was 3.35%
is to say that the improvement in the circumstances of the country as a
whole is comparable to the improvement in the standard of living of a
family of four people in 1961 when its income increases from $4000 to
$20000 per year. Economic growth is like a raise in salary. This analogy
between personal income and national income is important because it

enables us to interpret income statistics in the light of personal experience and because it serves as a guide to the design of measures of real income and economic growth in more difficult and realistic cases to be taken up later on.

The second way to depict real income is as a distance on an indifference curves diagram as illustrated in Figure 2.2. Think of a representative consumer whose tastes are invariant over time in the sense that he evaluates bundles of goods consumed in different years with respect to a single, unchanging set of indifference curves. The limitations of two dimensional geometry compel us to suppose that there are only two commodities, bread and cheese, quantities of which are indicated on the vertical and horizontal axes of the figure. Several indifference curves are shown; these are labelled U^a, U^b, U^c, U^d, U^e, and U^f. For economic growth to have taken place, the production possibility curve of the economy must have shifted outward over time because, otherwise, since taste is invariant, the quantities consumed would have remained the same, year after year. The production possibility curves

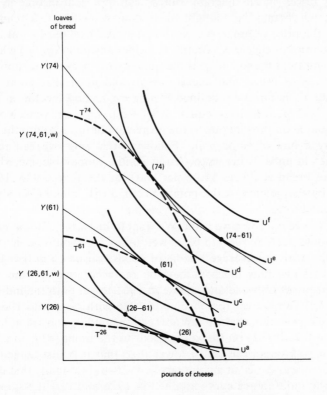

Figure 2.2 Taste, technology, and income in a two-good economy

for the years 1926, 1961 and 1974 are indicated by the broken curves labelled as T^{26}, T^{61} and T^{74}. Each year the representative consumer chooses the point on that year's production possibility curve yielding the greatest possible utility. As is well known from the theory of demand, this is the point at which the production possibility curve is tangent to an indifference curve. Suppose it turns out that the highest utility attainable in 1926 is that indicated by the indifference curve U^a, the highest utility attainable in 1961 is that indicated by the indifference curve U^c, and the highest utility attainable in 1974 is that indicated by the indifference curve U^e. We label the points of common tangency between T^{26} and U^a, T^{61} and U^c, and T^{74} and U^e respectively as (26), (61) and (74). In this economy without excise taxes or other distortions in the price mechanism, the relative price of cheese each year is the common rate of substitution in production and in use between bread and cheese as indicated by the slopes of the common tangents of the utility curves and production possibility curves at the points (26), (61), and (74). We cannot depict money income directly because we cannot represent money prices on the diagram. But we can represent income in units of bread, which may be thought of as money income in circumstances where the price of bread is constrained to be \$1.00 per loaf at all times but the price of cheese is variable. Consider any point (q_b, q_c) where q_b is the quantity of bread and q_c is the quantity of cheese, and suppose that the prices of bread and cheese are p_b and p_c at that point. Money income, Y, as normally defined is $p_b q_b + p_c q_c$, and income in units of bread is Y/p_b which is equal to $q_b + q_c(p_c/p_b)$ and which may be represented on the diagram as the projection of (q_b, q_c) onto the vertical axis by a line of slope p_c/p_b. Following this rule, we can represent incomes in units of bread (or, equivalently, money income where the price of bread is always \$1.00 per loaf) for the years 1926, 1961 and 1974 by the heights of the points $Y(26)$, $Y(61)$ and $Y(74)$ above the horizontal axis.

But it is real income we want. We want to know the amount of money one would need in 1961 to be as well off as one would be in 1926, for instance, with the average bundle of goods consumed in that year; we want to know how much money the representative consumer would need at prices of bread and cheese in 1961 to get onto the indifference curve U^a. To discover real income in 1926 with respect to 1961 as the base year, we take what we can now call the budget constraint for 1961, the line from $Y(61)$ on the vertical axis to the point (61), and, without changing its slope, raise it or lower it so that it is just tangent to the indifference curve U^a at a point labelled (26–61) to signify that the point is on the indifference curve attained in 1926 and that the slope of the indifference curve at that point reflects the relative price of cheese in

1961. The intersection of this line with the vertical axis is labelled $Y(26, 61, w)$. The measure of real income in 1926 when 1961 is the base year is the height of $Y(26, 61, w)$ above the horizontal axis, for $Y(26, 61, w)$ signifies the amount of money one would require to be as well off as an average person in 1926 if the price of bread were \$1.00 per loaf and the relative price of cheese was the same as in 1961. The w in the expression $Y(26, 61, w)$ is mnemonic for welfare; it signifies a welfare measure of real income as distinct from other measures to be discussed presently. Similarly, real income in 1974 with respect to 1961 as the base year is the height of the intersection with the vertical axis of the tangent, with slope equal to the relative price in 1961, to the indifference attained in 1974. It is labelled $Y(74, 61, w)$. Since 1961 is the chosen base year, real income in 1961 and money income in 1961 are one and the same.

We can now draw a correspondence between Figures 2.1 and 2.2. If the price of bread were really \$1 per loaf in 1961, then the values of $Y(26, 61, w)$, $Y(61)$, and $Y(74, 61, w)$ would be \$1000, \$3000, and \$5000 respectively because the conceptual experiments used to obtain the measures of real income in Figures 2.1 and 2.2 are exactly the same. However, if the price of bread differed from \$1 per loaf, we should have to multiply the values of $Y(26, 61, w)$, $Y(61)$, and $Y(74, 61, w)$ respectively by the price of bread in 1961 to get real incomes expressed in 1961 dollars.

The third representation of real income is as a property of the indirect utility function. Suppose now that there are n, rather than just two, commodities in the economy. The representative consumer maximizes his utility function

$$U = U(q_1, \ldots, q_n) \tag{1}$$

subject to a budget constraint

$$Y = \sum_{i=1}^{n} p_i q_i \tag{2}$$

where q_i is the quantity of the i good, p_i is its price and Y is money income. He chooses quantities q_i such that their marginal utilities are proportional to market prices

$$p_i = \lambda \frac{\partial U}{\partial q_i} \quad i = 1, \ldots, n \tag{3}$$

for some scalar λ. From the set of $n + 1$ equations (2) and (3), we may derive the complete set of demand functions

$$q_i = D_i(p, Y) \tag{4}$$

where p without a subscript denotes the vector of prices of all n goods. Substituting the demand curves back into the utility function, we obtain what is called the indirect utility function

$$U = U(D_1(p, Y), \ldots, D_n(p, Y)) \tag{5}$$

$$= U(p, Y)$$

which may be inverted to yield what is called the cost function

$$Y = C(p, U) \tag{6}$$

where Y in equation (6) is now interpreted as the minimum cost at prices $p_1, p_2, \ldots, p_n$ of attaining a level of utility U. Though we have postulated a budget constraint in equation (2), the derivation of the indirect utility function is not really dependent upon it. The effective constraint may be a production possibility curve as in Figure 2.2. All we really need to assume is that relative prices reflect rates of substitution in use at the chosen output. Then Y in equation (6) becomes the income required to attain utility U at prices p regardless of the original constraint.

But that is exactly what we have been defining as real income! All we need to do to complete the correspondence with Figure 2.2 is to specify the years to which the utility function and the reference prices belong. For instance, if 1961 is the base year so that p in equation (6) is the vector of 1961 prices and if U in equation (6) is the utility attained in the same other year, say 1974, then we can write

$$Y(74, 61, w) = C(p^{61}, U^{74}) \tag{7}$$

where the superscripts on p and U signify the years to which they belong. Figure 2.2 is the two-dimensional representation of this definition.

It follows immediately from the definition of real income in equation (7) that real income as we have defined it is simply one among many ways of measuring utility. In the theory of demand we say that utility is ordinal, and by this we mean that if a function $U(q_1, \ldots, q_n)$ is a representative of utility then so too is $f(U)$ where f is any monotonically increasing function of U. The function $C(p^{61}, U)$ is a monotonically increasing function of U and is, therefore, as good a utility indicator as U itself.

This identification of real income and utility suggests a paradox which we had better dispose of now, lest it interfere with the development of the analysis of real income later on. The paradox goes as follows: it is the essence of an ordinal as opposed to a cardinal measure that we can speak of an ordinal measure as increasing or decreasing but that we cannot attach numbers to a change in any unique or meaningful way. Thus, for instance, one can by experiment show which of two substances is the harder, and all known substances have been given numbers on a scale from zero to ten such that the hardest known substance is ten, the softest is zero, and all other substances have numbers in between, the harder the substance the higher the number. This is an ordinal measure of hardness because the numbers zero and ten are completely arbitrary (any other pair of numbers would have done just as well) and because there is no principle for attaching numbers to new substances other than that its hardness value shall be less than that of harder substances and greater than that of softer ones. Utility is similar. The sequence of indifference curves U^a, U^b, U^c, ... in Figure 2.2 could have been given the values 1, 2, 3, ..., or the values -876, -23, 1079, ..., or any increasing values whatsoever. To measure real income is to attach values to a sequence of indifference curves. The values in Figure 2.1 are ordered correctly in that larger numbers correspond to higher indifference curves, but the values we attach in this roundabout way have no priority over other values we might have attached in some other way. Consequently, all that measures of real income can ever tell us is whether we are better off now than people were at other times or at other places. No significance can be attached to the numbers themselves. Growth rates, on this reasoning, are completely meaningless. If our numbers tell us that real income per head in Canada grew at 3% per year from 1926 to 1961 and at 4% per year from 1961 to 1974, we would know that people in 1974 were better off than people in 1961 and that people in 1961 were better off than people in 1926, which is neither more nor less than we would know if the growth rates had been reversed, if the economy grew at 4% from 1926 to 1961 and at 3% from 1961 to 1975; for a monotonic transformation of the time series of real income could have converted the earlier 3% growth rate into a 4% growth rate and the later 4% growth rate into a 3% growth rate.

To resolve the paradox, let us consider for a moment the concept of temperature. Before the introduction of the thermometer, temperature *was* an ordinal measure. I could say that it is hotter today than yesterday, but I could say not attribute numbers to the difference in any satisfactory way. I could say that today is 10 and yesterday was 5, but you could equally well say that today is 30 and yesterday was −16. The thermometer changed all that. The identification of temperature with the height of a column of mercury enabled us to attach numbers to temperature in a commonly-acceptable way, and converted temperature into a cardinal measure. The difference between cardinality and ordinality in this case was simply that one among the many possible ways of attaching numbers to temperature was singled out as being of primary interest, and all other ways were forgotten. (The difference between Fahrenheit and Centigrade is irrelevant in this connection.)

In general the difference between cardinal and ordinal measures is not that you cannot attach numbers to ordinal measures but that you can do so too easily and in too many different ways. As soon as you find one method of attaching numbers to an ordinal concept that is clearly better than all the rest or that corresponds uniquely to some human concern, then the concept ceases to be ordinal from that day on. The method we have used to construct real income can be interpreted as a proper cardinalization of utility. Just as temperature is cardinalized by the analogy with distance in a thermometer, so too is utility cardinalized by the analogy between the welfare of people at different times and places and the spectrum of money incomes in any given base year as illustrated on the income thermometer of Figure 2.1. Utility is cardinalized by linking it to money incomes in the base year, and with respect to that linkage we can meaningfully say that the growth rate of real income in the years 1961 to 1974 is greater or less, as the case may be, than the growth rate of real income in the years 1926 to 1961.

B. THE CHOICE OF BASE YEAR

A small terminological ambiguity ought to be cleared up before we proceed. The term base year is often used to denote the year for which the value of an index is set at 100. One speaks, for instance, of a cost of living index as being, say, 142 for some given year with respect to 1961 as the base. This is not the sense in which the term is used here so far. In choosing 1961 as the base year we are not adjusting a time series by a scale factor. We are comparing the heights of indifference curves by means of lines (or planes in the n-dimensional case) with slopes equal to relative prices in the chosen base year. This concept is sometimes referred to as a standard rather than a base, but our choice of the latter term should not give rise to confusion because it will always be clear from the context how the term is being used. Frequently, one wants to use the term in both senses at once: a time series is evaluated at prices in a given year *and* scaled up or down so that its value in that year is 100. That is why it is convenient to have the double meaning of the term.

Now let us consider the base year itself. In defining real income we chose 1961 as the base year without giving any justification for our choice. Would it have made a difference if we had chosen another year instead? If so, is there any reason for preferring one base year to another? These are the questions to which we turn.

The choice of the base year has no effect upon the measure of economic growth if relative prices remain constant over the entire period of the time series or if indifference curves are homothetic. In the former case, it can make no difference at all which year is chosen as the base because, referring back to Figure 2.2, all budget constraints are parallel. If all prices remain constant, a change of base from 1961 to 1974, for instance, could have no effect on the measure of economic growth because

$$Y(26, 74, w) = Y(26, 61, w) \qquad (8)$$

since both would be equal to $Y(26)$ itself and

$$Y(74, 74, w) = Y(74, 61, w) \qquad (9)$$

since both would be equal to $Y(74)$ itself. Otherwise, if relative prices are constant but absolute prices are changing, the values of $Y(26, 74, w)$ and $Y(74, 74, w)$ will exceed the values of $Y(26, 61, w)$ and $Y(74, 61, w)$ by the extent to which prices have increased from 1961 to 1974 (the same for all goods since relative prices are constant) but the rates of economic growth will be unaffected.

That the rate of economic growth is independent of the choice of the base year when indifference curves are homothetic follows directly from simple properties of homothetic functions. To say that a set of indifference curves is homothetic is to say that each curve is a scaled up or scaled down version of every other. Thus, the slopes of all indifference curves must be the same along any ray from the origin of the figure. Figure 2.3 is like Figure 2.2 except that the indifference curves U^c and U^e are assumed to be homothetic so that their slopes at A and B on the ray OAB are required to be the same. So too are their slopes at C and D on the ray OCD, though the common slopes at A and B and at C and D will not, of course, be the same. It also follows from the definition of homotheticity that the ratios of distances between indifference curves are the same along all rays from the origin, so that OA/OB and OC/OD are necessarily equal. It now follows from properties of similar triangles

CONSUMPTION

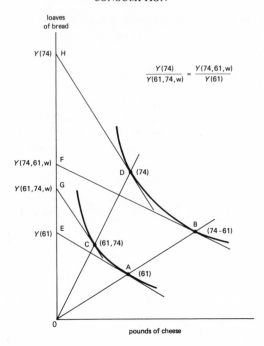

Figure 2.3 Comparison of real income when indifference curves are homothetic

that the ratios of distances along the vertical axis OH/OG and OF/OE are also equal, where E, F, G and H are projections of A, B, C and D at the corresponding slopes. Now, if we let A represent quantities consumed in 1961 and D represent quantities consumed in 1974, we see that C becomes the cheapest bundle of goods at 1974 prices which yields the same satisfaction as the bundle of goods actually consumed in 1961, that B becomes the cheapest bundle of goods at 1961 prices that yields the same satisfaction as the bundle of goods actually consumed in 1974, that OH becomes $Y(74)$, OG becomes $Y(61, 74, w)$, OF becomes $Y(74, 61, w)$ and OE becomes $Y(61)$. And the equality between the ratios OH/OG and OF/OE, gets translated into the statement that $Y(74)/Y(61, 74, w) = Y(74, 61, w)/Y(61)$, which is precisely what we want to establish, for if the ratios of real incomes are independent of the base year, then so too must be the rates of economic growth. Note that the argument, though framed in a comparison between two particular years, 1961 and 1974, is actually quite general and holds for any pairs of years or for any time series. It can also be shown that the proposition, established here for an economy with two commodities, is actually true for an economy with any number of commodities.[1] On the other hand, it should be borne in mind that indifference curves are not normally homothetic, for homotheticity implies that all income elasticities of demand are equal to one. Every empirical study of demand I know of has shown this not to be so.

These special cases aside, the rate of economic growth does depend to a greater or lesser extent on the choice of base year. To see this we need only to redraw Figure 2.3 for a case where the indifference curves are clearly not homothetic. The indifference curves in Figure 2.4 are drawn so that the income elasticity of demand for bread is considerably greater than 1, and the income elasticity of demand for cheese is considerably less than 1. Clearly, the ratio of the real income in 1974 to the real income in 1961 is greater when 1961 is the base year than when 1974 is the base year, that is $Y(74)/Y(61, 74, w)$ is less than $Y(74, 61, w)/Y(61)$.

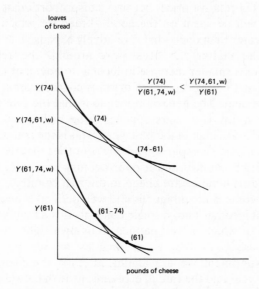

Figure 2.4 The effect of a change in the base year on a comparison of real incomes when elasticities of demand differ from 1

What does this mean? Is it a contradiction or ambiguity in the concept of economic growth, or does the change in the base year have real economic significance? To get to the bottom of the matter, let us reconsider the conceptual experiment by which real income was

[1] This is proved by Samuelson and Swamy in the article cited at the end of this chapter.

defined. We set 1961 as the base year and asked the representative consumer to tell us how much income he would need in 1961 to be as well off as he would be with the bundle of goods consumed in 1974. To change the base year is to run another conceptual experiment entirely. If, for instance, we change the base year to 1974, we are asking the representative consumer to compare the actual income in 1974 with the amount of money he would need in 1974 to be as well off as he would be with the bundle of goods consumed in 1961, or, what amounts to the same thing, when he is given the average income in 1961 and confronted with 1961 prices for the goods he buys. These different experiments ought to yield different rates of economic growth. We see in Figure 2.4 that bread is relatively cheap in 1974 and cheese is relatively dear. Consequently, starting from any given indifference curve, such as that attained in 1961, a given percentage increase in money income makes the representative consumer worse off at 1961 relative prices than he would be at 1974 relative prices because a disproportionate share of his extra income will be spent on the good—bread for which the income elasticity is greater than one—that is relatively expensive at 1961 prices. Or, to put the matter the other way around, the representative consumer needs a smaller increase in income to augment utility by any given amount at 1974 prices where bread is cheap, than at 1961 prices where bread is dear. The general principle is that the rate of economic growth between any two years appears to be high when the relative prices of luxuries are high in the base year. This is the counterpart of the proposition in income comparison among countries that the ratio of real incomes of a rich country and a poor country is greater at the poor country's prices if luxuries are cheap in the rich country.

Thus real income is unambiguous and well defined if one interprets it correctly. Real income is not a single concept. It is a family of concepts, each member of which is well defined in its own right. As long as we specify the base year, that is, as long as we say precisely which conceptual experiment we are aiming at, then the measure of real income in any year and the rate of economic growth between any pair of years are exact within the terms of reference of the assumptions of this chapter.

That is not quite the end of the story, for it is of little use to describe real income as a family of concepts unless we have a criterion for choosing among the members of the family in any particular instance of income comparison. Real income might as well be an ambiguous concept if we have an infinity of different interpretations to choose from. That is the position we are in if we treat the measurement of economic growth from a strictly technical or analytical point of view. To narrow down our options we must consider the purpose of the exercise. Why, we must ask, are we measuring real income at all? The answer would seem to be that we want to compare our situation with that of our parents or grandparents at some time in the past, and to do so with reference to a standard with which we are familiar. We want to know who today might reasonably be compared with our parents or grandparents, not who in 1926, for instance, might our parents or grandparents have compared with us. We can, therefore, say that the appropriate base year for income comparison is the current year because the measure with that base supplies the answer to the question we are asking.

The implication of this line of reasoning is that time series of real income should be constructed fresh each year with the current year treated as the base. We do not do so in practice, because the computation would be enormous, because users of the statistics do not want their time series revised every year, and because income elasticities of demand are close enough to unity and relative prices sufficiently stable over short periods of time that the year to year revisions in the series would probably be quite small. Most national income offices adjust their bases about once a decade.

C. A FIRST ATTEMPT AT MEASURING REAL INCOME WITH TIME SERIES OF PRICES AND QUANTITIES

Real income has been defined as the outcome of a conceptual experiment similar to that used to generate indifference curves in the theory of demand. We ask the representative consumer to compare bundles of goods available in different circumstances or at different periods of time, and we say that real income in 1974, for instance, is the cheapest bundle at base year prices that the representative consumer considers to be at least as desirable as the average bundle of goods consumed in 1974. But though we can define real income in a psychological experiment, we cannot measure it in that way. There is no representative consumer and we cannot send him back in time. In practice, we have no choice but to construct the time series of real income with the time series of prices and quantities that the economy provides. The question to which we now turn is whether these data are sufficient for measuring real income as we have defined it, exactly or to a tolerable degree of approximation.

Real income may be expressed as the sum of two components, one directly measurable from statistics of prices and quantities, and the other not. Consider real income in 1974 with respect to 1961 as the base year—the term Y (74, 61, w) in equation (7) above. It follows immediately that

$$Y(74,\ 61,\ w) = \left[\sum_{i=1}^{n} p_i^{61} q_i^{74} \right] + \left[C(p^{61},\ U(q^{74})) - \sum_{i=1}^{n} p_i^{61} q_i^{74} \right] \quad (10)$$

We shall refer to the expression $\left[\sum_{i=1}^{n} p_i^{61} q_i^{74} \right]$ as "the Laspeyres measure,"

and we shall refer to the expression $\left[C(p^{61},\ U(q^{74})) - \sum_{i=1}^{n} p_i^{61} q_i^{74} \right]$ as "Surplus". Then equation (10) becomes

$$\text{Real Income} = \text{the Laspeyres measures} + \text{Surplus} \quad (11)$$

The Laspeyres measure is obviously computable from statistics of prices and quantities. Surplus, on the other hand, depends on the form of the unknown function C, but we are assured that Surplus is negative because $C(p^{61}, U(q^{74}))$ is defined as the cheapest bundle of goods that can be purchased at prices p^{61} to yield no less utility than the bundle of goods q^{74}, and this in turn guarantees that the Laspeyres measure is an overestimate of real income itself.

The use of the word surplus may seem strange in this context because the word is normally used (as in the phrase "consumer's surplus") to denote certain gains or losses from changes in tax rates or in project evaluation. In fact, our usage of the word is almost identical to the usage in public finance and benefit-cost analysis, as may be seen when the

surplus in equation(10) is approximated by the expression $-\dfrac{1}{2} \sum_{i=1}^{n} \Delta p_i\ \Delta q_i$,

where the Δq_i are changes in q_i along the indifference curve attained in 1974 in response to changes in relative prices from those in 1961 to those in 1974 and the Δp_i are the corresponding changes in money prices with total money income held constant at $C(p^{61},\ U(q^{74}))$. If only one quantity or only one price changes, the measure of surplus becomes $1/2\ \Delta p \Delta q$ which may be interpreted as an approximation to the area under a compensated demand curve.[2]

---

[2] Define q^* as the set of quantities the representative consumer would choose if had an income $C(p^{61},\ U(q^{74}))$ to spend at prices p^{61}. The quantities q^* are represented by the point (74–61) in Figure 2.4. Expand $C(p^{61},\ U(q^{74}))$ in a Taylor series around q^*.

$$C(p^{61},\ U(q^{74})) \equiv C(p^{61},\ U(q^* + \Delta q))$$

$$= C(p^{61},\ U(q^*)) + \sum_{i=1}^{n} \frac{\partial C}{\partial q_i} \Delta q_i + 1/2 \sum_{i=1}^{n} \sum_{j=1}^{n} \frac{\partial^2 C}{\partial q_i \partial q_j} \Delta q_i\ \Delta q_c + R^3$$

The connection between real income and consumer's surplus may be illustrated in the two-good economy. Figure 2.5 is a reproduction of part of Figure 2.2 together with a transformation of the content of the diagram from the space of indifference curves to the space of demand curves. On the top half of the diagram, bundles of goods consumed in 1961 (the base year) and in 1974 are labelled accordingly, real income in 1974, which we shall refer to for short as Y, is labelled $Y(74, 61, w)$, and the Laspeyres measure of real income in 1974 is labelled as L. Clearly, L is greater than Y because both L and Y are projections onto the vertical axis of points on the indifference curve attained in 1974 at an angle equal to the relative price of cheese, and Y is defined to be the lowest of all such projections. As in Figure 2.2, the tangent to the indifference curve attained in 1974 at an angle representing prices in 1961 is labelled as (74–61). For convenience, several points on the diagram are indicated by letters.

To display the connection between real income and consumer's surplus, we transform the indifference curve through the point (74) into the demand curve on the bottom half of the diagram. The horizontal axis remains the same, but the vertical axis becomes the relative price of cheese. The demand curve itself is compensated, in the sense that the height of the demand curve for any given quantity of cheese is the price of cheese as it would be if that quantity of cheese were consumed together with enough bread to make the representative consumer as well off as he is in 1974.

Now the relation among real income Y, the Laspeyres measure L, and consumer surplus is plain. The difference between L and Y is the distance CB on the top diagram which translates exactly into the area

where R^3 is the sum of the third and higher order terms in the series. From equations (3) and (6) it follows that $\dfrac{\partial C}{\partial q_i} = p_i^{61}$ in which case $\dfrac{\partial^2 C}{\partial q_i \partial q_j} = \dfrac{\partial p_i}{\partial q_j}$, and $\left(\sum\limits_{j=1}^{n} \dfrac{\partial^2 C}{\partial q_i \partial q_j} \Delta q_j \right)$ becomes a second order approximation to Δp_i. It also follows from the definition of the expenditure function that $C(p^{61}, U(q^*)) = \sum\limits_{i=1}^{n} p^{61} q^*_i$. Combining all this, ignoring R^3, and noting that $q^*_i + \Delta q = q^{74}$ by definition, we see that $Y(74, 61, w) = \sum\limits_{i=1}^{n} p_i^{61} q_i^{74} + 1/2 \sum\limits_{i} \Delta p_i \Delta q_i$

The Δp_i and Δq_i are not directly measurable from time series of prices and quantities because the location of q^* cannot be observed. The location of q^* may, however, be estimated to a degree of approximation by the techniques, described briefly in chapter 9, for constructing complete sets of demand functions.

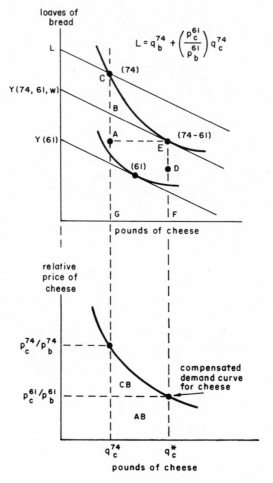

Figure 2.5 The bias in the Laspeyres index interpreted as consumer's surplus

CB on the bottom one.[3] But the area CB is what one normally speaks of as consumer's surplus. It is the area under the demand curve over and above the value of the increase in the quantity of cheese consumed at a new lower price—not, however, the actual increase in the quantity of cheese between 1974 and 1961, but the increase as it would have been if the consumer had been as well off in 1961 as in 1974 but had

---

[3] The area CB on the bottom diagram is equal to the integral

$$\int_{q_c^{74}}^{q_c^*} (p - p^{61})\, dq_c$$

experienced the decline in the relative price of cheese nonetheless, as, for instance, would be the case if the money price of cheese declined, the price of bread remained constant, and money income declined just enough to compensate for the decline in the price of cheese.

This unexpected appearance of consumer surplus in the middle of our discussion of the concept of real income suggests that there is close connection between the measurement of real income and the measurements one makes in benefit–cost analysis. To see how close the connection really is, we can interpret our diagram as follows. Suppose a planner is deciding whether to shut down a cheese factory and to divert the resources saved to the production of bread. We can draw correspondences between the initial situation and what we have been calling the base year, 1961, and between the new situation as it would be if the factory were closed down and the year 1974. But to do so we have to assume that the increase or decrease in utility between the two situations, as opposed to the change in proportions of bread and cheese consumed, has no effect on the relative price of cheese, in other words, that the point we have been calling (61) takes up a position D at which consumption of cheese, q_c^* is the same as it would be at the point (74–61). (Note that though D is illustrated as being lower than the point E, it could in fact be either higher or lower, and, indeed, the planner's problem is to decide which of these possibilities is really the case.) The closing of the cheese factory reduces output of cheese from q_c^* to q_c^{74} changing total output from the point D to the point C. The planner might choose to evaluate these bundles of goods at initial prices. That would be equivalent to a comparison between L and $Y(61)$ and to closing down the factory if and only if $L > Y(61)$. (Keep in mind that we have moved (61) to D.) That would be an inappropriate way to proceed because it would not take account of the loss of consumer's surplus in cheese. To evaluate the reduction in the output of cheese, one would

---

where p is the relative price of cheese,

$$p = \frac{p_c}{p_b} = -\frac{\partial q_b}{\partial q_c}$$

observed along the indifference curve through the point (74).
The integral is therefore equal to

$$\int_{q_c^{74}}^{q_c^*} \left(\frac{\partial q_b^{61}}{\partial q_c^{61}} - \frac{\partial q_b}{\partial q_c} \right) dq_c = p^{61}(q_c^* - q_c^{74}) - (q_b^* - q_b^{74})$$

But, we see from the top diagram that $p^{61} = AB/AE$, $q_c^* - q_c^{74} = AE$, $q_b^{74} = CG$ and $q_b^* = EF$. Therefore, the area CB on the bottom diagram is equal to $CG - EF - BA$ which is precisely the distance CB on the top diagram.

need to subtract the appropriate area, CB, under the compensated demand curve from the value of output after the closing of the cheese factory. In other words, the benefit–cost analysis of the closing of the cheese factory boils down to a comparison between $Y(74, 61, w)$ and $Y(61)$. Benefit–cost analysis is nothing more than a comparison of real incomes before and after the introduction of a given project. The difference between total benefit and total cost is the amount by which real income has increased.

Thus one may treat benefit–cost analysis as an application of the theory of income comparison or income comparison as an application of the benefit–cost analysis depending on where one's main interest lies. The difference between these branches of economics is not in the theory but in the circumstances to which the theory is applied, the comparison of situations before and after the introduction of projects in one case, and the comparison of situations in different places or at different times in the other.

The partly arbitrary choice of a base year for the measurement of economic growth has its counterpart benefit–cost analysis in the distinction between 'equivalent variation' and 'compensating variation' as concepts of consumer's surplus. The difference between these concepts is simply that to measure consumer's surplus as equivalent variation is to compare real incomes before and after the introduction of the project (or the imposition of the tax, or the change in the price of a commodity—whatever the cause of the change may be) by treating the situation before the change as the base year; while to measure consumer's surplus by the compensating variation is to compare real incomes by treating the situation after the change as the base year. Typically, the choice of the base year does not make a great deal of difference in benefit–cost analysis because most prices are unaffected, or affected only slightly by the project. It is otherwise in comparisons of real income over long periods of time within which all relative prices may change to a significant extent.

Returning now to our main theme, the significance of equation (11) is that real income in any year can be looked upon as the sum of the Laspeyres measure and the consumer's surplus, that the consumer's surplus is negative and, one hopes, small by comparison with the Laspeyres measure, and that the Laspeyres measure is a simple expression consisting of prices and quantities which can in principle be observed. Thus, the Laspeyres measure will serve as a first approximation to real income that can be constructed from prices and quantities directly without any input from the representative consumer himself. In fact, when we come to measure real consumption in Chapter 10, we shall approximate real income in each year t by the Laspeyres measure

$$Y(t, 61, w) \simeq \sum_{i=1}^{n} p_i^{61} q_i^t \qquad (12)$$

ignoring consumer's surplus altogether. Other, possibly more accurate, approximations will be discussed in Chapter 9.

D. A REVIEW OF THE ASSUMPTIONS WITH A VIEW TO THE DEVELOPMENT OF THE CONCEPT OF REAL INCOME IN THE REST OF THE BOOK

As mentioned at the outset of this chapter, real income is defined in the first instance in an exceedingly simple model of the economy. Some of the assumptions of the model can and will be relaxed, so that measures of real income later on in the book will be more realistic and closer to the detail of the economy than this chapter might lead one to suppose. Other assumptions can be relaxed only partially if at all. They may be discussed, examined and criticized, but not replaced. Thus, there will always remain something forced and artificial about our statistics of real income. The raw data are processed and the computations are interpreted as though the data pertained to the simple world in our models rather than to the complex world from which the data actually came. This is inevitable, and we must accept it if we are to use statistics at all. The main assumptions are these:

(a) The demand side of the economy can be looked upon as though the economy consisted of only one person (or, equivalently, of many people who are identical in every relevant respect) whose tastes remain invariant over time. This means that bundles of goods consumed in different years can be evaluated with reference to the supposedly invariant utility function of the representative consumer, and that observed prices represent rates of substitution in use among goods in accordance with this utility function. The implications of this assumption will be examined in the next chapter, but the assumption itself will be maintained in the rest of the book.

(b) Real income is a measure of welfare. This is not so much an assumption as a statement of our object in measuring real income. There is a substantial body of literature based on the premise that real income should reflect, not the welfare of the community, but the productive capacity of the economy. Referring to Figure 2.2 again, economic growth between 1926 and 1974 should, on that view, reflect the outward shift of the production possibility curve from T^{26} to T^{74}. Productive capacity is discussed in Chapter 4.

(c) Real income can be approximated by a Laspeyres measure. We shall make extensive use of this approximation because of its simplicity, because it makes minimal demands on data, and because the advantages of other measures, discussed in Chapter 9, are in many cases dependent upon assumptions which may be violated in the circumstances of income comparison.

(d) All goods are consumed in the current year. This assumption will have to be relaxed to take account of saving and investment. We will discuss investment and the related concept of depreciation in Chapters 5 and 6. It will turn out that the concept of investment in real terms is much trickier, and much more open to a variety of interpretations than is generally supposed.

(e) There are n distinct goods. A great deal of attention will be paid to this assumption at various places throughout the book. Any attempt to measure real income must come to grips with the fact that the apportionment of the flow of income into exactly n goods with properties presumed to be invariant over time is a statistician's construct imposed on a world where no two items are really alike, where what we call goods are gradually but steadily changing their characteristics over time, where new goods appear and old ones are forced out of the market, where a distinction must be made between public goods and private goods, and where outputs of some goods cannot be observed at all. The specification of commodities is the subject of Chapter 8.

(f) Utility depends on goods alone. In fact, much of the change in the well-being of people depends on developments that cannot properly be classified as increases or decreases in quantities of goods consumed. Pollution may become more or less of a burden. Crime may become more or less prevalent. Mortality rates may rise or fall. We examine the effect on utility of features of the economy that cannot reasonably be classified as increases or decreases in quantities of goods consumed under the heading of the theory of imputations, discussed in general in Chapter 7 and with particular reference to mortality rates in Chapter 11.

NOTES FOR FURTHER READING

The definition of real income in this chapter is based upon the economic theory of index numbers as developed in the nineteen twenties and thirties. Two important landmarks are H. Staehle, 'A Development of the Economic Theory of Index Numbers', *Review of Economic Studies* (1934–35), pp. 163–88; and R. Frisch, 'Annual Survey of General Economic Theory: The Problem of Index Numbers', *Econometrica* (1936), pp. 1–37. An extensive, though not quite complete, bibliography is to be found in P. A. Samuelson and S. Swamy, 'Invariant

Economic Index Numbers and Canonical Duality: Survey and Synthesis', *American Economic Review*, **64** (1974), pp. 566–93. R. G. D. Allen's, *Index Numbers in Theory and Practice* contains a satisfactory introduction to the economic theory of index numbers.

The definition of real income by way of the indirect utility function is now almost standard in the literature. See for instance, L. Phlips, *Applied Consumption Analysis*, North Holland, 1974, Chapter V. The analysis leading to the identification of real income as the sum of the Laspeyres measure and consumer's surplus follows the standard definition of surplus in benefit–cost analysis: H. Hotelling, 'The General Welfare in Relation to Problems of Taxation and of Railway and Utility Rates', *Econometrica*, **6** (1938), pp. 242–69, and A. C. Harberger, *Taxation and Welfare*, Little, Brown and Company, 1974, Chapters 1 and 2. The connection between real income and consumer's surplus is also well known. It was discussed in J. R. Hicks' early papers on index numbers, for instance, 'Consumers Surplus and Index Numbers', *Review of Economic Studies*, **9** (1941–42), pp. 126–37.

3

Consumption: The Welfare of the Community

We have now defined real income as a measure of the welfare of the representative consumer and we shall adhere to this definition in the rest of the book, treating average consumption per head as his consumption and observed prices as his rates of substitution in use. I believe that this definition of real income, drawing as it does on the analogy between countries and persons and between economic growth in a country and the increase in money income of a person or family, rationalizes statistical procedure in the national accounts and reflects what we have in mind when we speak of economic growth. Yet it must be recognized that the deliberate suppression of difference among consumers may obscure important aspects of change in the economy. It is, therefore, useful to subject the representative consumer to a critical examination so that we may know precisely what we are assuming away when we suppose him to exist, and, more important, we may acquire a sense of when to mistrust our analysis because what we assume away is important for the problem at hand. How do we go about evaluating the assumption that the taste of the community may be summarized as the taste of a representative consumer? There would seem to be two ways, both of which are employed in this chapter. We can consider the realism of the assumption, that is, we can ask what we need to postulate about the economy for the observed time series of prices and quantities to conform to a utility function that we may identify as the utility function of the representative consumer. Or, since we are going to measure real income one way or another, we can compare the definition of real income we have used so far with alternative definitions that seem to make allowance for the multiplicity of people in the economy; we can investigate whether the assumptions required in the alternative definitions are more acceptable and whether a reasonable time series of real income to reflect these definitions can be constructed with the information at hand.

Let us consider once again what we mean by real income. We have so far treated real income per head as the answer to a question addressed to the representative consumer: how much income would you need in the base year to make yourself as well off as you would be with the average bundle of goods consumed in the current year? We shall contrast this definition with three alternatives. In the first, we ask essentially the same question to each consumer separately. We ask each man in the current year how much money he would require in the base year to be as well off as he is in the current year, and we measure real income per head as the simple average of all of the answers. In the second alternative, we make use once again of the representative consumer but we ask him a different question. We ask him to imagine, not that he consumes the average bundle of goods in the current year, but that he is put in a risky situation where he has an equal chance of being each consumer in the current year. We ask him how much money, if he had that income with certainty in the base year, would make him as well off as he would be in a lottery where every possible outcome corresponds to the income of a consumer in the current year. In the third alternative, we evaluate the real income of each person in the current year and transform these evaluations into a measure of real income of the community by an imposed social welfare function. These four definitions of real income will be examined in turn, each in a separate section headed by a statement of the question to which statistics of real income per head, so defined, would supply the answer. Bear in mind, however, that we are not yet relaxing the assumption that the whole of income is consumed, and that the different definitions become considerably more complicated if we try to take saving into account.

A. WHAT WOULD IT COST IN THE BASE YEAR TO MAKE THE REPRESENTATIVE CONSUMER AS WELL OFF AS HE IS WITH QUANTITIES CONSUMED IN THE CURRENT YEAR?

To define real income, as we have done in the preceding chapter, as the answer to this question requires that we make two large assumptions about the representative consumer and his relation to the economy as a whole: that his consumption is the average consumption per head in the economy and that his rates of substitution in use among commodities are reflected in observed relative prices. The second of these assumptions is especially troublesome though it is indispensible in justifying the Laspeyres approximation to real income or any other construction in which real income as the welfare of the representative consumer is measured by means of observed prices and quantities. For strictly speaking, the assumption is false. A rational consumer buys a unique set of goods at any given income and prices and, conversely, has a unique set of rates of substitution in use for any given bundle of goods consumed. A community of rational consumers can arrive at any of a large number of sets of relative prices for a given aggregate bundle of goods consumed depending on the distribution of income. Contrary to our assumption, there is for the community no unique relation between relative prices and quantities consumed.

Though this would be irrational in an individual, it is entirely possible for a community of rational consumers, to consume the same quantities $q_1, \ldots, q_n$ in each of two years at prices $p_1, \ldots, p_n$ in one year and at different prices $p'_1, \ldots, p'_n$ in the other. A simple example will show how this may come about. Total output of the economy is 100 pounds of cheese and 100 loaves of bread per head, and there are two types of consumers, those who eat relatively more bread than cheese at any given price and those who eat relatively more cheese. The relative price of cheese in terms of bread will depend on how income is divided between these groups. The larger the share of national income accruing to the cheese-eaters, the greater will be the relative price of cheese, despite the fact that total quantities of bread and cheese consumed are constant and that each consumer's behaviour is in conformity to his own utility function. We need not even have assumed there to be two sorts of people. We could instead have assumed that every man's utility function is the same, but that some people are rich and others poor, and that income elasticities of demand are such that rich people consume relatively more cheese. Now a transfer of income from poor to rich will raise the relative price of cheese, even if there is no change in total quantities consumed, though, of course, there would be if cheese could be substituted for bread in production or in trade. Clearly, we cannot maintain that observed quantities and prices will always be in strict conformity with a utility function.

But strict conformity is really more than we require to make sense of the national accounts. The important question is not whether the taste of the community can be accurately represented by the utility function of the representative consumer—for it cannot—but whether the resultant ambiguity in the concept of real income is such as to render the concept useless for all practical purposes. It is important in this connection that there are two sets of conditions under which observed prices and quantities would conform to a utility function. The first is where all consumers have the same tastes and equal shares in the ownership of all factors of production. In that case, observed prices and quantities per head have to be consistent with the utility function of the representative consumer because each man is, in effect, the representative consumer. The second case is where all consumers have the same tastes (so that the bread-eater, cheese-eater example is ruled out) and all income elasticities of demand are equal to one (so that the rich–poor example is ruled out too). In that case, no transfer of income among consumers can affect relative prices because the consumers who receive the income are prepared to buy precisely what the consumers who lose income forgo, without any change in relative prices. We have to recognize, of course, that these cases where relative prices are unique functions of quantities consumed in the community as a whole are themselves extreme cases. Normally income elasticities are not equal to one, the distribution of income is unequal, and tastes are not identical. But we may be content with a good deal less. The real question is whether income elasticities are close enough to unity, the distribution of income is stable enough (and it is stability rather than equality that one needs to keep prices and quantities in a relation that looks like it might be generated by a utility function) or tastes are similar enough for statistics of real national income to be usefully interpreted as pertaining to the welfare of the representative consumer. It is as though prices and quantities conformed to a utility function with a randomly distributed error term, as though the utility of the representative consumer were of the form

$$U = U(q_1, \ldots, q_n, u) \tag{1}$$

where u has a mean value of zero and some given variance. The reader should be warned that this is just an analogy, and that there is no real, immutable relation which is observed erroneously. Our model, like all models, does not quite fit the facts, and the question is whether it fits closely enough for practical purposes.

Do observed time series of prices and quantities conform closely enough to a function which could be interpreted as the utility function of the representative consumer to justify our use of this construction in interpreting and in modifying the national accounts in real terms? It is hard to say what constitutes 'closely enough'; for 'closely enough' is a matter of judgement and opinion. That there is some conformity is beyond dispute, for the whole of the corpus of empirical applications of the theory of demand can be interpreted as evidence for the existence of the representative consumer. Every demand curve that seems to fit the data, every price or income elasticity that comes out with the right sign is evidence for the proposition that the demand side of the economy can be usefully looked upon as a reflection of his behaviour. Even our doubts about the existence of the representative consumer have their counterpart in the theory of aggregation where it is shown conclusively that, strictly speaking, community demand curves do not and cannot exist, except under conditions that correspond more or less to the existence of a utility function of the representative consumer. The fact that these curves do exist in the sense that elasticities come out with the right sign, that prediction is sometimes possible and, what is particularly interesting from our point of view, that consumer surplus computed from such curves does not seem to be altogether meaningless, gives weight to our interpretation of real national income as a measure of his welfare.

B. WHAT WOULD IT COST IN THE BASE YEAR TO MAKE EACH MAN AS WELL OFF AS HE IS IN THE CURRENT YEAR?

Instead of asking the representative consumer how much income he would need in the base year to be as well off as he would be with the average income in the current year, we ask each man in the current year how much income he would need in the base year to be as well off as he himself was in the current year, and we add up the answers to get real income in the country as a whole. From here on, it will be convenient to alter our notation slightly. Instead of choosing specific years, such as 1961 and 1974, as the base year and the current year, we shall refer to the base year as 0 and to the current year as t, and we shall drop the term w from the expression representing real income, except when it is necessary to differentiate a welfare interpretation of real income from another interpretation altogether. Suppose there are N people in the community. For each man j, define $y^j(t, 0)$ to be the amount of money he would need in the base year 0 (that is, at prices in the year 0) to be as well off as he is in his circumstances in the current year t. Real national income per head is then defined as

$$Y(t, 0) = \frac{1}{N} \sum_{j=1}^{N} y^j(t, 0) \qquad (2)$$

This definition of real incomes dispenses entirely with the difficulties discussed in the preceding section over the correspondence of observed prices and quantities to something like a utility function for the community as a whole, for nothing in this definition requires such a function to exist. The bread and cheese example loses its force entirely. The welfare of bread-eaters and cheese-eaters, of rich and poor is always measurable as dollars of income in the base year. We have even dispensed with the representative consumer, though we could restore him by redefining the function $y^j(t, 0)$ to be the amount of money he would require in the base year to be as well off as he would be if he had the same income as Mr j in the current year. It may be advantageous to think of real income in this way to avoid having real income higher in one year than in another merely because of differences in the tastes of the inhabitants of the economy in the different years.

The main difficulty with this definition of real income is that it requires more information about the economy than we are likely to possess. The conceptual experiment with the income thermometer in the preceding chapter has to be conducted for each person individually, and the characteristics of his utility function need be accounted for in deciding what his real income $y^j(t, 0)$ is to be. We could simplify the process if we assumed every man's utility function to be the same, in which case it would be sufficient to know prices in the base year and in the current year, the distribution of money income in the current year, and the form of the supposedly common indirect utility function. One might introduce demographic weights to this function so that, for instance, a given level of utility to a child could be obtained with less expenditure than would be required to provide that level of utility for an adult. However, the introduction of a common utility function brings back many of the problems we hoped to avoid with this definition, for the only evidence we have is the time series of prices and quantities, and we would have to infer the form of the common utility function from these data, just as though we had postulated a representative consumer in the first place.

We can circumvent these problems if we are prepared to use a Laspeyres approximation, which is, in fact, as good an approximation for this definition of real income as it is for the definition based upon the representative consumer. Regardless of the form of his utility, each man's real income can be approximated as discussed in the preceding chapter by a Laspeyres index of the goods he consumes, and these individual indexes can be aggregated up to an index for the economy as a whole. We need not know the values of the individual indexes because the aggregation properties of the Laspeyres index number are such that the index for the economy as a whole is necessarily equal to the sum of the indexes for each person in the economy.[1]

[1] If $p_1(0), \ldots, p_m(0)$ are base year prices of the m goods consumed, and if Mr j consumes quantities $q^j_1(t), \ldots, q^j_m(t)$ in the year t, then each consumer's Laspeyres index of real income is

$$L^j(t, 0) \equiv \sum_{i=1}^{m} q^j_i(t)p_i(0)$$

The sum of these indexes for all consumers is

$$\sum_{j=1}^{N} L^j(t, 0) = \sum_{j=1}^{N} \sum_{i=1}^{m} q^j_i(t)p_i(0) = \sum_{i=1}^{m} q_i(t)p_i(0)$$

where $q_i(t)$ is total quantity consumed of the good i in the year t, and the right-hand expression is the Laspeyres index of real consumption for the economy as a whole.

A second difficulty with this definition is that the measure of real income for the economy as a whole can rise or fall with changes in the distribution of income. This might be a desirable characteristic if there were a systematic relation between the measure of real income and the degree of equality in the income distribution, but the effect of distribution in this instance is of an entirely different sort. The difficulty is best explained with the aid of a box diagram (see Figure 3.1). Again the goods are bread and cheese, amounts of which are measured as vertical and horizontal distances respectively. There are two consumers, A and B, and we draw their indifference curves from the southwest and

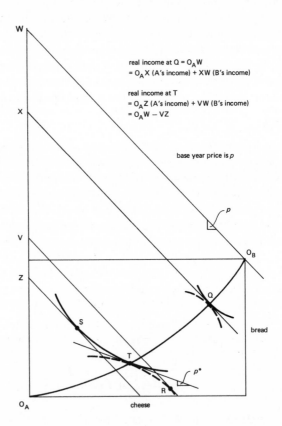

Figure 3.1 How the measure of real national income as the sum of the real incomes of every person may be affected by a Pareto optimal redistribution of goods

northeast corners of the box, the points labelled O_A and O_B respectively. The contract curve, the locus of all Pareto optimal allocations of bread and cheese between A and B is labelled $O_A Q O_B$. Ideally, our measure of real income should attribute the same real income to every point on the contract curve, and should attribute less real income to points off the contract curve because any such point is inferior for both parties to some point on the contract curve. Or, to put the matter in another way, we would like our measure of real income to be a function of quantities consumed per head, regardless of how quantities are distributed among people, provided only that the distribution is efficient in the normal sense of that term. The definition of real income we are examining in this section does not possess this property.

To represent real income on this diagram, we must know the distribution of bread and cheese between A and B, and we must choose a base year. The relevant characteristic of a base year on this diagram is not time, for the diagram is timeless; it is a reference price of cheese in terms of bread. Let the base year price be p, indicated on the diagram as the slope of the line $O_B W$. As a rule there will be some point on the contract curve at which the common rate of substitution of cheese for bread just happens to be equal to the base year price. Call that point Q. At Q, the real income of A with respect to bread as the numeraire is $O_A X$, the real income of B is XW, and their sum is $O_A W$ which is the value at base year prices of total quantities consumed.

What we would like our measure of real income to do—and what it does not do—is to show the same value, $O_A W$, of real income with respect to base year price p for any other point on the contract curve. Consider any other point T at which going price p^* differs from the base year price p. The real income of A is now $O_A Z$ (the income in units of bread that A would require, if the price were p instead of p^*, to be as well off as he is at T), the real income of B is VW, and their sum, $OZ + VW$, is less by an amount VZ than real income at Q. The simple economics of this disparity is that if the base year price of cheese is higher than the current price, a redistribution of income from bread-eaters to cheese-eaters will increase real national income because the extra income accruing to cheese-eaters is worth more at base year prices than the loss of income to the bread-eaters.

One should not make too much of this failing. It would, of course, be convenient to have a measure of real income invariant to movements along a contract curve, but we can get along without that property. In particular, it should be recognized that the definition of real income in this section as the sum of equivalent incomes at base year prices is well defined and free of internal contradiction. That it may be influenced by movements along the contract curve is unfortunate but not unbearable.

The definition of real income as the consumption of the representative consumer is both better and worse in its response to changes in the allocation of goods: better because all allocations on the contract curve count as the same amount of real income, worse because allocations off the contract curve also count as the same amount of real income when, ideally, they should count for less.

C. HOW MUCH WOULD IT COST IN THE BASE YEAR TO MAKE A MAN AS WELL OFF AS HE WOULD BE IF HE HAD AN EQUAL CHANCE OF OCCUPYING ANY POSITION IN THE ECONOMY IN THE CURRENT YEAR?

Imagine a comparison of real incomes between a society with a king who earns $100.00 and 99 serfs who earn $1.00 each, and a society of 100 equal citizens who earn $1.99 each. As long as there is no difference in price levels between the societies, their real national incomes as normally measured are equal because the total values of goods and services are the same. But one could argue that the national incomes ought not to be counted as equal because people are on average less well off in the first society than they are in the second. Disregard the class structure and consider only the incomes themselves. A risk averse person who could choose which society to live in and who would have an even chance of occupying any position in the society he chooses (that is, a 99% chance of having an income of $1.00 and a 1% chance of having an income of $100.00 if he chooses the first and a certainty of having an income of $1.99 if he chooses the second) would surely choose the second, for his expected utility would be higher there. As an example of a risk averse utility function, suppose the utility of $1 is 10, the utility of $1.99 is 15, and the utility of $100 is 25. Then the expected utility in the first society is $[(10 \times 99) + (25 \times 1)]/100$ equal to 10.5 while the expected utility in the second is 15.

In this section we redefine real national income so that incomes in two societies would only be the same if the representative consumer is indifferent between the prospect of having an equal chance of occupying any position in the first society and an equal chance of occupying any position in the second. Formally, we need to make two assumptions about the representative consumer. The first is that his utility in a risky situation is the expected value of the utilities in every possible outcome. Specifically,

$$U^c(t) = \frac{1}{N} \sum_{j=1}^{N} U^j(t) \tag{3}$$

where $U^c(t)$ is the certainty equivalent utility in the risky situation t, $U^j(t)$ is his utility in the event that the outcome is j, and there are N equally likely outcomes. The second assumption is that the utility of the representative consumer is a unique function of income at base year prices,

$$U = U(y) \quad U' > 0 \tag{4}$$

A negative second derivative of U would correspond to risk aversion on the part of the representative consumer, and a positive second derivative would imply a willingness to accept risk at worse than fair odds. With appropriate substitutions, we can write

$$U(y^c(t, 0)) = \frac{1}{N} \sum_{j=1}^{N} U(y^j(t, 0)) \tag{5a}$$

or

$$y^c(t, 0) = U^{-1}\left(\frac{1}{N} \sum_{j=1}^{N} U(y^j(t, 0))\right) \tag{5b}$$

which expresses certainty equivalent real income assessed at prices in the year 0 as a function of the incomes, $y^j(t,0)$ associated with each possible outcome j. On this definition, we can compute real income per head if we know the distribution of income in the current year and the utility function of the representative consumer inclusive of his behaviour toward risk.

There arises at this point a conundrum which is not unlike the cardinal–ordinal paradox discussed in the last chapter. So far we have defined real income as a measure of utility. Now, in equation (3), we define utility as a function of real income. How, it may be asked, can both definitions hold good at the same time? The solution to this conundrum lies, I think, in the realization that any monotonically increasing function of a utility function is a utility function as well. What we are talking about is a relation between equally valid representations of utility, one being dollars worth in the base year and the other being that monotonically increasing function of the first representation for which equation (3) holds, for which the consumer maximizes expected utility in risky situations. The point to keep in mind is that the ordinality of utility does not mean that you cannot attach precise numbers to the function; it means that you can do so too easily and in too many different ways. It turns out that the cardinalization appropriate to rationalize behaviour in risky circumstances is different from that appropriate for measuring real income of an individual or a representative consumer in dollars worth in the base year.

To show the significance of the distinction between average income and certainty equivalent income, we shall compare the implied rates of economic growth in Canada between the years 1964 and 1973 for which comparable data on the decile shares of income are readily available. The data are presented in Table 3.1, and three additional assumptions are required: that, within each decile, all incomes are equal; that the real income of each individual in 1961 dollars is adequately represented by the average income in 1961 dollars scaled up or down according to how his share of total income in the current year exceeds or falls short of the average (this assumption is not strictly true because the proportion between income in current dollars and real income in 1961 dollars would normally be different for the rich than for the poor); and, most important, that the elasticity of the marginal utility of income is constant. This last assumption enables us to rewrite equation (5) as

$$y^c(t, 0)^e = \frac{1}{N} \sum_{j=1}^{N} y^j(t, 0)^e \qquad (6)$$

where the parameter e is the elasticity of utility with respect to income. The representative consumer is risk averse if and only if $e < 1$, for in that case y^c will be less than the simple average value of y^j over the population as a whole. Actually, the interpretation of e as the elasticity of utility with respect to income only makes sense for values of $e > 0$, but equation (6) as a whole makes sense over the whole range of e from $-\infty$ to ∞. A value of e of $-\infty$ means that the representative consumer identifies the certainty equivalent income as the lowest value of y^j among all j, while a value of e of ∞ means that he identifies the certainty equivalent as the highest value of y^j among all j.

Table 3.1   Decile shares of total national income in Canada, 1965 and 1973

year	first	second	third	fourth	fifth	sixth	seventh	eighth	ninth	tenth	real income per head ($1961)
1965	1.21	3.23	5.08	6.69	8.27	9.68	11.23	13.26	15.99	25.36	2334
1973	1.02	2.82	4.48	6.23	7.97	9.68	11.49	13.66	16.61	26.04	3439

Source: The decile shares have been compiled by the Economic Council of Canada. Real income is defined here as the sum of consumption and saving converted to 1961 dollars by the national income deflator for consumption goods. [The number 1.21 in the top left-hand corner of the table means that the poorest 10% of the population consumes only 1.21% of total income, amounting to $282 per head in 1965.]

Our procedure now is to work out certainty equivalent incomes and rates of economic growth for alternative values of e and to suggest a conceptual experiment which would enable the reader to decide for himself which value of e is reasonable. The calculations are presented in Tables 3.2 and 3.3.

Table 3.2 Real income per head and rates of economic growth under alternative assumptions about risk aversion

	1965 (1961 dollars)	1973 (1961 dollars)	average rate of growth (% per year)
average income	2334	3439	4.84
lowest income	282	351	2.73
highest income	5919	8955	5.18

elasticity of utility with respect to income (e)	certainty equivalent income per head (1961 dollars) y^c		rate of economic growth (% per year)
	1965	1973	
∞	5919	8955	5.18
4	3562	5389	5.16
3	3214	4852	5.15
2	2805	4209	5.07
1.5	2579	3841	4.98
1	2334	3439	4.84
0.50	2066	2993	4.63
-0.50	1468	2005	3.90
-1	1183	1559	3.45
-2	784	990	2.91
-3	593	739	2.76
-4	499	621	2.73
$-\infty$	282	351	2.73

The data in Table 3.1 and in the top section of Table 3.2 show that economic growth as normally measured—the growth rate of average income per head—was 4.84% per year, but the distribution of income worsened so that the growth rate of incomes of people in the lowest decile was only 2.73% per year while the growth rate of people in the top decile was 5.18% per year. The bottom half of Table 3.2 shows certainty equivalent income, y^c (as assessed in accordance with equation (6) where the y^i are computed from the data in Table 3.1) growing between 2.73% and 5.18% as e, the elasticity of utility with respect to income, varies between $+\infty$ and $-\infty$. To put a value on e, the reader needs only to ask himself how large an income he would accept

Table 3.3 Certainty equivalents of equal chances of incomes of $10,000 and $20,000 for alternative values of the elasticity of utility with respect to income

elasticity of utility with respect to income (e)	certainty equivalent income ($ thousand) y^c
∞	20.0
4	17.1
3	16.5
2	15.8
1.5	15.4
1.0	15.0
0.5	14.6
-0.5	13.7
-1	13.3
-2	12.6
-3	12.1
-4	11.7
$-\infty$	10.0

as being equivalent to an equal chance of finding himself in each decile of the income distribution. The answer to that question is his value of y^c which may be used to compute his value of e from equation (6). Once his value of e is determined, the reader can select his assessment of the rate of economic growth from the bottom half of Table 3.2. But the calculation is complicated, and it is perhaps better to try to elicit one's value of e in an artificially simplified situation.

Imagine yourself having to choose your income for the rest of your life between two options. In the first option a fair coin is tossed, and you get $10,000 per year if it comes out heads or $20,000 per year if it comes out tails. In the second, you get an income of $x per year regardless of whether the coin comes up heads or tails. The example is set in terms of alternative streams of income for life to avoid complications that might otherwise arise from the possibility of borrowing to cover a shortfall of income in any particular year. Now ask yourself what value of x in the second option would leave you indifferent between these options. If x is $15,000, you are risk neutral and your value of $e = 1$; if x is less than $15,000 you are risk averse and your value of e is less than 1; if x exceeds $15,000 you enjoy risk and your value of e is greater than 1. The exact relation between x and e (computed from equation (6) where $N = 2$, $y^1 = 10,000$ and $y^2 = 20,000$) is presented in Table 3.3; for each value of e there is a corresponding value of y^c varying from a maximum of $20,000 when $e = \infty$ to a minimum of $10,000 when

$e = -\infty$. You can see from Table 3.3 that if you are indifferent between an equal chance of $10,000 and $20,000 and a certain income of, for instance $12,600, then your value of e is about -2.00, implying according to Table 3.2 that your assessment of the rate of economic growth in Canada from 1965 to 1973 is about 2.91% as compared with the usual measure of 4.84% for this period.

This example is intended to demonstrate that real income can, in principle, be measured as a certainty equivalent, but the actual numbers in Table 3.2 ought not to be taken very seriously if only because the inference we have drawn from Table 3.1 that the income distribution is worsening over time may be mistaken. The variance of the observed distribution of income may widen for reasons that have nothing to do with genuine inequality of income among people. The distribution of family income can widen because old people or young people become prosperous enough to form households apart from their children or parents, because married women enter the labour force, as the market compensates for the fact some commodities such as medicine are being provided in equal amounts to everyone by the state, or simply because of changes in the age distribution of the population. Despite the evidence we have presented, it may be that the dispersion of incomes corrected for family size, transfers, taxes and goods provided equally to everyone by the state has not widened for any particular age group.[2] It is the opinion of economists who have studied the Canadian income distribution in detail that the apparent widening over the last decade is wholly or partly spurious in the sense that inequality as we feel it ought to be measured has not worsened or has worsened less than Table 3.1 would suggest, and that statistics revised to account for institutional and demographic change would present a more satisfactory picture. Our adjustment to the measure of economic growth in Table 3.2 should be thought of as an exercise in method, and not as a statement about economic growth in Canada.

Nor have we any evidence to justify the assumption that the elasticity of utility with respect to income is the same for all values of income. It could, for instance, be negative at low incomes and positive at high incomes, or the relation between utility and income might be humped as is suggested by the Friedman–Savage hypothesis. In principle, the shape of the utility of income schedule could be discovered from a complicated series of questions of the same general type as those used to infer the value of e, and the resulting function, $U = U(y)$, could be used to compute certainty equivalents in accordance with equations (3) and (4).

---

[2] I am indebted for these warnings to Robin Rowley who supplied me with the data in Table 3.1.

It should also be noted that one's attitude to inequality may be what it is for selfish or altruistic reasons, and that we have been concerned with selfish reasons exclusively. Our representative consumer (if $e < 1$) evaluates a distribution of income at less than the mean because he would get more displeasure from having his income fall a given amount below the average than he would get pleasure from having his income rise the same amount above the average. But one may have an aversion to income inequality *per se*. One may be happier in a community of equals than one would be in a community of unequals, even if one is guaranteed the mean income in each case. Alternatively, one may be personally risk averse but prefer to live in a society with clear gradations of rank, status and income. These possibilities are not taken into account in our example.

Over and above these technical considerations—the uncertainty about the meaning of the distribution of income, the possibility that e is variable, and the distinction between selfish and altruistic concern for inequality—our attitude to this measure of economic growth should depend primarily on what we mean by economic growth. We may feel that our sense of the meaning of the term is captured by a measure of the certainty equivalent of an equal chance of enjoying each income in the current year. We may, on the other hand, feel that real income is one thing and its distribution is another; and that the two should be kept distinct, conceptually and in our measurements. Or, just as economic growth itself is a summary measure of changes that are of interest in their own right, so too may we wish to keep separate measures of the size of real income and of the distribution of income, but to try nonetheless to amalgamate these into a more comprehensive measure of welfare as a whole.

D. HOW MUCH WOULD IT COST PER PERSON IN THE BASE YEAR TO OBTAIN THE VALUE OF THE SOCIAL WELFARE FUNCTION THAT IS ATTAINED IN THE CURRENT YEAR?

Suppose we have a social welfare function

$$W = W(y^1, \ldots, y^N) \tag{7}$$

where y^j is the real income of the person j with respect to prices in the base year. As there is no obvious way of linking up all income recipients in different years (Mr Smith may have been present in 1965 and 1973, but Mr Jones was present only in 1965, and Mr Brown was present only in 1973), it is best to suppose that the welfare function is anonymous in the sense that its value is independent of a reordering of the arguments (that is, the value of W is unchanged if there is an interchange of incomes between Mr Smith with an income of \$15,000 and Mr Jones with an income of \$23,000), and that the value per head of the welfare function is independent of scale in the sense that a doubling of population leaves welfare per head unchanged if average income and the shape of the income distribution are invariant. Suppose also that the welfare function is biased toward equality in the sense that

$$W(\bar{y}, \ldots, \bar{y}) \geq W(y^1, \ldots, y^N) \tag{8}$$

where $\bar{y}$ is the average of the incomes $y^1, \ldots, y^N$, and the inequality holds strictly unless $y^1, \ldots, y^N$ are all equal.

Real income, Y, corresponding to the distribution of income $y^1, \ldots, y^N$, can now be defined as

$$Y = W^{-1}[W(y^1, y^2, \ldots, y^N)] \tag{9}$$

Analytically, the definition of real income in equation (9) is a generalization of the definition in equation (5) in the preceding section, and the social welfare function in equation (7) can be looked upon as a generalization of the expected utility hypothesis. The application of this concept of income requires, of course, that we identify someone, be he the general will, parliament, the planner, or God himself, to whom the overall welfare function applies. In the only attempt I know of to measure economic growth assessed by means of an imposed social welfare function, it was assumed that

$$W = \frac{\sum_{j=1}^{N} y^j W^j}{\sum_{j=1}^{N} W^j} \tag{10}$$

where W^j is a weighting set equal to 1 for the richest member of the community, 2 for the second richest and so on, down to N for the poorest member of the community. It is a simple matter to measure economic growth when real income is defined in accordance with equations (9) and (10) from the data shown in Table 3.2. As long as we maintain the assumption that there is complete equality of income within each decile class, the appropriate weights to be attached to incomes of each decile class are 9.5 for the poorest, 8.5 for the next, up to 0.5 for the highest decile. The effect of this welfare measure is to reduce the rate of economic growth by just under half of one per cent.

*

That completes our discussion of how the distribution of income and the diversity of taste among consumers might be accounted for in measuring real income and economic growth. From now on in the remainder of the book, we shall adhere to the simple definition of real income per head as the amount of money that makes the representative consumer as well off as he would be with the average bundle of goods consumed in the current year, and, where necessary, we shall identify prices in the current year as his rates of substitution in use. We are, therefore, keeping to the hard and fast distinction between the size of income and the distribution of income. We shall not attempt to impose a social welfare function onto the spectrum of incomes or to take account in any way of differences in taste among consumers or of special characteristics of the rich or the poor. We define income as we do for two reasons. On a theoretical plane, it does, I think, make sense to distinguish between the size of income and its distribution. The statement that 'real income has increased but its distribution has become more unequal', be it true or false in a given situation, is not nonsense. It is, therefore, reasonable to construct statistics to represent the size of real income, leaving distribution entirely aside. On an empirical plane, it has to be recognized that adequate time series of the distribution of money income are not available over long periods of time, that, with a few interesting exceptions, we cannot in practice account for differences in utility functions among consumers, and that allowance for changes in the distribution of income would complicate matters greatly when we come to consider real saving, imputations, quality change and other modifications to the circumstances in which real income is defined. We should not feel that our definition of income is inadequate merely because it is based on assumptions that are descriptively false. Any concept is embedded in a model, and all models falsify the world in some respects. The issue is whether a particular falsification is expedient for the problem at hand. Whether the assumption that there is a representative consumer is, in fact, expedient must be judged from its implications throughout the book.

NOTES FOR FURTHER READING

Much of the literature on the theory of how to measure the real income of a community of people has been devoted to a problem that is peripheral to our main concern. We know that an individual j is necessarily better off in the year t than he was in the year 0 if

$$\sum_{i=1}^{n} p_i(t)q_i^j(t) > \sum_{i=1}^{n} p_i(t)q_i^j(0)$$

That follows directly from equation (10) in the last chapter. The point at issue in this literature is whether and in what sense the same can be said for the economy as a whole, that is, whether the economy is 'better off' if the equation holds when all $q^j_i(t)$ and $q^j_i(0)$ are replaced by total quantities consumed. The starting point of the debate was J. R. Hicks', 'The Valuation of the Social Income', *Economica*, 1940, pp. 105–24. Other contributions were S. Kuznets, 'On the Valuation of Social Income-Reflections or Professor Hicks' Article', *Economica*, 1948, pp. 1–16 and pp. 116–31 (with Professor Hicks' comments on pp. 163–72), I. M. D. Little, 'The Valuation of the Social Income', *Economica*, 1949, pp. 11–26, and P. A. Samuelson, 'Evaluation of Real National Income', *Oxford Economic Papers*, 1950, pp. 1–29. Samuelson, summarizing the debate, shows that you cannot infer from the inequality that everyone is better off in the year t than in the year 0, that everyone could be made better off by a redistribution of goods and services, or even that everyone could be made better off by a combination of a shift in the composition of output in accordance with the given production possibility curve and a redistribution of the output of goods and services. It is proved in J. S. Chipman and J. C. Moore, 'Why an Increase in GNP Need Not Imply an Improvement in Potential Welfare', *Kyklos*, 1976, pp. 391–418, that the inequality is sufficient to guarantee that everyone could be made better off in year t than he was in year 0 if and only if utility functions are identical and homothetic. The argument surrounding Figure 3.1 is based, with modifications, on R. Boadway, 'The Welfare Foundation of Cost–Benefit Analysis', *Economic Journal*, 1974, pp. 926–36.

The idea that the representative consumer might be given an equal chance of being anybody in the economy he is to evaluate seems to have originated in J. C. Harsanyi, 'Cardinal Welfare, Individualistic Ethics, and Interpersonal Comparisons of Utility', *Journal of Political Economy*, 1955, pp. 309–21. It was brought to the forefront of current economic analysis after it was taken up in J. Rawls, *A Theory of Justice*, Harvard University Press, 1971. Equation (6) is really a variant of a measure of inequality introduced in A. B. Atkinson, 'On the Measurement of Inequality', *Journal of Economic Theory*, 1970, pp. 244–63. Its use in the measurement of economic growth was suggested to me by Wilfred Beckerman who uses a similar equation to impute for changes in the distribution of income in a study of economic growth in the OECD countries, *Measures of Leisure, Equality and Welfare*, OECD, 1978. Rankings of real incomes among the states of India have been computed using the weighting system in equation (10) in A. K. Sen, 'Real National Income', *Review of Economic Studies*, 1976, pp. 19–39.

The use of demographic weights in the construction of price indexes, measures of inequality and the estimation of demand relationships has been studied by J. Muellbauer in 'Inequality Measures: Prices and Household Composition', *Review of Economic Studies*, 1974, pp. 493–504 and 'Prices and Inequality, the United Kingdom Experience', *Economic Journal*, 1974, pp. 32–55.

4

Consumption: The Productive Capacity of the Economy

In Chapters 2 and 3 and in the remainder of this book, real income is looked upon as a measure of welfare exclusively. There was some discussion in Chapter 3 about whose welfare should be represented and about how to average welfare in a community, but it was taken as a starting point that welfare rather than some other property of the economy is to be reflected in the time series of real income. Not all national accounts and economists are inclined to look upon real income in this way. There is a substantial body of opinion that statistics of real income ought to reflect productive capacity instead. The purpose of a time series of real income is on this view to reflect the outward shift over time in the production possibility curve rather than the location of the indifference curve attained. In this chapter, we digress from our main theme to consider the productive capacity approach to the measurement of real income. We do so to explain why it has been advocated in the literature, to explain why it is not adopted in this book, and to clarify the welfare interpretation of real income by contrast with the alternative. In fact, there is no clear-cut, right or wrong choice to be made between these concepts. The choice depends in the end on what one wants to mean by real income and what the statistics are to be used for, as we shall see in our comparison of these concepts once real income as a measure of productive capacity has been formally defined.

A. THE DEFINITION OF REAL INCOME AS PRODUCTIVE CAPACITY

Figure 4.1 is a development of Figure 2.2; the taste or demand side of the economy is represented as an invariant set of indifference curves, and the production or supply side is represented as a production possibility curve which shifts outward in the course of time. Concentrate for a moment on the points K and L. The point K is the equilibrium in the year 1961, defined by the property that the production possibility curve T^{61} happens to be tangent to an indifference curve at that point. The point L is the comparable equilibrium for the year 1974. The

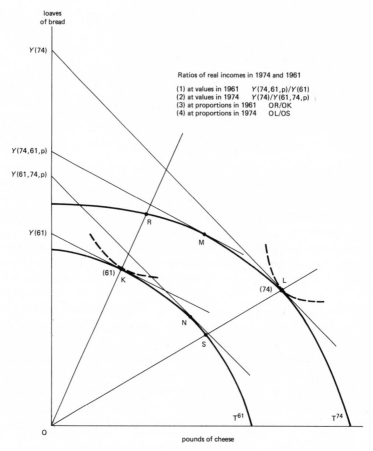

Figure 4.1 Real income as a measure of productive capacity

relative prices of cheese in 1961 and 1974 are p^{61} and p^{74}, illustrated as
the slopes of the common tangents of indifference curves and production possibility curves at K and L. Money incomes in the years 1961 and
1974, again with bread as the numeraire, are the projections of these
tangents onto the vertical axis at heights $Y(61)$ and $Y(74)$ above the
horizontal axis.

There are in fact two types of measures of real income as productive
capacity. Real income may be assessed at base year values or at base
year proportions between the goods produced. The first type is analogous to the welfare measures discussed in Chapter 2 with production
possibility curves playing the role of indifference curves in this derivation. Suppose 1961 is chosen as the base year. Real income in 1961 is
just $Y(61)$, for real income and money income in the base year are one

and the same as long as bread is the numeraire. Real income in 1974 is defined as the maximum value at base year prices of goods and services that could be produced in accordance with the production possibility curve T^{74}; it is the height of the intersection with the vertical axis of the tangent to the production possibility curve T^{74} with slope equal to the relative price of cheese in the base year. The point of tangency itself is M. Real income in 1974 is designated as $Y(74, 61, p)$ where the first argument refers to the year in which quantities are observed, the second refers to the prices at which quantities are converted to income, and the letter p in the third place is mnemonic for productivity. Similarly with 1974 as the base year, the real incomes in 1961 and 1974 are designated as $Y(61, 74, p)$ and $Y(74)$. Note that real incomes in 1961 and 1974, each with respect to itself as base year, could have been designated as $Y(61, 61, p)$ and $Y(74, 74, p)$. The ratio of real incomes in 1974 and 1961 is $Y(74, 61, p)/Y(61)$ when 1961 is the base year, and is $Y(74)/Y(61, 74, p)$ when 1974 is the base year. These definitions are easily extended from 2 to N commodities, and a time series of real income with respect to any given base year can be constructed for any number of years.

Like the measure of real income as welfare, the measure of real income as productive capacity may be approximated by a Laspeyres index, but the direction of bias is opposite because of the opposite curvatures of indifference curves and production possibility curves. With 1961 as the base year, the relation among the index of real income as welfare, the index of real income of productive capacity, and the Laspeyres index is

$$\frac{Y(74, 61, w)}{Y(61, 61, w)} \le \frac{\sum_{i=1}^{N} p_i^{61} q_i^{74}}{\sum_{i=1}^{N} p_i^{61} q_i^{61}} \le \frac{Y(74, 61, p)}{Y(61, 61, p)} \tag{1}$$

The first of these inequalities has already been established in Chapter 2. To establish the second, observe that the denominators of all three ratios are the same, for they are all equal to $Y(61)$ which is the money income in 1961 with bread as the numeraire. Now it only remains to show that $\sum_{i=1}^{N} p_i^{61} q_i^{74} \le Y(74, 61, p)$. This follows from the fact that $Y(74, 61, p)$ is the highest of all projections from T^{74} onto the vertical axis at the slope representing the relative price of cheese in 1961. Look at Figure 4.1 again. The value of $\sum_{i=1}^{N} p_i^{61} q_i^{74}$ is the projection, not shown, at the point L onto the vertical axis by a line with slope equal to p^{61}. Clearly, from the curvature of T^{74}, it follows that the point M is above this line so that $Y(74, 61, p)$ must be greater than $\sum_{i=1}^{N} p_i^{61} q_i^{74}$, establishing the second inequality in equation (1). Comparable results are easily established for the case where 1974 is chosen as the base year. We could go on to identify the difference between the values of $Y(74, 61, p)$ and $\sum_{i=1}^{N} p_i^{61} q_i^{74}$ as a measure of producers' surplus, just as we identified consumer's surplus in equation (10) of Chapter 2, but the demonstration is straightforward and we will not have occasion to use that fact in the rest of the book.

The other type of measure of real income as productive capacity is simpler to define but less analogous to the welfare measure developed in Chapter 2. The question to be answered by the measure is: What multiple of output in the base year could be produced in the current year? Output in 1961 consists of amounts of bread and cheese as indicated by the point K. All bundles of bread and cheese in the same proportion are indicated as points on the ray through the point K; above K more bread and cheese are produced, below K less bread and cheese are produced. The amounts of bread and cheese in this proportion that could be produced in accordance with the production possibility curve in the year 1974 are indicated by the point R, which is the intersection of this curve with the ray through K. The ratio of real incomes with respect to proportions of bread and cheese produced in 1961 is therefore OR/OK. The corresponding ratio when 1974 is the base year is OL/OS. These ratios can also be approximated by Laspeyres indexes, and the direction of the bias can be inferred from the curvature of production possibility curves.

B. HOW WE CHOOSE BETWEEN WELFARE AND PRODUCTIVE CAPACITY MEASURES OF REAL INCOME

It may not matter for some purposes whether real income is thought of as welfare or as productive capacity because both may be approximated by a Laspeyres index and because the Laspeyres index is more or less representative (at this level of generality) of the statistical procedure used to construct the time series of real income in the national accounts. The national accountant can get on with his day to day work without having to bother much about what he is 'really' measuring. We cannot adopt so agnostic a stance because our object is not to measure real income according to established rules but to explain why the rules are what they are and to suggest how they might be modified. To identify real income in the first instance as what is no more than a convenient approximation would be like trying to aim without a target, and would cut us off from the possibility of improvement. We need a clear objective when we try to construct a better approximation than the

Laspeyres index in Chapter 9 and when we extend the definition of real income to impute for leisure and other aspects of the environment in Chapter 7.

We could try to construct two parallel families of measurements of real income, one as welfare and the other as productive capacity. I have not done so, partly because it would be cumbersome but primarily because the welfare concept is what I choose to mean by real income and, I think, what is most often meant when statistics of real income are used in economic analysis. In the remainder of this chapter, the two concepts of real income are compared to show how they differ in their implications about economic growth and how they hold up when we pass from the simple model in which they are both well defined to more complex and realistic situations.

(1) The productive capacity concept avoids interpersonal comparisons of utility. All of the difficulties discussed in the last chapter associated with the identity of the representative consumer and the precise nature of the conceptual experiment to which he is subjected are obviously overcome if we can define real income as a property of the technology of the economy.

(2) There is no unique production possibility curve for final goods and services. Imagine a closed economy with an eastern province where all the cheese is produced, a western province where all the bread is produced, and a trucking industry to bring cheese to western consumers and bread to eastern consumers. The production possibility curve for bread, cheese and transport is illustrated in Figure 4.2. Note particularly that the production possibility curve for bread and cheese alone is a slice of the three-dimensional production possibility curve taken parallel to the bread–cheese axis at a distance reflecting resources devoted to transport, and that the amount of transport required depends on the volume of trade which in turn depends on how well easterners like bread and westerners like cheese. No resources need be devoted to transport if all cheese is consumed in the east and all bread is consumed in the west. Resources devoted to transportation will be at a maximum if all cheese is consumed in the west and all bread is consumed in the east.

It follows at once that the size of real income in this economy is not a property of its technology alone but is taste dependent, even when real income is defined in the first instance as an indicator of productive capacity. The reason is that real income includes only final goods and services, bread and cheese but not transport, so that any change in demand for transport affects real income accordingly. Real income increases if there is a change in taste in the west in favour of bread or in the east in favour of cheese. It is influenced by the changes in the distribution of income if, for instance, the rich in the east and in the west

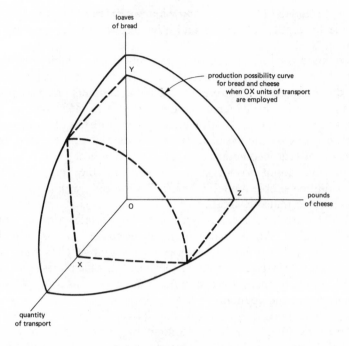

Figure 4.2 The production possibility frontier for bread, cheese, and transport

tend to consume the same proportion of bread and cheese while the poor in each region tend to consume disproportionate amounts of the local product. Thus, where transport is important, we cannot define the relevant production possibility curve as a property of technology alone and many of the problems we encountered in trying to define real income as welfare are with us again. There is some question in my mind about the empirical significance of the influence of the distribution of income and of changes in taste upon the location of the production possibility curve. I suspect that the problem is less acute for the productive capacity concept of income than for the welfare concept of income.

(3) The productive capacity concept of real income can be extended in a simple way to include investment goods as well as consumption goods. Consider Figure 4.1 again. The definition of real income as productive capacity at base year values or at base year proportions would be exactly the same if we had labelled the horizontal axis tractors instead of cheese, for real income, on this definition, depends on how much is produced rather than on what the output is used for. The indifference curves, on the other hand, would lose their meaning if the

horizontal axis were changed from cheese to tractors because utility is defined to be a function of consumption goods alone, and real income as welfare would have to be defined in a roundabout way if it could be defined at all.

Discussion of this issue is best postponed until the next chapter which is devoted entirely to the problem of extending the definition of real income from a world where all output is consumed in the current year to a world where output consists of investment goods as well as consumption goods. It is shown there that the extension of the productive capacity concept of income to investment goods, while simple and straightforward, may be inexpedient because an outward shift of the production possibility may not in that case represent an improvement in the circumstances or opportunities of the average consumer.

(4) Only the welfare concept of real income can be extended in a natural way to account for the appearance of new kinds of goods and services. Suppose a new commodity, the television for instance, is invented between 1961 and 1974. The production possibility curve in 1961 is

$$T^{61}(q_{bread}, q_{cheese}) = 0 \qquad (3)$$

and the production possibility curve in 1974 is

$$T^{74}(q_{bread}, q_{cheese}, q_{TV}) = 0 \qquad (4)$$

where q_{TV} is the quantity of television sets consumed.

The impact of the invention of the television upon the measure of real income would depend critically upon whether the base year occurs before or after the invention. In the former case the price of television sets would not be included among the set of base year prices (television sets could not be priced because they could not be made at all) and real income in the year 1974 would have to be evaluated in accordance with the amounts of bread and cheese that could be produced if there was no output of television sets, a procedure that could easily show real income in 1974 to be smaller than real income in 1961 despite the fact that all consumers would prefer the bundle of goods produced in 1974 to the bundle of goods produced in 1961. Even in the latter case where television sets are priced in the base year, the productive capacity measure of real income in 1961 may turn out to be greater than the productive capacity measure of real income in 1974 because of the greater capacity to make bread and cheese in 1961 and despite the fact that all consumers are better off in 1974.

In principle, there is no comparable problem of welfare measurement because newly invented goods can be evaluated in accordance with tastes in the base year even if they cannot be produced at any cost. If television sets are available in 1974 but not in 1961, then real income as a measure of welfare in 1974, the term $Y(74, 61, w)$, is defined indirectly by the equation

$$U(Y(74, 61, w), p_{bread}^{61}, p_{cheese}^{61}) = U(Y(74), p_{bread}^{74}, p_{cheese}^{74}, p_{TV}^{74}) \quad (5)$$

where it is understood that $Y(74, 61, w)$ can only be used to buy bread and cheese while $Y(74)$, the actual money in the year t, can be used to buy bread, cheese and television sets. Similarly, if television sets were for some reason available in 1961 but not in 1974 and if the base year continues to be 1961, then real income as a measure of welfare in 1974 is defined indirectly by the equation

$$U(Y(74, 61, w), p_{bread}^{61}, p_{cheese}^{61}, p_{TV}^{61}) = U(Y(74), p_{bread}^{74}, p_{cheese}^{74}) \quad (6)$$

where it is understood that $Y(74, 61, w)$ can be used to buy bread, cheese and television sets while $Y(74)$ can only be used to buy bread and cheese. The difference between the welfare and productivity measures lies in the fact that a representative consumer can evaluate any bundle of goods regardless of whether or not all of the bundle can be produced. The productive capacity concept is less flexible and less adaptive than the welfare concept as we move out of our simple bread and cheese economy because there is no fundamental conceptual experiment to guide us in a wide range of conditions.

(5) Only the welfare concept of real income can be extended to account for technically dissimilar goods that are close substitutes in use. Suppose that wheat is the only good produced, that different varieties of wheat are produced in 1961 and 1974, that the variety grown in 1961 will not grow in 1974, that the variety grown in 1974 will not grow in 1961, and that the varieties are perfect substitutes in use. If we designate 1961 to be the base year, we should have to say that the productive capacity measure of real income in 1974 is zero, that there is no real income in 1974, because there is no output of the only good that is priced in 1961. Similarly, if we designate 1974 to be the base year we should have to say that the productive capacity measure of real income in 1961 is zero, that there is no real income in 1961, because there is no output of the only good that is priced in 1974. Strictly speaking, the productivity measure of real income in any year should be very low if the economy in that year were not geared up to produce the sorts of goods that were produced in the base year, regardless of what else can be produced. In practice, of course, we could agree to treat similar

goods as though they were the same good. If biologically different varieties of wheat are grown in 1961 and 1974, and if the varieties are interchangeable in use, we could treat the two varieties as one good in the evaluation of real income. We would not do the same for all possible varieties of mushrooms, though varieties may be as similar biologically and as close substitutes in production as varieties of wheat.

The principle beneath this example is that the identification of similar goods as one good for the purpose of measuring real income as an indicator of productive capacity is not an aspect of technology. It is an aspect of taste or utility incorporated surreptitiously at the stage in the process of measurement where quantity data are being prepared for incorporation into our index number formulae. In practice, we can rarely if ever compare the productivities of two economies without introducing considerations of taste or demand at some stage of the analysis. What passes as a measure of productive capacity is always a hybrid between technology and taste. Taste, on the other hand, may stand alone. Output changes over long periods of time, not only in the proportions consumed of the different commodities, but in the commodities themselves. It is as though output in 1961 consisted of bread and cheese and output in 1974 consisted of lettuce and meat, with bread and cheese being prohibitively expensive in 1974 and lettuce and meat being prohibitively expensive in 1961. In this extreme case there is no basis for comparison of productive capacity and no way for deciding which of the two production possibility curves constitutes the greater real output. Nevertheless, the representative consumer can be sent from one economy to another and he can be expected to tell us how much money he would need in the base year to be as well off as he would be in any other time or place.

(6) The welfare concept of income tends to be compatible with statistics of social indicators. It is easier and more natural to compare the growth of income as a flow of goods and services with changes over time in indicators of leisure, mortality rates, environmental conditions and the like, if income is a measure of welfare than it if is a measure of productivity. This point is discussed in Chapter 10.

(7) The utility function, if it exists at all, is more amenable to measurement than the sequence of production possibility curves because the utility function remains invariant over time while the production possibility curve can change its shape substantially from year to year. The complete time series of prices and quantities of all goods consumed is in principle consistent with a single set of indifference curves, the shapes of which are reflected to a degree of approximation whenever we construct a set of demand curves for all commodities at once. But we have only one observation of prices and quantities for each

production possibility curve, and there is no reason for believing that the process of technical change which pushes out the production possibility from one year to the next does so in a systematic fashion. This year there is an improvement in bread production. Next year there is an improvement in cheese production. Each improvement extends the frontier, but its slope at any proportion between outputs of bread and cheese may change this way or that in an entirely unpredictable fashion. There is, in other words, every reason to believe that the supply curves will be unstable even in circumstances where the demand functions are stable. It is therefore extremely difficult to predict the locations of points like N, S, M or R on Figure 4.1. Unlike indifference curves, production possibility curves may even cross, in which case real income may increase with respect to one base year and decrease with respect to another. Welfare and productive capacity measures of real income are different in this respect. A change in the base year may affect the rate of growth of real income as welfare, but it cannot reverse the sign, turning growth to decline or vice versa.

(8) One's own concept of real income can be discovered by examining cases where real income as welfare increases and real income as productive capacity declines. Suppose, as illustrated on Figure 4.3, that the production possibility curve shifts outward from 1961 to 1974 so that real income as productive capacity has unambiguously increased.

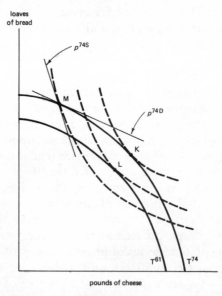

Figure 4.3 An example of how real income as a measure of welfare may decrease despite the increase in real income as a measure of productive capacity

Suppose also that the outward shift in the production possibility curve coincides with the introduction of a distortion into the economy; the demand price in 1974 exceeds the supply price, $p^{74D} > p^{74S}$, and output is at M where the quantity of cheese demanded at p^{74D} equals the quantity supplied at p^{74S} rather than at K where utility is maximized. The distortion is assumed to be so marked that the indifference curve through M lies below the indifference curve through L, where L represents quantities consumed in 1961. As the figure is drawn the equilibrium output M is on the surface of the production possibility curve T^{74}, but it could be below, as would be the case if the distortions were in the factor market rather than in the product market. This would make no difference to the example, the essence of which is that the economy is on a lower indifference curve in 1974 despite the fact that the production possibility curve in 1974 is unambiguously superior. What do we want to say about real income in this case? Do we want to say that real income has increased but that people are worse off nonetheless or do we want to say that real income has declined despite the improvement in productive capacity? I am inclined to think that most people would say the latter. We often speak of real income increasing because resources are being deployed more efficiently. We certainly speak of real income declining as labour and other factors of production become unemployed. Be that as it may, the reader is not logically compelled to prefer one definition over the other, and each man weighing the pros and cons of the two definitions may choose as he thinks best. I choose to discuss the welfare measure in the remainder of this book.

NOTES FOR FURTHER READING

The distinction between the welfare and productive capacity, demand and supply, interpretations of real income was first proposed in J. R. Hicks, 'The Valuation of Social Income', *Economica*, 1940, pp. 105–24. The starting point of Hicks' analysis was the controversy between Colin Clark and A. L. Bowley as to whether money income ought to be measured at market prices or at factor cost. Hicks argued that valuation at market prices is appropriate when income is looked upon as an indicator of economic welfare, and that valuation at factor cost is appropriate when income is looked upon as an indicator of the productivity of the economy. He defined an improvement in productivity to be an outward shift of the production possibility curve and he defined an improvement in economic welfare to be a movement to a higher indifference curve. The concept of real income as productive capacity has been developed and advocated by R. Moorstein ('On Measuring Productive Potential and Relative Efficiency', *Quarterly Journal of Economics*, 1961, pp. 451–66) and by A. Bergson (*The Real National Income of Soviet Russia since 1928*, Cambridge, Harvard University Press, 1961, Chapter III, pp. 25–41). It is also discussed in F. M. Fisher and K. Shell, *The Economic Theory of Price Indices*, Academic Press, 1972.

Many national accountants have advocated the productive capacity interpretation of real income because they feel that aggregate welfare is too soft a foundation for the national accounts in real terms. See particularly, E. F. Denison, 'Welfare Measurement and the G.N.P.', *Survey of Current Business*, 1971, pp. 1–9; A. M. Okun, 'Should the G.N.P. Measure Social Welfare?', *The Brookings Bulletin*, **8,** No. 3, Summer 1971, pp. 4–7; F. T. Juster, 'A Framework for the Measurement of Economic and Social Performance', in M. Moss (ed.), *The Measurement of Economic and Social Performance*, National Bureau of Economic Research, 1973, pp. 25–84, and G. Jaszi's comments on the above on pp. 84–99.

5

Investment

Return now to the original problem as posed in the introduction. Suppose that the national accounts as we know them did not exist and we are trying to construct time series of a statistic, which we choose to call real income, to reflect the economic progress of countries over long periods of time. In constructing the series, we must take account of the fact that goods and services have different temporal status. Some goods are intended to be consumed as soon as they are produced. Other goods contribute to consumption in the future or steadily over long periods of time. Our problem in this chapter is how to deal with goods of the latter sort, how, that is, to define real income inclusive of investment and consumption. The essence of the problem is to specify a function, comparable to the utility function in the definition of real consumption, such that statistics of real income may be designed to reflect the value of function and the function itself reflects whatever desirable objective we have in mind when we say that real income has increased.

In this chapter we develop two related propositions. The first is that real investment is a genus with many species and subspecies. This should not be surprising. If the simple concept of real consumption has two species, welfare and productive capacity, may not the complex concept of real investment have even more? We shall identify four main species which we shall call: (i) increase in real wealth; (ii) output of new capital goods; (iii) increase in real capital; and (iv) real saving; reserving the term real investment to refer to all of these concepts collectively, to the genus as a whole. We shall study each of these species of real investment one by one, comparing their properties and their suitability to serve in a measure of economic growth.

The second proposition, which is contentious, is that of all these species of real investment the most appropriate for our purposes is real saving, defined as the alternative cost of investment in units of consumption goods forgone. This proposition is contentious because the statistical routine it implies differs from the practice in the national accounts. Real investment is measured in the national accounts by deflating the money value of investment each year by a price index of investment goods themselves, just as though investment goods were a second type of consumption goods. Real saving, on the other hand, is measured by deflating the value of investment by the price index of consumption goods. It should be borne in mind, however, that to allege real saving to be the most appropriate concept for the purpose of measuring economic growth is not to allege it best for all purposes. A case can be made that other species of real investment are better for short or medium term forecasting of the economy, for budgeting, or for the study of business cycles. All we are asserting is that real saving is best for inclusion in a definition of real income for charting the progress of an economy over long periods of time.

To speak of economic growth—not just as a mix of events, but as something that can be represented as the growth rate of a single variable—is to look upon the economy through the distorting lens of a one-sector model. Let us consider that model for a moment. In its simplest form, it consists of a production function

$$Y = f(K, L) \tag{1}$$

where Y is income measured in loaves of bread, K is capital measured as a number of machines that last forever, and L is the labour force assumed to be constant; an identity

$$Y = C + S \tag{2}$$

where consumption C and savings S are both measured as loaves of bread; a production function for capital goods

$$pM = S \tag{3}$$

where M is output of new capital goods and p, the price of capital goods, is constant; a growth-of-capital equation

$$\dot{K} = M \tag{4}$$

where, of course, K and L are stocks and $\dot{K}$, M, S, C and Y are flows; and an intemporal utility functional

$$U = U(C(t)) \tag{5}$$

that guides the representative consumer in his choice of C at each moment of time. The representative consumer selects a time path of $C(t)$ to maximize U in equation (5) subject to equations (1) and (4) as constraints. From the time path of C we can compute his wealth with regard to current consumption as the numeraire

$$W = \int_0^\infty C(t)e^{-r(t)t}\, dt \tag{6}$$

where 0 is the present and $r(t)$ is the subjective rate of discount of the representative consumer over the period from 0 to t; the function $r(t)$ is defined indirectly from equation (5) as follows

$$\left.\frac{dC(t)}{dC(0)}\right|_U = e^{-r(t)t} \tag{7}$$

We may now define economic growth as the rate of appreciation of Y/L. It follows as a matter of arithmetic that economic growth can only be sustained, that Y/L can only increase at a constant rate, if at least one of the functions in equations (1) and (3) is allowed to change over time, that is, if f in equation (1) if a function of time or p in equation (3) steadily declines. This point will be important later on in the chapter and especially in Chapter 12, but we ignore it for the moment.

The four main species of investment in real terms are associated with properties which hang together as long as we remain within the one-sector model of equations (1) to (5) but which go their separate ways, each giving rise to distinct definitions of real investment and real income, in the more complex models to be discussed below. Real income can equally well be looked upon as:

(i)   Maximum sustainable consumption: the amount that can be consumed this year consistent with the community being as well off at the end of the year as it was at the beginning—the maximum C such that $\dot{W} = 0$.

(ii) A measure of total output: the value at constant prices of the output of consumption goods and capital goods together—$C + pM$.

(iii) The value at constant prices of consumption and the increase in the size of the capital stock during the year—$C + p\dot{K}$.

(iv) Potential consumption: the value at constant prices of actual consumption and consumption forgone in the process of investment—$C + S$.

The corresponding measures of investment are $\dot{W}$, pM, $p\dot{K}$, and S which are equal only as long as we remain within the one-sector model. In the more complex model to follow, time series of $\dot{W}$ and pM, for instance, may change at different rates at any given time, obliging us to choose among the alternative definitions of income and investment in real terms, retaining what we consider the most important property for the purpose at hand and reluctantly discarding the rest.

How do we choose among the alternative definitions? Ultimately, as in the choice between welfare and productive capacity interpretations of real consumption, we must simply decide what we want the term to mean; we must decide which among the definitions captures most of what we want the time series of real income to tell us about the progress of the economy. We can, however, facilitate the choice by comparing properties and implications of the different definitions, so that we will know what our choice really entails. We shall study these definitions individually, but before we do so, we state the criteria on which they will be compared and outline a more complex intertemporal model within which the different concepts of real investment may be separately and distinctly defined.

The definitions will be compared on the following criteria.

(1) What information does the measurement of real investment require? Is it information readily available in or shortly after the current year? Does the information pertain to functions that are in principle observable in the current year but are in fact difficult to observe? Or does the information pertain to events that may or may not occur in the future, so that only a prophet could measure real investment accurately?

(2) What is the effect on the measure of real investment of anticipated technical change? Does technical change affect real income when it is first anticipated? Does technical change affect real income when, and only when, it results in increased production of consumption goods? Or does technical change affect real income frivolously in the sense that changes with the same effect on the time stream of consumption may get incorporated in income in different years depending on irrelevant characteristics of the technology of the economy?

(3) What counts as an investment? Need an investment result in a tangible asset at the end of the year? Or is it sufficient to be counted as investment that an expenditure be designed to increase future consumption in some direct or roundabout way?

(4) Can one be sure that a positive investment makes the representative consumer better off tomorrow than he is today?

(5) Does the definition of real investment supply a clear guide to the statistician as to how it ought to be measured?

(6) Does the choice of the base year have a major influence upon the time series of real investment and real income?

(7) Is the magnitude of real income in any given year independent, in a fully employed economy, of the behaviour of consumers in their choice between consumption and investment? We would like to think of real income in any year as a constant amount to be divided as one pleases between consumption goods and investment goods. This property holds for some species of investment but not for others.

Table 5.1 summarizes the analysis to follow and shows how the different definitions of real investment perform in the light of this list of criteria. Actually we consider five definitions of real investment because the third on our original list, the increase in the capital stock, subdivides into two definitions with somewhat different properties. The reader is warned that the assignment of characteristics to definitions of real investment is to some extent arbitrary, and that his judgement about the characteristics of the different definitions may differ from my own in a few cases. The choice of the characteristics themselves is, of course, arbitrary, though it seems to capture most of what authors in the fields of capital theory and the national accounts consider important when they advocate this or that definition. The meaning of some of these charac-

Table 5.1 A comparison of the characteristics of alternative definitions of real investment

species of real investment / characteristics	(i) the increase in wealth	(ii) the output of new capital goods	(iii) the increase in the capital stock — instantaneous capital stock	long run capital stock	(iv) real saving
(1) information					
(a) readily available					√
(b) available in principle		√	√		
(c) not available in the current year	√			√	
(2) affected by technical change					
(a) when anticipated	√				
(b) when consumption increased					√
(c) frivolous		√	√	√	
(3) scope of investment					
(a) tangible assets only		√	√	√	
(b) forward-looking expenditure	√				√
(4) necessarily associated with improvement in welfare?	yes	no	no	no	no in one sense, yes in another
(5) relatively free from influence of statistical judgement?	no	no	no	no	yes
(6) free from excessive dependence on choice of the base year?	yes	yes	no	no	yes
(7) the measure of income independent of behaviour of consumers?	no	no	no	no	no

teristics—notably (5), (6), (7)—may not yet be entirely evident, but it will become so when we examine the definitions in detail.

We now set out an intertemporal model in which the different definitions of real income may be compared. The representative consumer chooses a stream of consumption commencing immediately and continuing into the indefinite future. In the year t, he maximizes

$$U(u(C^t), u(C^{t+1}), \ldots, u(C^{t+\tau}), \ldots) \tag{8}$$

where U is intertemporal utility and u is annual utility. The utility function U is maximized subject to the constraint of a sequence of annual technologies

$$f^\tau(C^\tau, M^\tau) = g^\tau(K^\tau, L^\tau) \quad \tau = t, t+1, t+2, \ldots \tag{9}$$

$$K^{\tau+1} - K^\tau = M^\tau - \zeta K^\tau \tag{10}$$

where the function f may be thought of as the production possibility curve and g may be thought of as the production function, and C, M, K and L are vectors;

$$C^\tau \equiv \{q_1^\tau, \ldots, q_n^\tau\} \tag{11}$$

is a vector of outputs of the n types of consumption goods consumed in the year τ;

$$M^\tau \equiv \{m_1^\tau, \ldots, m_s^\tau\} \tag{12}$$

is a vector of outputs of the s types of capital goods in the year τ;

$$K^\tau \equiv \{k_1^\tau, \ldots, k_s^\tau\} \tag{13}$$

is a vector of stocks of the s types of capital goods available during the year τ;

$$L^\tau \equiv \{l_1^\tau, \ldots, l_r^\tau\} \tag{14}$$

is a vector of the amounts of r types of labour available during the year τ; the vectors K^t and L^t are given for the year t; the labour force L^τ remains constant over time; and ζ is a diagonal matrix of rates of depreciation on the s types of capital goods. The technologies f^τ and g^τ are made dependent on τ to allow for the possibility of technical change. By substituting equations (10) to (14) into equation (9), the supply side of the economy can be condensed into an intertemporal production possibility curve

$$T(C^t, C^{t+1}, \ldots, C^{t+\tau}, \ldots) = 0 \qquad (15)$$

and the whole economy can then be looked upon as though the representative consumer chooses time streams of the different consumption goods to maximize his intertemporal utility curve of equation (8) subject to the constraint of his intertemporal production possibility curve of equation (15).

This model incorporates a very general specification of technical change. The dependence of the functions f^s and g^τ on time means that these functions can shift in any way whatsoever in the course of time. But we maintain the assumptions of the simple model of equations (1) to (5): (a) that the future is known with certainty; and (b) that the nature of goods remains constant over time. In what follows we shall have to consider the implications of relaxing both of these assumptions, for definitions of real investment that might be quite satisfactory if these assumptions held may turn out very badly when they do not.

A. REAL INVESTMENT DEFINED AS THE CHANGE IN WEALTH OVER THE YEAR

Of all the definitions we shall consider, this is the best in theory and the worst in practice, where the distinction between theory and practice turns on what can be measured to a reasonable degree of accuracy and what cannot. Wealth is the intertemporal analogue of consumption. Suppose the future is known with certainty as postulated in the model of equations (8) to (14). The money value of wealth in the year t is

$$W(t) = \sum_{\tau=0}^{\infty} \sum_{i=1}^{n} p_i^{t,\tau} q_i^{t+\tau} \qquad (16)$$

where $q_i^{t+\tau}$ is the quantity of the good i consumed in the year $t + \tau$, and $p_i^{t,\tau}$ is its forward price defined by the relation

$$p_i^{t,\tau} = D^{t,\tau} p_i^{t+\tau} \qquad (17)$$

where $p_i^{t+\tau}$ is the spot price of the good i in the year $t + \tau$ and D is a discount factor such that

$$D^{t,\tau} = \frac{1}{1 + r^{t+1}} \frac{1}{1 + r^{t+2}} \cdots \frac{1}{1 + r^{t+\tau}} \qquad (18)$$

and r^{t+i} is the one year rate of discount on money between the year $t + i - 1$ and the year $t + i$, defined as in equation (7) with the appropriate adjustment for the difference in initial and terminal dates over which interest in computed.

Real wealth could be defined analogously to real income in Chapter 2 as the minimum amount of money required at base year prices (including forward prices in this case) to make the representative consumer as well off as he would be with the actual time path of consumption goods. Set the year 0 as the base year. Real wealth would then be

$$W(t, 0) = \min \sum_{\tau=0}^{\infty} \sum_{i=1}^{n} p_i^{0,\tau} \bar{q}_i^{t+\tau} \qquad (19)$$

such that $U(\bar{q}_i^{t+\tau}) = U(q_i^{t+\tau})$ where the minimization process consists of choosing the cheapest time stream of consumption goods $\bar{q}_i^{t+\tau}$ at base year prices that yields as much satisfaction in the long run as the actual time stream of consumption goods, and where $p_i^{0,\tau}$ is the forward price of the good i taken τ years ahead of the base year 0 rather than of the present year t as was done in the definition of the money value of wealth in equation (16). But it is convenient for our purposes to consider what might be called the Laspeyres approximation to real wealth

$$W(t, 0, \mathrm{L}) = \sum_{\tau=0}^{\infty} \sum_{i=1}^{n} p_i^{0,\tau} q_i^{t+\tau} \qquad (20)$$

which differs from the true measure of real wealth by the substitution of actual quantities $q_i^{t+\tau}$ for the hypothetical quantities $\bar{q}_i^{t+\tau}$ in equation (19).

We must be exceedingly careful about timing. Let it be assumed that wealth each year is assessed on 1 January but that consumption takes place on 31 December. We make this assumption to ensure that the formulae which will be derived from a model with discrete units of time come out as though we had used a continuous model, and to avoid having to discount units of consumption occurring at different times within the current year. Note that the Laspeyres measure of this year's wealth may be defined as this year's consumption plus the discounted value of next year's wealth, i.e.

$$W(t, 0, \mathrm{L}) = \sum_{i=1}^{n} p_i^0 q_i^t + \sum_{\tau=1}^{\infty} \sum_{i=1}^{n} p_i^{0,t} q_i^{t+\tau}$$
$$= \frac{C(t, 0, \mathrm{L})}{1 + r^1} + \frac{W(t+1, 0, \mathrm{L})}{1 + r^1} \qquad (21)$$

where $C(t, 0, L)$ is the Laspeyres approximation to the true measure of real consumption defined as $C(t, 0) = \Sigma_{i=1}^{n} p_i^0 \bar{q}_i^t$.

Now we can define real income as

$$Y(t, 0) = C(t, 0) + W(t + 1, 0) - W(t, 0) \tag{22}$$

Income, on this definition, can be interpreted either (in the words of Professor Hicks) as 'the maximum value which he (the income recipient) can consume during the week and still be expected to be as well off at the end of the week as he was at the beginning' or as the annual return to accumulated wealth. The first interpretation follows directly from equation (22) because $W(t,0) = W(t + 1,0)$ whenever $Y(t,0) = C(t,0)$. The second interpretation is an approximation obtained by substituting $W(t,0,L)$ for $W(t,0)$ in equation (22). It then follows immediately from equation (21) that

$$Y(t, 0) = r^1 W(t, 0, L) \tag{23}$$

An analogy can therefore be drawn between property income as a return to capital and total income as a return to total wealth. This is the basis of the old term 'social dividend' by which real income was at one time denoted. Note that the validity of equation (23) does not require that the economy be in a steady state, but it does require that future consumption be correctly anticipated.

The increase in real wealth $W(t + 1,0) - W(t,0)$ consists of the sum of the value at base year prices of new capital goods produced and capital gains. Thus, the attempt to measure real investment as the change in wealth over the year amounts in practice to adding an estimate of capital gains to the usual measure of real investment in the national accounts. This is a major addition to income. Robert Eisner has estimated that, over the period 1946 to 1975, the average annual capital gains in the United States in excess of that attributable to inflation amounted to 42.4 billion dollars a year as compared to a net investment as conventionally measured of 66.2 billion, that is to say, about 39% of the increase in real net worth over the period is attributable to capital gains.[1]

It is particularly important in evaluating this species of real investment to be conscious of our purpose in measuring real income in this book. We are concerned exclusively with the construction of long time series of statistics for monitoring the progress of an economy. This needs

[1] R. Eisner, 'Capital Gains and Income: Real Changes in the Value of Capital in the United States, 1946–75', in D. Usher (ed.), The Measurement of Capital, Studies in Income and Wealth, Conference on Income and Wealth, National Bureau of Economic Research, 1980, Appendix Table 4.

emphasis because there is a strong case to be made for including capital gains as part of income for tax purposes. Suppose I make a great deal of money through the appreciation in value of a piece of land or a common stock I possess. It is considered appropriate that I should be obliged by the tax system to share my good fortune with the rest of the population, and this is done by counting capital gains as part of the tax base. But the question at issue here is not whether individual capital gains should be taxed but whether national capital gains should be included as part of current national income. We shall discuss the pros and cons presently. For the moment it is sufficient to appreciate there is nothing illogical in treating capital gains as part of income in one case but not in another.[2]

We must also take care to distinguish between true and anticipated capital gains. True capital gains is the change over the year in the size of real wealth minus that portion of the change attributable to the net acquisition of capital goods. It is dependent, as we see from equations (19) and (22), on the whole time series of consumption until the end of the world, and it is representative, if it is positive, of the benefit accruing from the fact that a future better than the present is becoming one less year farther away. But statisticians are not clairvoyant. Unable to observe true capital gains directly, they have no choice but to measure capital gains as the change in the market's evaluation of capital goods and other titles to future income streams. Many of the undeniable advantages of a measure of true capital gains may be lost if the market's anticipation of capital gains is all that we can observe.

There are several theoretical and statistical problems with the use of anticipated capital gains as part of a measure of real investment:

(i) The market does not supply us with a measure of capital gains in real terms. We can observe changes over the year in the money value of wealth and in the price level of currently available goods and services, and we can use this information to construct a measure of wealth in constant dollars. However, this measure differs from the definition of wealth in constant dollars in equation (19) because it allows wealth to increase if real rates of interest fall, even in the absence of any change in the time stream of future consumption. It is as though we knew that income with bread as numeraire has increased but we could not tell whether the increase is due to greater consumption of bread and cheese or to a rise in the price of cheese with no change in quantities consumed.

---

[2] The classic statement of the case for a comprehensive tax base inclusive of capital gains is Henry Simons', *Personal Income Taxation*, University of Chicago Press, 1938. It is significant that Simons explicitly denies on p. 47 of that book that capital gains belongs as a component of national income.

(ii) We have no data on capital gains in human capital. The change in discounted future consumption in the measure of wealth in equation (19) would normally accrue in part to labour and in part to capital. Only the latter part is recorded in the market's assessment of capital gains. The excluded part may well be the larger of the two because labour's share of income is larger than capital's share. Nor is it clear how capital gains to human capital might be estimated because much of the gain accrues to people who are yet to be born.

(iii) The market's valuation of assets may change during the year, not because of events occurring within the year, but because of changes in expectations about future years. Suppose wealth increases overnight because we come to believe that there will be an important technical change ten years hence. Do we really want to consider this change as real income in the current year? Admittedly, our assessment of our wealth today is greater than our assessment of our wealth yesterday. But our wealth has not really increased, for our future, if only we knew it, was the same yesterday as it is today, and our wealth yesterday as assessed in the light of what we know today was not appreciably less than our wealth today. Whatever we mean by real income, we want the time series of real income to be such that a change in real income from one year to the next signifies that the years are genuinely different in what people produce and consume and not just in the way they anticipate the future.

(iv) The measure of income in accordance with equation (22) is fundamentally inconsistent with the one-sector model of the economy within which real income is originally defined. One cannot imagine real income in this sense of the term as being produced with labour and capital in accordance with equation (1). A simple example should make this clear. Imagine an economy where labour is the only factor of production and where there is no capital, no saving, no investment, and no growth of population, but technical change occurs at a rate λ. Real income in accordance with equation (1) is therefore

$$Y^t = C^t = Le^{\lambda t} \tag{24}$$

where C^t and L are the output of consumption goods and the number of men employed. Since L is constant, consumption grows at a rate λ, wealth each year is

$$W^t = \int_t^\infty \exp\left[-r(\tau - t)\right]C^\tau \, dt$$
$$= L\int_t^\infty \exp\left[-r(\tau - t) + \lambda\tau\right] d\tau = \frac{C^t}{r - \lambda} \tag{25}$$

and real income in accordance with equation (22) would have to be

$$Y^t = C^t + W^t = C^t + \frac{d}{dt}\left(\frac{C^t}{r-\lambda}\right) = C^t\left(1 + \frac{\lambda}{r-\lambda}\right) \qquad (26)$$

where the rate of interest r is assumed constant over time. The term $r-\lambda$ must be positive, for otherwise wealth would be infinite and a man could sell a share, no matter how small, of his earning power in perpetuity for an infinitely large sum. Forced to choose between abandoning the production function and abandoning the definition of real income as the sum of consumption and the change in wealth, I, and I think most economists, would have no hesitation in abandoning the definition of income as the sum of consumption and the change in wealth because the other usage of the concept of income is deeply imbedded in economic analysis while the definition of income as the sum of consumption and the change in wealth is a definition and no more.

B. REAL INVESTMENT DEFINED AS THE OUTPUT OF NEW CAPITAL GOODS

It is best to think of this definition of real investment in the context of the definition of real income as a whole. This definition is based on the productivity interpretation of real income where no distinction is made between capital goods and consumption goods. Money income in the year t is

$$Y(t) = \sum_{i=1}^{n} p_i^t q_i^t + \sum_{j=1}^{s} p_j^t m_j^t \qquad (27)$$

where q_i^t and m_j^t are quantities of the i type of consumption and the j type of capital goods produced, and p_i^t and p_j^t are their prices. With the year 0 as the base year, real income in the year t is

$$Y(t, 0, p) = \max\left(\sum_{i=1}^{n} p_i^0 q_i + \sum_{j=1}^{s} p_j^0 m_j\right) \qquad (28)$$

where p_i^0 and p_j^0 are base year prices and the vectors of consumption goods and capital goods, $C = \{q_1, \ldots, q_n\}$ and $M = \{m_1, \ldots, m_n\}$, are chosen to maximize $Y(t,0,p)$ subject to the production possibility curve for the year t

$$f^t(C, M) = g^t(K^t, L^t) \qquad (29)$$

The Laspeyres approximation to $Y(t,0,p)$ is

$$Y(t, 0) = \sum_{i=1}^{n} p_i^0 q_i^t + \sum_{j=1}^{s} p_j^0 m_j^t \qquad (30)$$

This definition of real income corresponds more closely than any of the other definitions we discuss to that now employed in the national accounts, and the Laspeyres approximation is the formula used in the national accounts for combining the main aggregates of consumption and investment into a measure of real income as a whole. There are, however, several problems with this definition as a basis for constructing time series of real income for the measurement of economic growth. (i) Unlike the measure of real consumption as productive capacity, the measure of real income in equation (28) carries no necessary implications about the welfare of the representative consumer because quantities of investment goods, m_j, are not arguments in the utility function. (ii) The definition of real income as the sum of real consumption and the output of new capital goods is frivolous in its response to technical change, in the sense that economically-equivalent technical changes may or may not lead to increases in real income depending on economically irrelevant characteristics of technical change. (iii) This measure of real income shares the defect of the measure of real consumption as productive capacity that it cannot take account of changes over time in the nature of goods and that a rule must be introduced extraneously to compare new and old types of goods on a common scale. We shall consider these problems in turn.

(i) The analogy between real income in equation (28) and real consumption in Chapter 4 is incomplete because there is no consistent set of indifference curves, tangent to each and every production possibility curve $f^t(C^t, M^t)$ at the chosen values of C^t and M^t. Suppose that bread is the only consumption good and tractors the only capital good. One can construct a sequence of production possibility curves for bread and tractors such as is illustrated in Figure 5.1, but there is no corresponding set of indifference curves because the number of tractors is not an argument in the utility function. Admittedly, the relative price of bread and tractors is a reflection of their rate of substitution in use, and in each year there may be constructed a set of, what might be called, pseudo-indifference curves, each of which is the locus of combinations of bread and tractors for which the intertemporal utility function of equation (5) is constant. What differentiates the intertemporal case illustrated in Figure 5.1 from the atemporal case discussed in Chapter 2 is that the pseudo-indifference curves in Figure 5.1 are not invariant over time even though taste itself is invariant in the sense that the intertemporal utility function of equation (5) preserves its form from year to year. Pseudo-indifference curves are incomparable from year to year because the rate of substitution in use between bread and tractors today depends upon the state of technology tomorrow and because technology is changing over time. Pseudo-indifference curves may cross as illustrated by the broken curves of Figure 5.1. One cannot infer from the positions of pseudo-indifference curves such as U^0 and U^1 in Figure 5.1 whether the representative consumer is better off in year 1 than he is in year 0, not even if one curve lies entirely outside the other.

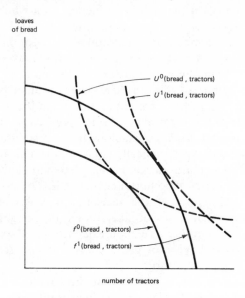

Figure 5.1 Genuine production possibility curves and pseudo-indifference curves for an economy with one consumption good and one intermediate product

In the atemporal model a representative consumer moving from a lower to a higher indifference curve is better off by definition, a uniform outward shift of the corresponding production possibility curve gives the representative consumer the opportunity to become better off, and he will do so unless the shift of the production possibility curve is accompanied by distortions in relative prices. By contrast, a uniform outward shift of the production possibility curve for bread and tractors in Figure 5.1 may not signify that the representative consumer has the opportunity to become better off, even in a perfectly competitive economy without taxes or other distortions in the price mechanism.

(ii) The second problem with the definition of real income as the sum of real consumption and the real output of capital goods is really an elaboration of the first. The source of the problem is that capital goods share many of the qualities of intermediate products. They are produced at the cost of consumption goods that might have been produced instead, and they yield extra consumption goods in due course. The difference between capital goods and intermediate goods is one of timing. Intermediate goods are created and used up in a single accounting period while capital goods continue to be useful for more than one accounting period; a statistician could transform goods from capital goods to intermediate goods, or vice versa, by lengthening or shortening the accounting period.

The sequence of creation and use of capital goods may be represented as $C \rightarrow K \rightarrow C$. Capital has two links to consumption. The first is between the consumption that must be given up to create capital goods and the amount of capital goods created; the second is between capital and the amount of consumption goods it can produce. Technical change may occur in either link of the chain. If it occurs in the second link, we are made better off without there being any increase in the quantity of capital goods produced; the capital goods we produce today become more productive, but we do not necessarily produce more capital goods than we would otherwise have done, and the measure of real investment need not show an increase. If technical change occurs in the first link, a given sacrifice of consumption goods today yields a larger supply of new capital goods, and there are corresponding increases in our measures of real investment and real income. The two types of technical change may be equivalent in their impact on the intertemporal welfare of the representative consumer, but one type is reflected as an increase in real investment while the other is not.

Consider the two-sector model formed by restricting the number of inputs and outputs in the intertemporal model in equations (9) and (10) so that there is one consumption good, C, one investment good, M, one type of capital, K (which is the same stuff as M), and one type of labour, L. In such a model, technical change in the $K \rightarrow C$ link of the chain from C to K to C affects the production function g exclusively and may be said to be C-augmenting. If technical change in the year t is C-augmenting at a rate $\ln \lambda^1$, then

$$g^t(\lambda^1 K, L) = g^{t-1}(K, L) \qquad (31)$$

where $\lambda^1 < 1$ signifies that the change is beneficial. Technical change in the $C \rightarrow K$ link of the chain from C to K to C affects the production possibility curve, f, exclusively and may be said to be K-augmenting. If technical change in the year t is K-augmenting at a rate $\ln \lambda^2$, then

$$f^t(C, \lambda^2 M) = f^{t-1}(C, M) \tag{32}$$

where $\lambda^2 > 1$ signifies that the change is beneficial. Since the measure of real income in equation (28) is an indicator of the outward shift of the f function alone, an increase in λ^2 compensated by an increase in λ^1 sufficient to leave the representative consumer no better off than he was before would lead to a spurious increase in real income, an increase that does not correspond to an improvement in the standard of living or in the prospects of the representative consumer.

In the machine industry, technical change is K-augmenting if two machines can be produced this year with the resources needed to produce one machine last year, while technical change is C-augmenting if we learn how to get twice as much output from any given machine. In the automobile industry, technical change is K-augmenting if two cars can be produced this year with resources needed to produce one car last year or if a new car, that costs no more to produce than a car of the old type, goes twice as fast and is twice as safe as an old one, while technical change is C-augmenting if, for instance, the development of a new type of gasoline enables all cars to go twice as fast or to be twice as safe as they were. In the economy as a whole, technical change is K-augmenting if the growth over time of consumption per head is accompanied by a large increase in the capital stock, while technical change is C-augmenting if the identical growth of consumption per head is accompanied by a relatively smaller increase in the capital stock with no less capacity to produce consumption goods.

The situation is illustrated in Figure 5.2 where, once again, the consumption good is bread and the investment good is tractors. Figure 5.2 describes two economies, A and B, in a two-period world. People in both economies are equally well off in that consumption is the same in both economies in each of the two years. The difference between these economies is that economy B has a 'better' production possibility curve, f, while economy A has a compensatingly 'better' production function, g; and, as a result of this economically-irrelevant difference, economy B has the greater real income according to equation (28) in the first period even though the real incomes of the two countries are the same in the second. The broken curves pertain to economy B exclusively, and the full curves pertain either to economy A or to both economies in the event that the two economies have properties in common. The world comes to an end at the end of period 1.

The productive capacities of economies A and B for making bread and new tractors in the year 0 are illustrated in the 'atemporal'

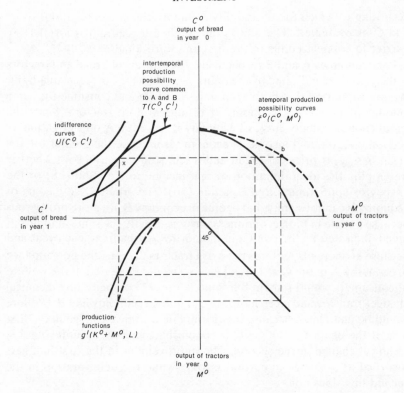

Figure 5.2 How the form of technical change can influence the measure of real income as productive capacity

production possibility curves, $f^0(C^0, M^0)$, in the northeast quadrant. In the diagram, economy B appears unambiguously more efficient because the production possibility curve of B lies everywhere outside of the production possibility curve of A. Production functions, $g^1(K^0 + M^0, L)$, connecting amounts of capital and outputs of bread in the year 1 are illustrated in the southwest quadrant. The curves do not begin at the origin of the diagram because capital is measured as the increase in the number of tractors attributable to investment in the year 0, not as the complete stock. Though economy B produces more tractors than economy A for any given output of bread, economy A is the more efficient in another sense. Its production function is such that the increment of bread in the year 1 is greater for any given output of tractors in the year 0. Finally, the northwest quadrant contains the intertemporal production possibility curve $T(C^0, C^1) = 0$ showing amounts of consumption that might be produced in each of the years 0 and 1. Also in this quadrant is a set of indifference curves, $U(C^0, C^1)$, according to which the desirability of the available combinations of C^0 and C^1 is evaluated. The line in the southeast quadrant is a reflecting barrier to connect points in the first and third quadrants.

For economies A and B respectively, the outputs of bread and tractors in the year 0 are indicated by the points a and b in the northeast quadrant. We are supposing that both economies produce and consume the same amount of bread, but economy B produces more tractors. Since the production possibility curve of economy B lies entirely outside of that of economy A, the real income of economy B must be the greater for any given base year prices of bread and tractors and regardless of whether we employ the ideal definition of real income in equation (28) or the Laspeyres approximation in equation (30). The greater real income of economy B cannot signify that people in economy B are more prosperous because people in both economies consume exactly the same amounts of bread, indicated by the point x in the northwest quadrant, each year and because economy B requires the extra tractors to equal the performance of economy A in the year 1. Real income would increase but the welfare of consumers would remain the same if a set of compensating technical changes transformed an economy like A into an economy like B. Welfare would be unaffected because the favourable technical change in the first link of the chain $C \rightarrow K \rightarrow C$ is counterbalanced by an unfavourable technical change in the second. The improvement in the first link gets recorded as a change in current income while the deterioration in the second link does not.

It is instructive to compare the northwest quadrant of Figure 5.2 with Figure 5.1. Both diagrams illustrate maximization at a point of tangency between an indifference curve and a production possibility curve. The indifference curves in Figure 5.2 are genuine in that they represent taste alone and that any northwest movement represents an unambiguous improvement in the circumstances of the consumer. The indifference curves of Figure 5.1 are spurious in the sense that they reflect productive capacity as well as taste so that a northeast movement does not necessarily make the consumer better off in the long run. We could construct pseudo-indifference curves corresponding to combinations of bread and tractors in the northeast quadrant of Figure 5.2, and the curve at B would lie above the curve at A despite the fact that the situation in economy A is neither better nor worse than the situation in economy B.

Thus contrary to our first expectation, the natural extension to an economy with consumption goods and investment goods of the model in Chapter 2 where a representative consumer maximizes utility subject to the constraint of a production possibility curve, is not to be found in the combination of pseudo-indifference curves with the atemporal production possibility curve. The intertemporal extension of these concepts is only to be found in the juxtaposition of genuine indifference curves with the intertemporal production possibility curve connecting amounts of consumption accruing at different periods of time. The alleged advantage of the productive capacity approach—that it generalizes nicely from consumption to income as a whole—is illusory. We cannot even discover the flow of consumption represented by the point of tangency between an intertemporal indifference curve and the intertemporal production possibility curve without far greater knowledge than can be assumed to be at the disposal of the national accountant. Where there are many consumption goods and many investment goods, the natural extension of the productivity interpretation of real consumption would be a measure of wealth rather than a measure of income; it would be an indicator of the outward shift in the course of time of the intertemporal production possibility curve of equation (15).

Though the example illustrated in Figure 5.2 was of a comparison of two economies in a two-period world, the principle in the example can be extended to the analysis of continuous economic growth over long periods of time. Consider a two-sector model in which outputs of the consumption good and the capital good are produced with labour and capital according to the functions

$$C = f^1(L_1, K_1, \lambda_C(t)) \quad \partial f^1/\partial \lambda_C > 0 \qquad (33)$$

and

$$M = f^2(L_2, K_2, \lambda_I(t)) \quad \partial f^2/\partial \lambda_I > 0 \qquad (34)$$

where $M = \dot{K}$ and where λ_C and λ_I are coefficients indicating the state of technology in the year t. Roughly speaking, a C-augmenting technical change is one that increases λ_C and λ_I in unison while a K-augmenting technical change increases λ_I alone. If λ_C and λ_I change together, a given rate of growth of consumption might be maintained together with approximately equivalent rates of growth of K and of real income assessed according to the formula

$$Y_0^t = C^t + p(0)M^t \qquad (35)$$

where $p(0)$ is the relative price of M and C in the chosen base year. However, if λ_I alone changes, a given rate of growth of consumption can only be maintained if M grows faster than C. We return to this example in Chapter 9 where the functions f^1 and f^2 in equations (33) and (34) are assumed to be Cobb-Douglas so that the growth rates of real income and consumption per head may be measured and compared.

(iii) The final problem with the definition of real income as the sum of real consumption and the output of capital goods is one that it shares with the definition of real consumption as an indicator of productive capacity. The problem is outside the framework of the model we have used so far, for it has to do with the appearance of new types of goods.

In principle, new types of goods can be accounted for in the measure of real consumption as an indicator of welfare because the representative consumer can tell us how much income in the base year would make him as well off as he would be in the current year when the new types of goods are available. There is no comparable test for the productive capacity measures of real consumption or real income, and some extraneous principle must be introduced to make things commensurate and to preserve the fiction, without which real income cannot be computed at all, that output in every year consists of amounts of n invariant types of goods. In our simple intertemporal model we supposed that there are exactly s kinds of capital goods, that no new types are invented, and that their qualities remain invariant over time. In reality, the types of capital goods are not invariant, new types of capital goods are invented, and the national accountant must draw the equivalence between amounts of old and new types of capital goods in some more or less arbitrary way. When a new type of machine is invented, he must decide which among the s kinds of capital goods it is, and, having allocated it to type j, he must decide how many units of the old machines of type j are to count as the equivalent of one new one. Clearly, the value of real income is affected by the national accountant's decision. If he equates one new machine to many old machines, he must record a relatively large real investment in the j type of capital goods. If he equates new machines to old machines in a less favourable ratio, he must record a relatively small real investment in the j type of capital goods.

The national accountant is understandably reluctant to make this kind of judgement. Instead, he relies on a procedure which appears to sort these matters out without too much intervention on his part. He assumes that the major categories of investment, categories such as housing and transport equipment, persist year after year, and he measures real investment in each category as the value of expenditure in that category deflated by the appropriate price index. The price index for each category is a weighted average of prices of a representative bundle of goods, the composition of which is adjusted from time to time as new types of capital goods appear and old types of capital goods become obsolete.

The deflation procedure makes new and old types of capital goods commensurate by restricting the coverage of the price index. Suppose that, in the year t, there is only one type of airplane available and that 1000 of these airplanes are acquired at $20,000 each. On the first day of the year $t + 1$, a new and better type of airplane is invented. In the year $t + 1$, 500 of the old type of airplane are acquired at \$25,000 each and 500 of the new type of airplane are acquired at \$50,000 each. The price of the new type of airplane cannot be included in the price index in the year $t + 1$ because there is no basis of comparison with the year t. Consequently, the price index of airplanes increases by 25% from the year t to the year $t + 1$, $[(25,000/20,000) - 1] \times 100$, the money value of investment increases by 88%,

$$\left(\frac{(500 \times 25,000) + (500 \times 50,000)}{1000 \times 20,000} - 1 \right) \times 100$$

and real investment increases by 50%, $[(188/125) - 1] \times 100$. If types of capital goods that were produced in the year t are no longer produced in the year $t + 1$, their prices may be dropped from the index or imputed from the secondhand market with due allowance for depreciation. The deflation procedure contains an automatic correction for quality change insofar as quality change among capital goods is assumed to be reflected in the relative prices of new and old types of capital goods.

Though, as a practical matter, the deflation procedure described above would appear to be the only method open to the national accountant for measuring the real output of capital goods, it should be recognized that this method of comparing new and old types of capital goods is not as automatic or mechanical as the example would suggest. In deflating money income to obtain real income, the national accountant must impose his own judgement upon the data in several important respects as may be seen in the following example. For many countries we have time series of real investment extending well back into the nineteenth century. Let us restrict our attention to transport equipment and suppose that we have at our disposal complete and detailed records of amounts and prices of every type of transport equipment produced each year from, say, 1850 to the present day. The difficulty in compressing these data into a time series of real investment in transport is that the types of equipment used in 1850 and today have very little in common but must nonetheless be treated as different amounts of the same stuff. The clipper ships of the nineteenth century and the jumbo jets used today have to be measured on a common scale despite the fact that they were used in entirely different technologies and were never used at the same time. The method of deflation is equivalent to comparing quantities of clipper ships and jumbo jets through a chain of substitutes by weighting of each adjacent pair of goods according to prices in the year that the more recent good was incorporated into the price index. It is as though the number of clipper ships deemed equivalent to a jumbo jet in the time series of real investment were determined by equating tonnage of clipper ships to tonnage of iron ships at their relative price in 1880, passenger capacity of iron ships to passenger capacity of propeller driven airplanes at their relative price in 1950, and passenger capacity of propeller driven airplanes to passenger capacity of jumbo jets at their relative prices in 1970. This example is not atypical of what goes on in the making of the national accounts, and of what must go on if a time series of real capital formation is to be constructed at all.

Though the national accountant does not compare clipper ships and jumbo jets directly, he cannot help but influence the final comparison because he must decide whether a new vintage of capital goods is or is not the same stuff as the old vintage and when to incorporate new capital goods into the price index. If the relative price of airplanes and iron ships is falling over time, the decision to incorporate airplanes in the price index of transport equipment at an early date tends to raise the relative weighting of jumbo jets and clipper ships in the time series of real investment as a whole. Furthermore, it is not always obvious how to allocate new types of capital goods among the old categories. A toy microscope might be classified as a toy or as a piece of optical equipment. If the price index of toys is rising less rapidly than the price index of optical equipment, then the measure of real income is higher if the national accountant classifies toy microscopes as toys than if he classifies them as optical equipment.

A second and equally serious problem with the deflation procedure is that it is grafted artificially onto the measure of real income in equation (28). The measure of real income is supposed to reflect the outward shift of the production possibility curve, but the relative price of new and old capital goods is as much a reflection of the demand side of the economy as of its capacity to produce. In fact, the relative price of new and old types of capital goods may at times be a reflection of their usefulness exclusively, regardless of their relative cost of production.

Consider the following modification of the airplane example discussed above. Suppose 1000 of the old type of airplanes are produced at $20,000 each in the year t. On 1 January of the year $t + 1$ a better airplane is invented, one that does twice the work of the old type but costs no more to produce. In the year $t + 1$, 1000 of the new type of airplanes are produced at $20,000 each, so that the money value of investment in that type of machine is the same in both years. Because the new airplane is better, the value of an old type falls to $10,000 in the year $t + 1$ despite the fact that it would cost $20,000 to make an airplane of the old type. Abstracting from depreciation, the rules of deflation would lead us to say that there has been a 50% reduction in the price index of airplanes, and that real investment in airplanes has doubled from the year t to the year $t + 1$ even though no extra resources are employed in the aircraft industry. This is not an unreasonable result because a technical change which renders today's airplane twice as effective as yesterday's airplane is economically equivalent to a technical change enabling us to make 2000 airplanes today with the same input of resources necessary to make 1000 equivalent airplanes yesterday.

What differentiates this example from the earlier one where 500 of the new type of airplane and 500 of the old type were acquired in the year $t + 1$, is that in the earlier example the ratio of the market prices of new and old airplanes reflected their rate of transformation in production as well as their rate of substitution in use while, in this example, the ratio of market prices reflects rates of substitution in use exclusively; in the earlier example, the market price was a reflection of the supply price as well as the demand price while in the present example the market price is a reflection of the demand price alone. There may even be independent evidence about the supply price. Suppose for instance, that the superiority of the new type of airplane is due to the invention of an improved gasoline which works very well in the new type of airplane but not in the old one. Suppose also that the new type of airplane could easily have been made in the year t, and would have been, if the improved gasoline had been available at that time. In that case, real investment in airplanes in the year $t + 1$ is twice what it was in the year t, not because more resources are put into the aircraft industry or even because of technical change in the aircraft industry, but because of technical change in the manufacture of gasoline. The example can be attenuated further by comparison with a situation where the invention of new gasoline affects all airplanes, new and old alike. Now, no distinction can be made between new and old types of airplanes, and we would measure real investment in airplanes in years t and $t + 1$ according to the number of airplanes produced regardless of the extent to which their performance is improving as a result of improvements in the quality of fuel.

If the national accountant knows that the new and old types of airplanes cost the same to produce in both years, he may well choose to depart from the formal rules of deflation as we have described them above, to ignore the fact that the use price of the old type of airplane is low in the year $t + 1$, and to decree that new and old types of airplanes constitute the same amount of real capital in the category of transport equipment.

The deflation procedure normally records an improvement in the quality of capital goods as an increase in real investment. This outcome seems reasonable from the standpoint of a comparison between a technical change that results in better capital goods and a technical change that lowers the alternative cost of capital goods of the old type. However, the outcome seems unreasonable from the standpoint of a comparison between a technical change that results in better capital goods and a technical change that makes all capital goods more useful, new types and old types alike. The invention of a better machine may be economically equivalent to the invention of a better way of using old machines, but the former increases the measure of real investment while the latter does not. The definition of real investment as the output of new capital goods becomes especially precarious because the national accountant can only identify the new machine as better if the old one becomes wholly or partially obsolete in the sense that the old machine sells at a greater discount with respect to the new machine than can be justified by normal depreciation.

The argument has come full circle. We began our critique of the definition of investment as the output of new capital goods by pointing out that economically-equivalent technical changes may or may not lead to an increase in real income depending on whether they are K-augmenting in f or C-augmenting in g. We then showed that the definition of real investment in equation (28) supplies no firm criterion to the national accountant for comparing new and old types of capital goods as amounts of the same stuff. It need only be added that the two problems are intimately related because a given technical change may show up as K-augmenting or as C-augmenting depending on how the national accountant chooses to construct his price indexes.

C. REAL INVESTMENT DEFINED AS THE INCREASE IN THE CAPITAL STOCK

Investment, like consumption, can be measured from the point of view of productive capacity or from the point of view of welfare. The productive capacity measure, discussed in the preceding section, is an indicator of the location of the production possibility curve of capital goods. The welfare measure we are now about to consider is an indicator of what the new capital goods can do. We shall see whether we can construct a pure use measure of real investment, a measure that increases if capital goods produced this year can do more than capital goods produced last year, regardless of the locations of the production possibility curves from which they themselves were created. An aggregate of quantities of different types of machines weighted according to their usefulness is commonly referred to as a measure of 'real capital stock' and is designated by the letter K. We shall now investigate whether real investment might be defined as the increase in K over the year. A Laspeyres measure of real income in this sense would be $(C^t + p^0 \dot{K}^t)$ where p^0 is the relative price of real capital with respect to the year 0 as the base year and to consumption goods as the numeraire. The question is whether a reasonable measure of real capital can be devised.

At the outset of this discussion, it is important to recognize that two separate and distinct concepts of real capital are employed in economic analysis. We shall refer to these concepts as 'instantaneous productive capacity' and 'long-run productive capacity', and we will illustrate them as properties of the simple intertemporal model in equations (8) to (14). Real capital stock as an indicator of instantaneous productive capacity will be designated as $\tilde{K}$ and real capital stock as an indicator of long-run productive capacity will be designated as $\bar{K}$.

When real capital stock is measured as an indicator of instantaneous productive capacity, we say that a mix of capital goods constitutes more real capital than some other mix of capital goods if the former can do what the latter cannot. Specifically, suppose that in some year 0 which we set as the base year, a mix of capital goods, $k_1^0, \ldots, k_s^0$ is producing a mix of outputs $q_1^0, \ldots, q_n^0, m_1^0, \ldots, m_s^0$ with the aid of labour inputs $l_1^0, \ldots, l_r^0$, so that

$$f^0(C^0, M^0) = g^0(K^0, L^0) \tag{36}$$

where C^0, M^0, K^0 and L^0 are the vectors defined in the statement of the intertemporal model of equations (8) to (14). We arbitrarily set the index of real capital stock in the year 0 at $\tilde{K}^0$. The index of real capital corresponding to any other mix of capital goods $k_1, \ldots, k_s$ is set at $\tilde{K}$ where

$$\tilde{K} \equiv \lambda \tilde{K}^0 \tag{37}$$

and where λ is chosen such that

$$f^0(C^0, M^0) = g^0(\tilde{K}/\lambda, L^0) \tag{38}$$

Notice that according to this definition, the amount of real capital embodied in a mix of capital goods depends not only on the amounts of these goods available but on the technology of the year 0, the amount of labour available, and the choice of outputs q_i^0 and m_i^0. It may well turn out that the mix of capital goods $k_1, \ldots, k_s$ constitutes more capital than the mix $k_1^0, \ldots, k_s^0$ with regard to the technology of the year t even though $k_1^0, \ldots, k_s^0$ constitutes more capital with regard to the technology of the year 0.

The second concept of real capital makes allowance for the durability as well as for the instantaneous productive capacity of the mix of capital goods. It would seem that the only way to account for durability in the definition of real capital—other than by appeal to wholly arbitrary statistical conventions—is to say that one mix of capital goods constitutes more real capital than another mix of capital goods if the representative consumer is better off with the first mix than he is with the second. From the system of equations in our simple intertemporal model, we can see that, for given supplies of labour, utility depends on the stocks of capital goods available. Since utility is a function of present and future consumption, and since consumption each year depends on the amount of capital goods available and on the amount of capital goods produced, the system of equations (8), (9), and (10) can be condensed into a type of indirect utility function

$$U = U(k_1, \ldots, k_s) \tag{39}$$

the exact form of which depends on the technology of the f-function and the g-function in the current year and in every subsequent year. If we designate the value in the year 0 of the intertemporal utility function of equation (8) as $\bar{U}$, then

$$\bar{U} = U(k_1^0, \ldots, k_s^0) \tag{40}$$

because, by definition, $\bar{U}$ is the utility attained with the mix of capital goods K^0. We may arbitrarily set the index of real capital stock in the year 0 at $\bar{\bar{K}}^0$ and designate the amount of real capital corresponding to any other mix of capital goods, $k_1, \ldots, k_s$ as

$$\bar{\bar{K}} = \gamma \bar{\bar{K}}^0 \tag{41}$$

where γ is determined implicitly in the equation

$$\bar{U} = U(k_1^0, \ldots, k_s) = U\left(\frac{k_1}{\gamma}, \ldots, \frac{k_s}{\gamma}\right) \tag{42}$$

The two concepts of capital, 'instantaneous productive capacity' and 'long-run productive capacity' are contrasted here to emphasize that it is the second, more complex concept that is appropriate in the context of measuring economic growth. Investment results in the appearance of new capital goods the values of which depend in an essential way on their durability as well as on what they can be used to make today. In principle, an index of real capital as long-run productive capacity can be constructed in the manner discussed above, but such an index would be of little or no value to the national accountant for four reasons. First, the index of real capital in equation (41) is defined with regard to a given utility function and a given current and anticipated technology. Suppose we decided to assess the magnitude of real capital with regard to the situation in year 0. Then, of two alternative bundles of capital goods K^* and K^{**} available in the year t, it may easily happen that K^* is counted by our rule as constituting more real capital despite the fact that K^{**} is the more useful bundle in conditions in the year t. Second, it is an essential characteristic of any measure of real investment that identical bundles of new capital goods be counted as the same amount of real investment. If output of new capital goods consists of one unit of k_1 and one unit of k_2 in year 0 as well as in year 1, we would want to say that real investment is the same in both years. Equation (41) does not work that way. An addition to capital of one unit of k_1 and one unit of k_2 would constitute different amounts of capital in circumstances where the capital stock is evenly divided between k_1 and k_2 than in circumstances where the capital stock consists mostly of k_1 or mostly of k_2. Similarly, one unit of k_1 and two units of k_2 might be more or less additional capital than one unit of k_2 and two units of k_1 depending on the proportions of k_1 and k_2 in the existing capital stock. Third, and this is a variant of the first objection, the concept of investment as the increase over the year in the real capital K is all but useless in an economy where technical change is altering the nature of capital goods. Recall that K is defined with regard to base year technology. In measuring real capital in the year t, the new types of capital goods, the semiconductors and the nuclear powered generators, could be thought of as being available without the technology necessary to work them (in which case they would be worthless) or as carrying the new technology on their backs in which case we should be counting technical change itself as part of capital formation, and the change in real capital would be indistinguishable from the change in wealth which we have already rejected as a definition of real investment. Fourth, even a perfect measure of real capital would not circumvent the problem of the interchangeability of K-augmenting and C-augmenting technical change discussed in Section B above.

D. REAL SAVING

The process of investment consists of the sacrifice of consumption goods, the resulting acquisition of new capital goods, the corresponding augmentation of the capital stock, and the ultimate increase in consumption in the future. The last three aspects of the investment process are each captured in one of the three species of real investment discussed above. The first aspect—the sacrifice of consumption goods—is captured in the concept of real saving.

We can measure real saving as the money value of saving (or investment) deflated by a price index for consumption goods. Consider again the simple economy illustrated in Figures 5.1 and 5.2 where bread is the only consumption good and tractors the only capital good. If a sacrifice of 100 tons of bread results in 10 new tractors last year and if the same sacrifice results in 20 new tractors this year, we say that real saving is the same in the two years. The appearance of the ten extra tractors would not be recorded as an increase in real saving this year, though their services would be reflected in the measure of real income next year when the tractors are used.

The concept of real saving fits particularly well into the one-sector model at the beginning of this chapter. Consider just the first two equations of the model, $Y = f(K, L)$ and $Y = C + S$. These two equations cannot hold simultaneously unless C and S, and therefore Y itself, are dimensionally the same. Thus the numeraire for S and Y in real terms has got to be consumption goods, and real income as the sum of real consumption and real saving can be represented as real consumption scaled up by the proportion between the money value of income and the money value of consumption. Equation (2) now becomes

$$Y \equiv C + S = C \frac{1}{1 - s} \tag{43}$$

where s is the rate of saving in the current year. To measure real income as the sum of real consumption and real saving is simply to look upon the time series of income in money terms and the price index of consumption goods as though they pertained to our one-sector model, and to disregard all evidence about quantities of capital goods produced.

There is another definition of real income which is related but not quite identical to the definition in equation (43) and which is reminiscent of the Hicks definition in equation (22). Within the confines of the one-sector model, real income may be thought of as 'the amount of consumption that could be obtained in the stationary state that would arise if technical change, net investment and population growth ceased today'. Clearly, if L is constant and if the production function f remains unchanged forever, then consumption would remain constant and equal to the value of Y in equation (1).

This alternative definition of income brings out the strong family resemblance between real saving and the increase in real wealth discussed in Section A. Both species of real investment are measured in units of consumption goods, and the two definitions would be identical in an economy accurately represented by the one-sector model of equations (1) to (6). They differ in their response to technical change. Suppose equation (1) were replaced by a sequence of production functions, each more efficient than the one before

$$Y = f(K, L, t) \quad \frac{\partial f}{\partial t} > 0 \qquad (44)$$

where t is time and the inequality signifies that Y would increase over time due to technical change, even if K and L remained constant forever. Real income as the sum of consumption and real saving is simply Y corresponding to the values of K, L and t in the current year. Real income as the sum of consumption and the increase in wealth is always larger than Y because wealth grows independently over time. The latter definition capitalizes technical change while the former does not.

My principal reason for preferring the definition of real income as 'maximum sustainable consumption if technical change and population growth were to cease' to all of the other definitions we have considered is that it seems to be the closest to what we really mean when we speak of real income in the context of assessing the progress of economies over long periods of time or when we prepare statistics of real income to serve as a basis for measuring the economic growth of nations. We do not wish to say that real income is large today because we expect technical change tomorrow. We do not wish to say that real income is large today because we are producing large amounts of capital goods which are very much cheaper and very much less useful than they were at some former time. We do wish to say that real income is larger if consumption is large or if a great deal of consumption is being sacrificed to produce new capital goods.

In addition, this species has the great negative virtues that it is the simplest to measure of all of the species we are considering and that it enables the statistician to escape from the impossible task of comparing amounts of new and old types of capital goods on the same scale. And because it does not involve us in trying to measure capital in its own units, this species of real investment enables us to broaden the definition of investment to account for intangibles of all kinds. Investment can be thought of either as the acquisition of tangible capital goods or as future-oriented expenditures, the latter including expenditure on research, mineral exploration, forgone earnings of students, and net foreign investment of all kinds. The attempt to impute for the intangible components of investment must be made within the context of a measure of real saving because we have no means whatsoever of measuring the output of intangibles in their own units. Any attempt to impute for intangibles in the measure of investment in real terms draws implicitly on a concept of real saving. The grafting of such imputation onto the official national accounts where investment in money terms is deflated by a price index of investment goods results in a hybrid concept, the meaning of which is obscure.

In the larger model of equations (8) to (14), we can define real income in the year t when year 0 is the base year as

$$\max_{q_i} \sum_{i=1}^{n} p_i^0 q_i \tag{45}$$

where $u(q_1, \ldots, q_n) \leq \bar{u}$ and where $\bar{u}$ is the greatest utility that can be attained in any stationary state commencing at once if the labour force remains constant and if the technology embodied in the production function f^t and the production possibility curve g^t remains in force from now on.

Unfortunately, our two definitions of real income, the sum of consumption attained plus consumption forgone and maximum sustainable consumption, part company when we pass from the simple to the more complex model. This difficulty may be illustrated in the two-sector model employed in discussion surrounding Figure 5.2. Figure 5.3 reproduces part of the northeast quadrant of that figure. As bread is the only consumption good, real income has to be measured as distance on the vertical axis. We can see at a glance that real income as maximum sustainable consumption is OD, the intersection of the production possibility curve with the vertical axis; while actual consumption is OC, the value (at the current relative price BC/AC of tractors and bread) of the output of tractors is CB, and real income, as their sum, is OB which is greater than OD. The definitions of real income differ because a rising supply curve for new capital goods causes each additional unit of tractors produced to represent a different amount of consumption forgone.

We might consider the definition of real income as maximum sustainable consumption as the primary definition and the sum of actual consumption and consumption forgone as an approximation. The former may be preferred because, as is obvious from Figure 5.3, the size of the latter measure can be influenced by changes in the propensity to invest. The decision to produce less bread and more tractors would

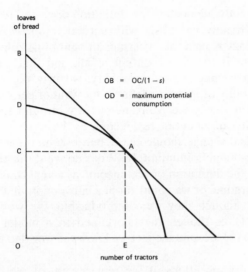

Figure 5.3 The difference between maximum potential consumption and the value of income measured in consumption units

affect the measure of real income. The point A would shift clockwise along the production possibility curve, the price of tractors would increase, and the real income OB would increase, too. The empirical significance of this point may be rather small because whatever bias is introduced into the measure of income by the divergence between OB and OD is maintained in the same direction over time. If it should happen that the proportion between OB and OD remains constant over time, as it may well do, then the measure of economic growth would be unbiased despite the bias in income itself.

Two further difficulties should be mentioned. The first has to do with the length of the run. Just as the slope of the supply curve increases with the length of the run, so too does the production possibility curve become straighter, for the one is the derivative of the other. The source of the difficulty is that the model within which real income is being defined does not take account of the distinction between fixed and variable factors of production. We have, in fact, postulated technologies where all factors of production are variable. This suggests that we should be defining real income with respect to very long run production possibility curves, in which case, incidentally, the importance of the distinction between our two definitions of real income in this section is minimized. It is not clear how, in practice, the longest run production possibility curve is to be identified. The problem is the same for all of the definitions of real income discussed in this chapter. We emphasize it here because we are advocating the definition discussed in this section.

The other difficulty has to do with natural resources. Suppose the current technology is such that a certain amount of petroleum has to be used up if there is to be any output at all, and that our petroleum reserves cannot be augmented. In reality, we may not be concerned about the possibility of income declining for want of petroleum because we are confident that we can invent our way around the impending shortage. But we cannot define real income as the maximum sustainable output if technical change should cease, because, on these assumptions, no output is sustainable indefinitely. What do we do in this case? We could revert to the definition of real income as actual consumption and consumption forgone, or we could adopt a convention that all assets are looked upon as though they were reproducible. We would, in effect, look at the data as though they pertained to a model like that in equations (1) to (5), despite the fact we know the world to be very much more complex.

The empirical implications of the replacement of real gross capital formation with real saving per head are illustrated on the accompanying charts. Chart 5.4 is a comparison of the indexes of real capital formation and real saving per head. The measure of real capital formation, taken directly from the national accounts, is the sum of 'gross fixed capital formation' and 'value of physical change in inventories', both expressed in real terms. Saving, on the other hand, is not expressed in real terms in

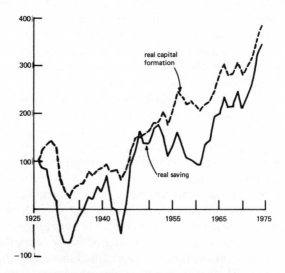

Figure 5.4 Indexes of real saving and real capital formation per head: Canada 1926–1974 (1926 = 100) Source: *National Income and Expenditure Accounts, Volume 1, The Annual Estimates, 1926–1974 Statistics Canada, 13–531*

the national accounts, but we may compute real saving as defined in this chapter by deflating the money value of saving by the implicit national accounts price deflator for personal consumption. Saving in current dollars is defined as 'gross fixed capital formation' plus 'value of physical change in inventories' plus the 'surplus of Canada on transactions with non-residents' minus 'capital consumption allowances and miscellaneous valuation adjustments'. Expressed in 1961 dollars, real capital formation increased from $226 per head in 1926 to $862 per head in 1974, while real saving increased from $150 per head in 1926 to $515 per head in 1974; and the corresponding growth rates over the 48 year period were 2.78% and 2.56% respectively.

Chart 5.5 is a comparison of the corresponding statistics of income, real gross national expenditure as the sum of real consumption and real capital formation, and real income as the sum of real consumption and real saving. Expressed in 1961 dollars, real gross national expenditure increased from $1079 per head in 1926 to $3513 per head in 1974, while real income increased from $899 per head in 1926 to $3504 per head in 1974; and the corresponding growth rates were 2.46% and 2.83%.

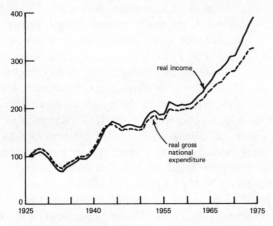

Figure 5.5 Indexes of real income and real gross national expenditure per head: Canada 1926–1974 (1926 = 100) Source: See Figure 5.4

NOTES FOR FURTHER READING

Classic statements of the definition of income by I. Fisher, H. C. Simons, J. R. Hicks, S. H. Frankel and others are contained in R. H. Parker and G. C. Harcourt, *Readings in the Concept and Measurement of Income*, Cambridge University Press, 1969. This book also contains N. Kaldor's valuable review of alternative definitions of income entitled 'The Concept of Income in Economic Theory' originally published as part of Kaldor's *An Expenditure Tax*, Unwin University Books, 1955. See also J. R. Hicks, 'The Measurement of Real Income', *Oxford Economic Papers*, 1958, pp. 134–85.

Irving Fisher's books, *The Nature of Capital and Income*, Macmillan, 1906, and *The Rate of Interest*, Macmillan, 1907, are still well worth reading. Fisher argues that the concept of income as the sum of consumption and investment is useless and that the twin concepts of consumption and wealth are all we need for economic analysis. This theme is taken up in P. Samuelson's 'The Evaluation of "Social Income": Capital Formation and Wealth', in F. A. Lutz and D. C. Hague (eds), *The Theory of Capital*, Macmillan, 1961. The argument surrounding Figure 5.2 is an extension of a similar argument in Samuelson's paper.

The incorporation of capital gains as part of income has been advocated for some time by R. Eisner. See his 'Capital Gains and Income: Real Changes in the Value of Capital in the United States', in D. Usher (ed.), *The Measurement of Capital*, Conference on Income and Wealth, National Bureau of Economic Research, Vol. 45, 1980. See also M. B. McElroy, 'Capital Gains and Social Income, *Economic Inquiry*, 1976, pp. 221–40. The contrast between the two concepts of real capital is discussed by Zvi Griliches in 'Capital Stock in Investment Functions: Some Problems of Concept and Measurement', an essay in C. Christ *et al.*, *Measurement in Economics*, Stanford University Press, 1963. There is a vast literature on the existence of an aggregate capital stock, much of which is referred to in T. K. Rymes, *On Concepts of Capital and Technical Change*, Cambridge University Press, 1971. The concept of real saving has not been given much attention in the literature but it has been advocated, somewhat casually by I. M. D. Little, *A Critique of Welfare Economics*, Oxford University Press, 2nd edn, 1958, pp. 235–6, and R. Stone, *Quantity and Price Indexes in the National Accounts*, OECD, 1956, p. 196, and with considerable enthusiasm by M. FG. Scott, 'Investment and Growth', *Oxford Economic Papers*, 1976, pp. 317–363. See also M. Weitzman, 'On the Welfare Significance of the National Product in a Dynamic Economy', *Quarterly Journal of Economics*, 1976, pp. 156–62.

6

Depreciation

In this chapter we discuss two closely related issues—how depreciation ought to be measured when real income is defined as the sum of real consumption and real saving, and how the measure of depreciation might usefully be extended beyond its normal scope, as the loss of value in the course of the year of the capital goods available at the beginning of the year, to take account of other ways in which economic activity this year is adversely affecting the future prosperity of the economy. We shall take up these issues in turn.

A. HOW TO MEASURE DEPRECIATION WHEN INCOME IS DEFINED AS THE SUM OF REAL CONSUMPTION AND REAL SAVING

Economic growth is the growth of net rather than gross income, for we do not wish to say that income is greater than consumption unless the capacity of the economy is being expanded by investment in the current year. If 100 new machines are produced and 40 old machines are taken out of service, we would wish to say that investment is 60 machines rather than 100. A country that produces no more machines than are needed to keep the capital stock intact is not investing at all, for it is no better off now or in the long run than another country with the same consumption, with no output of capital goods and with a capital stock that does not deteriorate over time. All this is straightforward and obvious as a general principle or in the context of the model set out in the last chapter where capital goods, regardless of their age, were assumed to disintegrate at fixed rates. The accounting for depreciation ceases to be straightforward when we begin to consider the multiplicity of kinds of capital goods and the many ways in which capital goods can lose or gain value over time.

It is best to begin with the firm rather than with the economy as a whole, for the issues are more easily sorted out in that case. The capital goods of a firm may lose or gain value over the year for any of six distinct reasons:

(1) *Changes in efficiency (deterioration)*

We assumed in Chapter 5 that capital goods do not deteriorate in the normal sense of the term, but that a given fraction of the stock of capital goods disintegrates each year, that the disintegration when it occurs is complete, and that the fraction disintegrating is entirely independent of the age of the capital good. This assumption of 'exponential decay' is particularly convenient because it implies that the rate of depreciation is entirely technological and, therefore, independent both of the behaviour of people in the economy and of the structure of relative prices of goods and factors of production. Once we abandon the assumption, we are obliged to recognize that the rate of deterioration is not purely technological. A capital good may become less efficient over time because it requires greater maintenance, more frequent repair, or more cooperating factors of production (more labour or more fuel) per unit of output. Each component of the loss of efficiency may itself be dependent on how intensively the capital good is used in the current year or on how intensively it was used earlier on in its life. Thus, the decline from one year to the next in the usefulness of a piece of capital equipment depends on the combined effect of all of these components of deterioriation, the weighting of the different components depends upon relative prices, and these in turn depend in a complex way on taste as well as technology.

(2) *Changes in relative prices (obsolescence)*

Deterioration is not the only source of decline in the net marginal value product of a capital good. The decline may also occur because of changes in prices of products the capital good is used to make, of purchased intermediate products, and of cooperating factors of production. In principle, price changes could raise or lower the net marginal product of a capital good, and both are observed from time to time, but one would suppose that the lowering of the net marginal product would generally predominate as a consequence of the rise over time in the real wage of labour, of the enlargement of the stock of capital goods of the same kind and, above all, of the invention of new and better kinds of capital goods leading to increased output and lower prices of the consumer goods that the capital is used to produce.

(3) *Durability*

The value of the capital good itself has a different time pattern of decline than the value of its net marginal product because the former is the present value of the latter over the remaining life of the capital good. The relation between stock prices and service prices is best illustrated in the case of the one-horse shay which has a life of n years and which remains in perfect working order until the day it disintegrates. When prices remain constant over time, the one-horse shay assumption is that the marginal value product of a capital good remains at some positive value x for T years and then falls to zero. If the rate of interest remains constant at r, the value of a new one-horse shay is $(x/r)(1 - e^{-Tr})$, the value of a t year old one-horse shay is $(x/r)(1 - e^{-r(T-t)})$, and the rate of depreciation of the one-horse shay is $r/(e^{r(T-t)} - 1)$ which is small at first but approaches ∞ as t approaches T. The point to emphasize is that the rate of decline in the value of the stock is derivable from the rate of decline in the value of the service, but the time patterns are nonetheless distinct.

The one case in which this distinction can be ignored is where depreciation takes the form of exponential decay, for in that case alone is the time path of future services per unit of a capital good independent of the time that has elapsed since the capital good was first employed, and in that case alone does the value of what is left of the capital good and the amount of services remaining decline at the same rate over time. This is another reason why exponential decay is such a convenient form for depreciation to take.

(4) *Changes in the real rate of interest*

Anticipated inflation resulting in an increase in the money rate of interest has no effect upon the price of capital goods today because the change in the money rate of interest just compensates for the expected rise in the money values of the marginal products of the capital goods. But the price of capital goods will fall if the rise in the money rate of interest is indicative of a rise in the real rate, due perhaps to an intensified preference at the margin for present over future goods which may in turn be due to the expectation of future technical change.

(5) *Tax rates*

The value of a capital good is the present value of the earnings over its life, where earnings are assessed net rather than gross of tax. From this it follows that the rate of depreciation, defined as the decline in value of the capital good over the year, has to be dependent on the tax laws we impose, including especially the rates of depreciation allowance in the corporation income tax. Other things being equal, accelerated depreciation in the tax code accelerates the rate of decline over time in the value of the capital good, because an old capital good is entitlement to a smaller reduction in the corporation income tax. Note, particularly, that the rate of allowable depreciation in the tax code and the rate of decline in the value of capital goods are not equal, except where the rates of depreciation in the tax code are designed to make them so.

(6) *Inflation*

Capital goods prices may rise or fall together with all other prices in a general inflation, and the value of depreciation rises or falls accordingly. But depreciation in constant dollars should be independent of the rate of inflation and should include only those changes in the value of capital goods over and above what can be accounted for by the general rise or fall in prices over time. The measurement of depreciation in constant dollars involves index number of problems similar to those we encounter in measuring real consumption.

Interactions among factors affecting the rate of change in the value of capital goods are illustrated in Figure 6.1. For a given type of equipment, the curve A shows its marginal value product in the year 0 as a function of its age; the height of the curve is the marginal value product

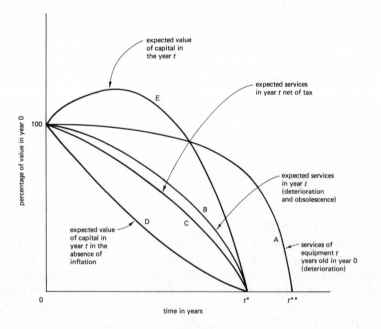

Figure 6.1

of t year old equipment expressed as a percentage of the marginal value product of new equipment. Suppose a firm buys a new piece of equipment in the year 0. Its expected return over the lifetime of the equipment may differ from the pattern in curve A due to anticipated obsolescence or other changes in prices affecting the future marginal value product of existing capital equipment. Expected marginal value products for every future year t are illustrated in curve B; the curve is drawn for the 'typical' case where obsolescence causes the capital good to be retired sooner than deterioration alone would require. The decline in the rent of the capital good net of tax is indicated by the curve C. The relation between B and C can be worked out from the detail of the tax code. The value each year of the capital good itself is shown by curve D. The height of D reflects the present value of the services net of tax as indicated by C; the rate of decline of D can be more or less rapid than that of C depending on how rapidly C itself declines, exponential decay being the intermediate case where the rates of decline are the same. The money values of the capital good could rise at first and then fall rapidly in inflationary conditions as shown in curve E. Changes in real rates of interest could affect curves D and E but not curves A, B or C.

Now let us return to the question of how to measure depreciation in a time series of real income designed for assessing the rate of economic growth of a country. The appropriate definition of depreciation of the capital stock of a firm is the decline over the year in the value of the capital goods owned at the beginning of the year. It is the combined effect of all the elements on our list except possibly the last which can be excluded by changing the numeraire from current to constant dollars.[1] But the definition of depreciation that is appropriate for the firm is not necessarily appropriate for the measure of economic growth. There will no doubt be a family resemblance, but some items on our list may be deleted and others added as we pass from the firm to the nation and as we change the purpose for which depreciation is measured. At a minimum we would want a measure of depreciation that is independent of changes in the tax code to avoid having to say that net income has declined from one year to the next merely because changes in the tax laws, that may have favoured labour as against capital, have reduced the present value of capital goods. Several considerations should be kept in mind as we attempt to define depreciation for the measurement of economic growth. It should be remembered that there is no measure of real net national expenditure in the official national accounts. The

[1] Actually, there is considerable dispute as to how to account for inflation in the assessment of profit and depreciation. The matter is not our concern in this book, but see Henry J. Aaron (ed.), *Inflation and the Income Tax*, The Brookings Institution, 1976.

practice in the national accounts is to measure depreciation in current dollars as capital cost allowance assessed for tax purposes, but depreciation is not converted to real terms as there does not seem to be an appropriate price index to do the job. That is why the commonly-used indicator of economic growth is the rate of increase of gross rather than net real income per head. Furthermore, it is at least probable that separate species of depreciation will be required for each of the separate species of investment discussed in Chapter 5. The change in units from one definition to another will require corresponding changes in the way depreciation is measured. Above, all, our measure of depreciation will in the end depend on what we want statistics of economic growth to tell us about the economy. Here we should remind ourselves of the ground rules of this book. We are not asking how real income is actually measured but how we would like to measure real income if we were building up our statistical-gathering institutions and establishing our rules of measurement all over again. We may in the end have to settle for a statistical procedure that is less than ideal because the ideal may be unattainable in practice, but it is important to know whether the procedure we choose is ideal or just the best we can do with the data at hand. Our task is made considerably easier for us by the fact that we have already come down in favour of a definition of real income as the sum of real consumption and real saving. It is sufficient, therefore, that we account for depreciation in that context alone and it need not disturb us particularly if it turns out to be difficult to define depreciation for other definitions of investment in real terms.

We shall now consider the different definitions of real investment and their corresponding definitions of depreciation. Real income as the sum of real consumption and the change in wealth is intrinsically a net rather than a gross concept, for wealth can only be said to increase, ignoring changes in expectations and the capitalization of future technical change, if the investment in the current year more than compensates for the depreciation of capital goods. In fact, we could avoid having to measure depreciation at all by estimating the net change in wealth from financial data. We would only need to measure depreciation if we wished to apportion the net change in wealth between net investment and capital gains. Here it is important to take note of the units in which these items are measured. Real capital gains, like real wealth, has to be measured in units of consumption goods; and net investment must also be measured in units of consumption goods if net investment and capital gains are to be commensurate. Thus gross investment is the value in units of consumption goods of the output of new capital goods, and depreciation is the value in units of consumption goods of the decline during the year in the efficiency of the capital goods that were available at the beginning. Which items on our list does this include? It certainly includes the first and third, deterioration and aging, but there is some question as to whether any of the other items ought to be accounted for because they might be more appropriately classified as a kind of capital loss. Obsolescence, for instance, can be looked upon as the result of a transfer of wealth from owners of old types of machines to owners of new types of machines, labour or consumers. The loss to the firm is genuine but the loss to the economy is counterbalanced by gains elsewhere. The case is even stronger for changes in the present value of capital goods resulting from changes in the tax laws. Clearly, from an accounting point of view, the loss to the firm is exactly balanced by a gain elsewhere and the measure of net investment in the economy as a whole should be unaffected.

The situation reverses itself completely when we measure real income as the sum of real consumption and the value of new capital goods. This concept of income is intrinsically gross rather than net because income is looked upon as the indicator of the location of the production possibility curve of consumption goods and investment goods combined and because the location of this curve is what it is regardless of the rate of deterioration of existing capital goods. The loss of value of old capital goods is not a species of new capital goods at all. These considerations, together with the fact that the official national accounts desist from measuring depreciation in real terms, give extra weight to the assertion in Chapter 5 that it is the output of new capital goods that national accountants themselves have in mind when they construct time series of investment in real terms.

It is different again when we measure real income as the sum of real consumption and the increase in the capital stock, and the appropriate measure of depreciation depends critically on whether the capital stock is being measured according to its instantaneous or its long-run productive capacity. In the former case where capital is treated as a measure of capacity to produce output today and where capital goods are therefore weighted by service prices rather than stock prices, it would seem that only deterioration should be accounted for in a measure of depreciation, and that all other items on the list should be ignored—even durability because the capacity of a machine today is independent of how long it is expected to remain in service. In the latter case where capital is treated as a measure of the usefulness over time of the whole mix of available capital goods within a given prospective history of technical change, one would certainly want to include aging as an element of depreciation and possibly obsolescence too, but not changes in tax laws, real rates of interest, or the price level.

Consumption forgone in the process of investment could in principle be measured net or gross, but the net measure would seem to be more appropriate in the time series of real income designed for computing a country's rate of economic growth. The measure of depreciation is very much like that used in apportioning the change in wealth between net investment and capital gains, for the numeraire is necessarily consumption goods rather than money or capital goods, and depreciation encompasses deterioration and aging but none of the other items on our list. Ideally, the difference between gross and net saving might be estimated as follows. Once a year on a set day, say 1 June, businessmen might be asked to prepare an inventory of all capital goods in existence at the start of the year, and to specify two prices for each capital good. The first is what the good would be worth on the day if it were in exactly the same condition and with the same life expectancy as on the first day of the year. The second is what the capital good would be worth in exactly the same condition it will be, assuming normal usage, on the last day of the year. The difference in the two prices is the money value of depreciation. Depreciation in different years may then be compared as components of net real saving by changing the numeraire from dollars to consumption goods, that is, by deflating by a price index of consumption goods. In practice we may not go too far wrong if we accept the accountant's measure of depreciation as adequate for our purpose. The measure is not ideal: it is affected in part by conventions or rules of thumb for setting rates of depreciation for different types of capital goods, it may not entirely abstract from obsolescence, and it is influenced to some extent by the tax laws in force in each year. One can only hope that the deviations from our ideal measure are not too important in the long run. We have, in fact, accepted the accountant's estimate of depreciation in current dollars when we measured real income as the sum of real consumption and real saving (converted from current to constant dollars by the national accounts price deflator for personal consumption) at the end of Chapter 5. We shall use this measure extensively in the remainder of the book. Our detour through alternative definitions of depreciation has been undertaken to avoid confusing this definition with other possible definitions of real net income and to specify precisely what aspects of the economy are accounted for when we define real net income in this way.

B. SOME EXTENSIONS OF THE CONCEPT OF DEPRECIATION

All of the definitions of depreciation we have so far considered have in common that depreciation is to be an amount deducted from gross investment sufficient to keep the existing capital stock intact. A case can be made, however, that these measures of depreciation are supplying answers to the wrong question. Our concern in measuring economic growth is not with the capital stock itself but with the capital stock per head. What we want to know is whether the process of accumulation in any year leaves the economy with a larger capital stock per head at the end of the year than there was at the beginning, for the average man is neither better nor worse off, other things being equal, if the population increases by 10% and the capital stock remains constant than he would be if the population remained constant and the capital stock declined by 10%. Consider the definition of real income as 'the amount of consumption that could be obtained in the stationary state that would arise if technical change, net investment and population growth ceased today', in the context of the simple one-sector model in which real income was first defined in Chapter 5, modified by the additional assumption that capital K depreciates at a rate d. The appropriate concept of income for the measurement of economic growth is no longer Y in equation (1). It is $Y - dK$ because that is all people can consume this year without being worse off next year. But if population were growing at $x\%$ per year the community would need to set aside an extra xK of investment to ensure that consumption per head is as large in the future as it is today, for the capital–labour ratio, which is the critical ratio for this purpose, is as much affected by the growth in population as by the deterioration of the capital stock. This suggests that we introduce a concept of the rate of depreciation per head as the sum of the rate of decline in the value of the capital goods available at the beginning of the year and the rate of increase in the population during the year. Real net income would then be $Y - (d + x)K$ instead of $Y - dK$ as it is usually defined.

To illustrate the concept of depreciation per head, we shall present some very crude evidence on the effect upon measured rates of saving of changing the definition of depreciation. This evidence is best combined with an extension in the concept of investment to include the creation of human capital through education because one of the principal costs of population growth is having to educate the extra children born. There are two ways of approaching this issue. We could measure the depreciation effect of population growth as the product of the rate of increase in population over the year and the (physical and educational) capital stock per head, or we could attempt to enumerate the costs and benefits of the increase in population over the year and treat the net cost as the depreciation effect of population growth. We shall adopt the first approach in our final discussion of Canadian economic growth in Chapter 13. The latter approach which we adopt in this chapter involves us in some dubious estimating procedures, but it has the advantage that it accounts, in principle, for the depreciation equivalent of changes in the age-composition of the population.

Imagine that there is born an extra pair of children who are to be cared for in childhood, educated, and, on reaching maturity, married and provided with their share of the nation's capital stock to be used for their support and for the support of their descendants in perpetuity, on condition that they participate in the support of the aged. There need be no other net transfer of income to or from the rest of the community because their descendants are cared for out of their earnings and their share of the community's capital stock. The cost of preparing a pair of children to take their places as members of the community is borne partly by their parents, partly by their brothers and sisters with whom they share their patrimony, and partly by the rest of the community with whom they share the public goods (the use of schools, roads, etc.) of the nation. Note particularly that the appearance of an extra pair of children can at once be an asset to their parents, who will get looked after in their old age, and a liability to society as a whole. The depreciation equivalent of population growth is the product of the cost to society per child born and the number of children born in the given year.

To the community of people who occupy a country on 1 January of any given year, the total depreciation in that year can be looked upon as the sum of the reduction over the year in value of capital goods in existence on 1 January plus the present value of all the costs and benefits associated with children born during the year, over and above the number of children required to maintain the population intact. The components of investment and depreciation are set out as credits and debits in Table 6.1. On the credit side are: (1) investment in physical capital as assessed in the official national accounts; (2) investment in education; and (3) the present value of the contribution to the aged made by the children born in the current year. This contribution will consist in part of support of their own parents and in part of contributions through tax payments to old age pensions for the population as a whole. The debit side consists of depreciation of capital and of costs associated with children born in the current year. Since education is counted as an investment, the loss of educational capital through retirement of people from the labour force or through the deterioration of skills must be included as part of depreciation. Capital consumption allowance is therefore the sum of: (4) deterioration of physical capital, and of (5) deterioration of human capital. The cost of children born in the current year is the sum of (6) the present value of expenditure by their parents or by the community as a whole on their food, clothing, shelter, etc., (7) of the present value of their education, (8) other

Table 6.1 The assessment of net saving inclusive of capital formation and population growth

Credits	Debits
Gross investment	Depreciation
(1) in physical capital	(4) of physical capital
(2) in educational capital	(5) of educational capital
Present value of benefits of births in the current year	Present value of costs of births in the current year
(3) future contributions by children born in the current year to the support of old people	(6) care of children born in the current year
	(7) education of children born in the current year
	(8) inheritance of children born in the current year
	(9) scale effect (ignored in Table 6.2)
	Trade debits
	(10) imports minus exports

transfers from the rest of the community, especially the inheritance they receive from their parents, and (9) a scale effect, which ought to be considered though we shall not take account of it in our calculations, consisting of the impact on output per head of diminishing returns to scale in labour and capital combined. This classification disregards the pleasure that parents derive from their children and the insurance motive that leads parents to want many children to make certain that some children survive to care for their parents in old age. The insurance motive is a consideration over and above support of the aged accounted for in item (3) in the table because, and only insofar as, a family without children cannot draw on children of other families for their support. The pleasure parents take in their children is excluded because it is not part of income as we choose to measure it. However, we must recognize that the decline in income due to the depreciation equivalent of children born in the current year may be considered a fair price to pay for the pleasure of having a large family.

The joint implications of widening the definition to include investment in education and of counting population growth as an extra source of depreciation are presented in Table 6.2 for ten countries chosen partly with a view to the availability of data but also to include rich and poor countries from several continents. The debits and credits from Table 6.1 are expressed as ratios of gross national product (GNP). A detailed account of how Table 6.2 is constructed is presented as an appendix to

Table 6.2 Effect of population growth on saving

country	year	natural increase of population (%)	investment in physical capital (1)	investment in education (2)	investment equivalent of extra support of aged (3)	Percentage of gross domestic product depreciation of physical capital (4)	depreciation of educational capital (5)	depreciation equivalent of care for extra children born (6)	depreciation equivalent of education of extra children born (7)	depreciation equivalent inheritance of extra children born (8)	exports–imports (9)	final net saving (10)
						(–)	(–)	(–)	(–)	(–)		(–)
Canada	1974	0.80	25.03	6.78	0.61	10.81	3.39	4.99	1.52	2.63	−1.57	+7.51
Chile	1971	1.91	14.19	8.30	0.75	8.83	4.15	12.72	5.43	7.28	−1.01	−16.18
Costa Rica	1973	2.32	24.00	5.09	1.60	5.58	2.54	17.48	2.40	6.79	−6.10	−10.20
France	1972	0.63	23.87	3.59	0.73	10.65	1.79	3.75	0.80	2.07	+0.99	+10.12
Japan	1971	1.26	36.52	4.37	1.24	13.13	2.18	6.35	1.97	4.14	+2.77	+16.92
Mauritius	1971	1.77	15.84	3.65	0.78	5.58	1.82	9.56	1.38	5.18	+1.03	−2.22
Singapore	1974	1.46	44.99	2.64	0.65	12.98	1.32	8.39	0.98	4.80	−18.78	+1.03
Sri Lanka	1968	2.41	16.99	3.71	1.49	4.87	1.85	13.66	1.99	7.17	−2.98	−10.33
Thailand	1970	3.24	25.00	3.47	1.26	7.56	1.74	16.90	2.28	9.35	−4.85	−12.95
USA	1974	0.59	18.00	6.47	0.79	11.70	3.23	4.08	1.31	1.95	−0.35	+2.64

Source: The details of how this table was constructed are presented as an appendix to this chapter.

this chapter. The main assumptions are the following. The age of maturity is set arbitrarily at 15 in poor countries and at 20 in rich countries. All expenditure on education is treated as investment, but, for want of data, depreciation of educational capital is set at one-half the total expenditure on education in the current year. The cost of caring for the extra children is assumed to rise from one-half consumption per head at birth to the full consumption per head at the age of maturity. The education of children is assumed to commence at age five and to continue till they mature, and the cost of education per child, estimated as the ratio of the total cost of education to the number of people in the age group from five years to maturity, is assumed to be the same for all children regardless of age. Each child is assumed to acquire his share of the nation's capital, inclusive of public capital, when he reaches maturity. The capital stock is estimated at 3.3 times GNP, on the assumption that capital's share of output is $\frac{1}{3}$, and the opportunity cost rate of interest is 10%. In estimating the contribution of newborn children to the support of the existing population in old age, it is assumed that consumption per head of the aged is the same as that for the population as a whole, that each man from the time he reaches maturity until he retires at age 65 bears an equal share of the cost, and that the ratio of retired people to working people will be the same in the future as it is today. Finally, each cost and benefit of population growth is adjusted for survival rates so that, for instance, the depreciation equivalent of inheritance is only half of what it might otherwise be if the probability of a newborn child living to maturity is only 50%.

The assumptions we have had to make in constructing Table 6.2 are too unrealistic to justify our placing much confidence in the results. One fact, and one fact only, does emerge from the calculation. There are many countries, principally poor countries with high rates of population growth, for which net saving rates are substantially negative in the sense that investment is insufficient to preserve the capital–labour ratio and only technical change stands in the way of a decline in income per head. Chile, Costa Rica, Sri Lanka and Thailand all have net rates of saving of less than -10%. The presentation of rates of final net saving with depreciation inclusive of the impact on the capital–labour ratio of population growth, is, I think, a forceful way of demonstrating the simple Malthusian proposition that population growth leads to impoverishment in the absence of substantial technical change. The numbers in the table, inaccurate as they may be, add weight to our proposition set out in the introduction to this volume that recent economic history may be looked upon as war between population growth and technical change.

An important aspect of the benefit–cost analysis of extra births, referred to in Table 6.1 as scale effect but overlooked in Table 6.2, is the impact on output per head of diminishing returns to scale in labour and capital combined. If output is a function with constant returns to scale in labour, capital and land, there must be diminishing return to scale in labour and capital alone. The extent of diminishing returns to scale in labour and capital would be small if the ratio of the value of land to the value of produced means of production were low, if the elasticity of substitution between land and capital were high or if technical change were somehow accelerated by population growth. I know of no evidence for these qualifications, and there is a widespread belief that the scarcity of land, broadly defined to include land *per se*, minerals, sources of energy, water and air, is a major impediment to further economic growth.[2]

Imagine an economy in which output (Y) is produced with three factors, labour (L), capital (K), and land (N). The aggregate production function is assumed to be homogeneous in degree one so that the sum of the elasticities of output with respect to each of the three factors is unity:

$$Y = f(L, K, N) \tag{1}$$

and

$$\varepsilon_L + \varepsilon_K + \varepsilon_N = 1 \tag{2}$$

where $\varepsilon_L = (\partial Y/\partial L)/(Y/L)$, etc. Suppose that the stock of land is fixed and unaugmentable. It is easily shown that the growth rate of capital in any year required to maintain output per head to compensate for population growth (population and labour force are assumed to be one and the same) is[3]

$$G_K|_{Y/L} = \frac{\varepsilon_K + \varepsilon_N}{\varepsilon_K} G_L \tag{3}$$

---

[2] A bit of evidence assembled by William Nordhaus and James Tobin ('Is Growth Obsolete', *Economic Growth*, Fiftieth Anniversary Colloquium, National Bureau of Economic Research, 1972) suggests that land-augmenting technical change may have been sufficient to preserve the land capital measured in efficiency units. However, they considered only land *per se* and not minerals, energy, water or air.

[3] Let $y = Y/L$ and for any variable x, let $G_x = (1/x)(dx/dt)$ where t is time. The growth rate of y is $G_y = G_Y - G_L = \varepsilon_L G_L + \varepsilon_K G_K + \varepsilon_N G_N - G_L$, because f is homogeneous in degree one. Since we are computing compensating growth rates of G_L and G_K, we may set $G_y = G_N = 0$ with the result that, $(\varepsilon_L - 1)$ $G_L + \varepsilon_K G_K = 0$, which transforms into equation (3).

In Table 6.2, the depreciation equivalent of the inheritance of the extra population is calculated according to the formula

$$G_K|_{Y/L} = G_L \qquad (4)$$

which would be correct if output were produced with labour and capital alone but which is an underestimate if land acts as a drag on economic growth when labour and capital increase proportionally.

The terms ε_K, ε_L and ε_N can be interpreted as shares of gross output accruing to capital, labour and land. These shares would remain constant over time if the production function f were Cobb–Douglas, but not otherwise. If the elasticity of substitution between land and capital were less than one, the term $(\varepsilon_K + \varepsilon_N)/\varepsilon_K$ in equation (3) would increase together with capital and labour force, and the rate of depreciation per head would grow even at a constant rate of population growth.

The concept of depreciation might also be extended to account for the using up of natural resources. A mineral deposit is like a factory in that both represent title to a flow of net income for some time to come. We say that the factory has depreciated if the present value of the flow is less at the end of the year than it was at the beginning. We could also say that the mineral deposit has depreciated if the present value of the remaining ore is less at the end of the year than it was at the beginning. There would seem to be three main problems in the assessment of the depreciation equivalent of the extraction of mineral resources: the determination of the price of used up minerals, the treatment of revaluations of mineral deposits in the course of the year, and the evaluation of the discovery of new minerals. The first problem is easy in principle though the appropriate data are often unavailable. In computing the depreciation equivalent of the extraction and usage of minerals, the quantity extracted should be evaluated at the shadow price of ore in the ground which for all practical purposes may be measured as the difference between the world price of ore and the cost of extraction, where the cost of extraction is measured net of tax, tariffs and royalties but inclusive of ongoing public expenditure, on police, maintenance of roads and so on, in assistance to the mineral-extracting industry. The world price is relevant because the loss of the world price is the alternative cost of leaving an additional unit of the mineral in the ground. This assumes, however, that the country does not have monopoly power in the export or import of the mineral; the determination of the shadow price of minerals in the ground becomes more difficult in that case.

Revaluation of minerals in the ground may or may not be counted as part of income depending on which concept of income is employed. It ought to be counted when income is defined as consumption plus the change in wealth, but it ought to be excluded from a measure of real income as the sum of actual consumption plus consumption forgone because no current consumption was sacrificed to effect the change in the price.

It is not obvious what to do about mineral discoveries. On the one hand, the discovery of a mineral deposit is like the production of an automobile factory, for both are the consequence of investment activity and both contribute to output accruing at some time in the future. On the other hand, production and discovery are not really on a par because minerals undiscovered today remain in the ground to be discovered tomorrow. A country that discovers a million barrels of oil and extracts a million barrels is worse off at the end of the year than it was at the beginning because the million barrels discovered would otherwise have remained in the ground to be discovered eventually, but the million barrels extracted is gone forever. Perhaps the theoretically correct procedure would be to compute net investment in the mineral industry as dependent on three elements: ordinary investment in plant and equipment, minus depletion evaluated at the shadow price of ore in the ground, plus discoveries evaluated at a price somewhat lower than the shadow price of ore in the ground to take account of the fact that ore not discovered today would be discovered eventually. There are serious difficulties with this procedure. The shadow price of minerals in the ground is difficult to obtain. Some mineral industries are monopolized. The world price may be less than the sum of the shadow price of minerals in the ground and the cost of extraction because insecurity of tenure or fear of increase in royalties may induce mining companies to produce more than would otherwise be warranted. There is no market for undiscovered oil.

Though we cannot estimate the full depreciation effect of depletion, a rough estimate for petroleum in Canada does suggest that the magnitudes may be considerable. By the end of 1973 the world price of petroleum in Canada (the potential well-head price) was about $11.70 a barrel and the cost of extracting oil was about $2.00 a barrel, leaving about $9.70 as the shadow price of oil in the ground. Of that $9.70, $5.20 was export tax and the rest could be accounted for by royalties collected by the provincial government, corporation income tax, and perhaps windfall profits of oil companies. Total Canadian production of oil in 1973 was 716.5 million barrels for which the value at the world price was $8.38 billion and the value at the shadow price was $6.95 billion.[4] This figure of $6.95 billion can be looked upon as the

[4] The numbers are from W. Gainer and T. Powrie, 'Public Revenue from Canadian Crude Petroleum Production', *Canadian Public Policy*, 1975, pp. 1–12.

depreciation equivalent of the reduction in Canadian reserves over the year. This is a very large number. The estimated $6.95 billion should be compared with the $13.38 billion of ordinary capital consumption allowance and $15.42 billion of total saving in Canada as a whole in 1973. The depreciation equivalent of production of all minerals would be larger still, though it is unlikely that the spread between world price and cost of production is as great for other minerals as for petroleum. Note that the change in accounting conventions in treating depletion as depreciation would involve an enormous reduction in the measured real incomes of the oil producing countries. Their net incomes would be small despite the fact that investment in tangible capital equipment is large and people living there are well off. The question is whether we should say that the income in these countries is high, or that consumption is high because they are living off their capital and that the extensive construction of plant and equipment reflects a change in the composition in their capital stock rather than an increase in the total.

The usage of natural resources creates a problem of a different kind when we define real income as sustainable consumption in the absence of technical change and population growth. Suppose there is a mineral—let us call it gold—that exists on earth in a limited supply, that cannot be recycled, and that is an indispensible ingredient of production; suppose, for example, that we use up one ounce of gold in the production of each billion dollars worth of GNP. This is an example of a 'limits to growth' situation in which no finite value of real income per year can be sustained indefinitely. In practice, we can usually depend on being able to invent our way out of such an impass, but that solution is specifically precluded by our definition of real income as stated above. The only way I can see around this problem is to extend our list of 'as if' qualifications by treating income as though it were generated within the one-sector model described at the beginning of Chapter 5 where a uniform stuff called Y is generated by labour and capital without the using up of natural resources. Thus, we can measure depreciation in current dollars as the loss in the value of assets of all kinds with due allowance for changes in known and unknown quantities of minerals in the ground as well as for the effect on capital per head of population growth in the current year. We can then replace the usual measure of depreciation with our revised measure to get revised net saving in current dollars which can then be translated into real net saving by deflating by the price index of consumption goods. We can treat the corresponding measure of real income as the potential consumption in a stationary state if technical change and population growth cease at the end of the year and if income can be looked upon as having been generated by labour and capital alone in accordance with the simple one-sector model.

APPENDIX ON THE CONSTRUCTION OF TABLE 6.2

The data are from various issues of United Nations Yearbook of National Accounts Statistics (YNAS), United Nations Demographic Yearbook (DY), UNESCO Statistical Yearbook (USY), and, for Canada only, 'Financial Statistics of Education', *Statistics Canada*, No. 81-208 (FS).

The numbered columns, expressed as percentages of gross domestic product, are constructed as follows:

(1) Gross investment in physical capital is measured as 'fixed capital formation' plus 'increase in stocks' (YNAS).

(2) Gross investment in educational capital is measured as total expenditure on education (USY and FS).

(3) Assistance of extra people in supporting the aged is measured according to the formula

$$\Delta L \sum_{t=T}^{64} \left[S(t)\left(\frac{1}{1+r}\right)^t \frac{C}{L} \frac{L(65+)}{L(T \text{ to } 64)} \right]$$

where L is mid-year population (DY). ΔL is mid-year population in the year specified in the first column of the table minus mid-year population in the preceding year. T is the age of maturity, set arbitrarily at 20 in Europe, North America and Japan and at 15 elsewhere. r is the use rate of interest, set arbitrarily at 5%. $L(x$ to $y)$ is population between the ages of x and y inclusive (DY). C is private and government consumption (YNAS) and $S(t)$ is the probability of a newly-born child surviving to age t.

The survival rate is measured according to the formula

$$S(t) \equiv \prod_{i=0}^{t} (1 - D(i))$$

where $D(i)$ is the mortality rate in the year prior to one's $i + 1$ birthday. The series $D(i)$ is estimated from population data and numbers of deaths by age groups; rates pertaining to intervals are applied to each year in the interval (DY).

(4) As statistics on capital consumption allowance appear to be unavailable for Singapore and Mauritius, we substituted the rates for Japan in 1974 and Costa Rica in 1973 (YNAS).

(5) Capital consumption allowance in educational capital is measured, *faute de mieux*, as half of gross investment in educational capital.

(6) Cost of caring for extra people as children is measured as

$$\Delta L \sum_{t=0}^{T-1} \left[\left(\frac{1}{2} + \frac{t}{2T} \right) \left(\frac{1}{1+r} \right)^t \frac{C}{L} S(t) \right]$$

(7) Cost of educating the extra people is measured as

$$\Delta L \sum_{t=5}^{T-1} \left[\frac{E}{L(5 \text{ to } T-1)} \left(\frac{1}{1+r} \right)^t S(t) \right]$$

where E is gross investment in education as indicated in item (2) above.

(8) Cost of inheritance of the extra people is measured as

$$\Delta L \cdot S(65) \cdot \frac{\text{GNP}}{L} \cdot \frac{1}{3} \cdot \frac{1}{2r}$$

where the term $2r$ represents the opportunity cost rate of interest assumed to be twice the use rate.

NOTES FOR FURTHER READING

The theory of how depreciation ought to be measured was studied extensively by economists in the nineteen thirties and forties when the national accounts as we know them were first being constructed. See particularly the pieces by Pigou, Hayek and Hicks on the maintenance of capital intact in R. H. Parker and G. C. Harcourt, *Readings in the Concept and Measurement of Income*, Cambridge University Press, 1969. Hotelling's article, 'A General Mathematical Theory of Depreciation', reprinted in Parker and Harcourt volume is still well worth reading.

Recently, there has been a good deal of work on the concept and measurement of 'economic depreciation'. Economic depreciation, as distinct from depreciation in the tax code, reflects the actual time path of decline in the value of assets as indicated by curve D in Figure 6.1. Rates of economic depreciation may be inferred from evidence on prices or rents of secondhand equipment or from the investment behaviour of firms. The procedure for estimating economic depreciation can be quite complicated because the actual and observable time path of the decline in the value of assets is affected by the tax laws in force and is therefore different from what would be observed if rates of economic depreciation were employed for setting capital consumption allowance in the tax code. See particularly, P. A. Samuelson, 'Tax Deductability of Economic Depreciation to Insure Invariant Variation', *Journal of Political Economy*, 1964, pp. 604–6; P. Taubman and R. Rasche, 'Economic and Tax Depreciation of Office Buildings', *National Tax Journal*, 1969, pp. 334–46; R. Coen, 'Investment Behavior, the Measurement of Depreciation and Tax Policy', *American Economic Review*, 1975, pp. 59–74; and A. H. Young 'New Estimates of Capital Consumption Allowances', *Survey of Current Business*, 1975, pp. 14–16.

The model used to account for the depreciation implicit in the decline in capital per head resulting from population is similar to that used in Enke's study of the economics of birth control: S. Enke, 'Economic Consequences of Rapid Population Growth', *Economic Journal*, 1966, pp. 44–56. The only attempt I know to account for the depreciation equivalent of the using up of natural resources is J. Soliday, 'The Measurement of Income and Product in the Oil and Gas Mining Industry', in D. Usher (ed.), *The Measurement of Capital*, Conference on Income and Wealth, National Bureau of Economic Research, Vol. 45, 1980.

7

Imputations

With the exception of the brief discussion of varieties of capital goods in Chapter 5, our study of real consumption and real income has so far been conducted as though the only problem in measuring economic growth is deciding how to combine time series of different quantities into one comprehensive index. It was taken for granted that the utility function depends on amounts consumed of a finite set of commodities, that money income is the value of these commodities at current prices, that expenditure of each commodity is the product of a quantity and a price, that all goods may be identified either as capital goods or as consumption goods, and that time series of quantities and prices are readily at hand. However, when one attempts to measure real consumption or real income, or when one watches the national accountant at work, one soon discovers that these suppositions about the nature of utility and the availability of data are deficient in two important respects. First, it is by no means obvious what quantities are to be included in income. Welfare depends on many things—apples, oranges, services of cars, hours of leisure, availability of recreational facilities, levels of pollution, the state of one's health, the maintenance of the law—and the national accountant in preparing his statistics must decide what to include in income and what to leave out. Second, we have derived rules for measuring real consumption and real income without considering where time series of prices and quantities originate and as though they were the outcome of direct observation untainted by economic theorizing or statistical manipulation. In reality the flow of income consists of an unlimited number of items, no two of which are exactly alike. The division of the flow of income each year into amounts of n allegedly homogeneous commodities is not a fact of nature, as we have so far supposed, but is imposed by the national accountant onto the available data. Economic analysis has as large a part to play in dividing the flow of income into a set of commodities and in identifying prices and quantities as in combining individual time series into big aggregates of consumption, investment and income. Most of the work of the national accountant and most of the tricky economic issues he has to resolve concern the development of the time series which we have taken as the starting point for our analysis. We shall discuss the first of these problems in this chapter, leaving the second to be discussed in the next.

Recall the conceptual experiment in which economic growth is measured. To determine the rate of economic growth between 1926 and 1974 with regard to 1961 as the base year, we instruct a representative consumer to tell us how much income he would need in 1961 to be as well off as he would be in 1926 with the average income in 1926, and how much he would need in 1961 to be as well off as he would be in 1974 with the average income in 1974. We designate these two sums of money in 1961 dollars to be the real income in 1926 and the real income in 1974, and we say that the rate of economic growth is whatever rate of appreciation is sufficient to raise the real income in 1926 to the real income in 1974 over a forty-eight year period. In discussing this experiment, we supposed that utility of the representative consumer is a function of amounts of a finite set of commodities, and that his money income is combined value of these commodities at current prices. Were we to attempt to conduct this experiment or to design statistics to reflect what we imagine its outcome would be, it would become immediately clear that the scope of income is not, as we have supposed, a fact of nature, but is instead a statistical convention we establish ourselves. If the representative consumer is to tell us how much income in 1961 makes him as well off as he would be in 1926 with the average income in 1926, we must first tell him what aspects of the economy and society in 1926 to take account of and what aspects to ignore, for the measure of real income does not necessarily encompass all conditions of life. For instance, we might instruct the representative consumer to work as many hours per day in 1926 as the average man worked in 1926, or we might instruct him to work as many hours per day as the average man worked in 1961. In the first case we would be accounting for leisure in the measure of real income while in the second case we would not. Similarly, we must give the representative consumer detailed specifications about his circumstances in 1926 with respect to conditions of sanitation, the environment in which he lives, working conditions, air pollution, crime rates, time spent in transport to work, and ownership of consumer durables. The statistician in preparing a time series of real income must decide which of these conditions of life to account for in the measure of money income and what imputations might be appropriate for the measures of real income and economic growth.

Recall also that the object of the income comparison is to connect the condition of the average man in each year of the time series with a particular income in the base year as illustrated in the income thermometer of Chapter 2, for the numbers alleged to represent real income each year have no meaning and no reference point other than the spectrum of personal incomes at a given moment of time. Thus, the ultimate criterion, both for the representative consumer in the conceptual experiment and for the national accountant in designing imputations for a measure of income to be used in assessing the rate of growth, is the common usage of the word 'income' in comparisons between people. Suppose I say that my income is larger than yours because, though we earn the same wages, I keep a garden where I grow vegetables, while you have to buy your vegetables at the shop. Is that a reasonable statement? If so, there is a case for imputing for home-grown food in the measure of income in the national accounts. Suppose I say that my income is greater than yours because, though we earn the same wages and enjoy the same services from our respective municipalities, you have to pay higher taxes since public buildings in your town are rented by the municipality, while public buildings in mine are owned and paid for. Is that a reasonable statement? If so, there is a case for adding imputed rents of roads and public buildings to the measure of income. Suppose I say that though you earn $20,000 and I earn $10,000, your income is not really twice mine because we both enjoy the same number of hours of leisure and have the same access to sunshine. Is that a reasonable statement? One might well say that it is not, for the term income was never intended to encompass leisure or sunshine, and your income, as the term is commonly understood, is twice mine despite the fact that we enjoy the same amount of leisure and sunshine. There should, therefore, be no imputation to the measure of real national income for quantities consumed of leisure or sunshine.

We posed the problem of income comparison in Chapter 2 as though income and welfare were synonymous at least to the extent that they encompassed the same range of commodities. Yet when we look at the composition of income more closeiy, it begins to seem as though welfare depends on two types of arguments some of which are included in income and some not. You and I compare our incomes against a backdrop of circumstances that we take for granted: leisure, health, sunshine, family life, good government. We exclude these from consideration when we compare incomes, not because they are unimportant—they may be more important than income itself—but because the word income is used in the first instance to designate what we earn and, by extension, what we buy with our earnings. There is an intrinsic connection between income and money. We might limit the word income to denote what is acquired in the market sector of the economy or we might extend the scope of income somewhat to account for goods and services acquired through barter, payment in kind or activity in the household, but we cannot extend the scope of income to cover the whole range of conditions that contribute to welfare without so distorting the term that it loses all connection with the original comparison among people.

We must recognize, however, that the background conditions do change over the years. People on average enjoy more leisure and longer lives, and it would be unfortunate to leave these changes out of account altogether, for they may well be more important to the representative consumer than the change in quantities of goods and services consumed. There might be a case for saying that my income broadly conceived is greater than yours if our money incomes are the same but I work less than you do. If you work nine hours a day and I work seven, it may be appropriate to make an adjustment to my income to account for the two extra hours of leisure I enjoy, though the leisure time we have in common may be disregarded. On the same principle, we might choose to measure real income per head in any given year as the amount of money the representative consumer would need in the base year to be as well off as he would be in the given year on the understanding that he works the average number of hours in each year, so that real income in the given year would be high if money income is high, if prices are low, and if average number of hours of work is less in the given year than in the base year. Thus, changes in hours of leisure would be allowed to affect the measure of economic growth, but the level from which these changes occur would not. A similar procedure could be adopted for pollution, life expectancy or any other aspect of the environment which is not in itself considered as part of income.

We shall therefore distinguish among three successively broader definitions of income: (1) the value of all final goods and services purchased during the year; (2) the above, plus the value of goods and services acquired outside the market but which might have been purchased with money under a different but plausible form of economic organization; (3) the above, plus the value of changes in the environment since the base year. There is a corresponding distinction between those imputations—to be called imputations of goods and services—that might reasonably be included in the second concept of income, and those imputations—to be called imputations for changes in the environment—that belong only in the third and broadest concept of income. It should be recognized at once that the definitions are not absolutely watertight. They are put forward as a guide to classifying imputations, but they do not relieve the statistician of having to decide in the end which imputations are appropriate and which are not. In this chapter, we shall present a list of possible imputations of goods and services, examine the concept of imputation for changes in the environment, and compute an imputation for changes in hours of leisure.

A. IMPUTATIONS OF GOODS AND SERVICES

Let us begin with a definition of income limited to final goods and services actually sold by one party to another, where 'final' refers to goods and services consumed during the year or to investment goods kept in use for more than one year. Starting from this definition, the scope of income may be widened or narrowed by imputations, or there may be imputations to components of income, as for instance, when current expenditure on higher education is reclassified from consumption to investment. Among the imputations that have at one time or another been computed are the following.

Home grown food

The food a farmer grows for his own use is as much a contribution to his welfare as the food his urban cousin buys in the shop. This imputation is normally included in the national accounts. A similar case can be made for the inclusion of the farmer's non-marketed investment in the improvement of his land, equipment and buildings, and for the inclusion of food that the city dweller grows in his backyard. It is hard to know where to draw the line. If I grow lettuce in my backyard and you grow roses, should my gardening be counted as income and yours not, or should flower-growing be counted as income too. Nor is it obvious how home-grown food should be evaluated. Some argue that it should be at farm-gate prices because food not consumed at home would presumably be sold. Others argue that it should be at retail prices because that is what people have to pay for food. The general problem to which we will return in the next chapter is what to do when prices are not the same for everyone in the economy.

Imputed rents

The man who owns the house he lives in is assumed in the construction of the national accounts to be both landlord and tenant. His imputed rent in his capacity as tenant is included as part of gross national expenditure. Without this imputation, we would have to say that the national income increases if I sell my house and rent it back from the purchaser.

Payment in kind

The most important instance is food and shelter provided to the military. The case for the inclusion of payment in kind in the national accounts is that a man who receives a low wage and payment in kind should not be counted as worse off than a man with a high wage and no payment in kind if the value of the goods received is equal to the difference in their wages. But what—to take a famous example—if the payment in kind is alcohol consumed by a diplomat at a cocktail party he is obliged to attend? Would it make a difference if the diplomat would have preferred to be a teetotaller? Ideally, goods received as payment in kind should be evaluated in the income of the recipient at the price the recipient would be willing to pay for an extra unit, a price which would equal market price if the recipient buys amounts over and above what he receives as payment in kind, but would normally be less otherwise. In practice, there is no alternative to evaluating payment in kind at market prices. Other examples of payment in kind are the businessman's lunch on expense account, the coffee provided by the firm during coffee break, and the vacation provided the professor 'attending conferences' or living abroad on sabbatical.

Forgone earnings of students

The usual definition of income includes the direct cost of education such as teachers' salaries, but excludes the alternative cost of the time the student devotes to study. A case can be made for including both costs, for the alternative cost of labour devoted to education has the same claim to be classified as investment as the alternative cost of labour devoted to the production of a machine. A similar case can be made for the inclusion of on-the-job training. A firm that trains workers has a joint product consisting of its normal output and the output of skilled workers. Both, so the argument goes, belong as components of real income.

Housework

Another famous conundrum in national accounting is of the man who causes the national income to increase by divorcing his wife and hiring her as a housekeeper. Her wages as a housekeeper would under present conventions be included as part of income, while the same housework performed by a wife would not. A way around this problem is to include all housework as income. The argument for doing so is not simply to avoid a conundrum. It is that real income should encompass the product of all labour, regardless of whether it is performed in the home or the office, as long as it can be said to contribute to the welfare of the community.

Volunteer labour

The case for the inclusion of volunteer labour in the national income is essentially the same as that for the inclusion of housework. Under present accounting conventions, work done in caring for the sick or disabled may or may not be included as part of national income depending, not on the work itself, but on whether the doer is paid for his activity.

Services of consumer durables

The purchase of a house is treated in the national accounts as an investment and an imputation is added to consumption for the services of owner-occupied houses. Other consumer durables might be treated in the same way. The purchase of a stove, now classified as expenditure on consumption, could be reclassified as investment. There would need to be a negative imputation for the depreciation of the existing stock of stoves, and the annual services of the stove would be imputed to consumption. The empirical significance of such imputations would depend upon the durability of the item.

Services of publicly-owned capital goods

Services of publicly-owned roads, bridges, hospitals and other public buildings tend to be excluded from income because these services are not actually sold in the current year. The city does not as a rule pay rent on the city hall. The value of the services of publicly-owned capital could be estimated either as the rent the government would need to pay if the capital used in the public sector were owned in the private sector and rented to the government on a long term contract, or as the interest the government would need to pay if the capital had been financed by perpetual bonds.

Research, development and exploration

There are, broadly speaking, two ways of classifying the expenditures of a firm into cost of production and investment. The first and simplest is to define an investment as a purchase of a tangible asset that persists beyond the end of the accounting year. The other is to say that expenditure is for investment if its effects persist beyond the end of the accounting year. Research, development and exploration are excluded from investment on the former definition but included on the latter; or, more generally, only tangible investments are included on the former definition while both tangible and intangible investments are included in the latter. The case for imputing for intangible investments is straight-forward. Consider once again the simple one-sector model set out at the beginning of Chapter 5. Recall that $Y = C + I$ where I augments K which in turn augments future Y. Whatever augments future in-come—buildings, machines, research, medicine or education—would seem to qualify as investment regardless of whether tangible physical goods are created. In constructing a time series of a country's rate of investment, it would seem appropriate to measure the rate of invest-ment as the proportion of income this year devoted to increasing income next year. Of two countries each of which consumes 70% of its income, if country A puts 15% of its income into research and 15% into constructing new plant and equipment while country B puts the full 30% of its income into constructing new plant and equipment, we would want to say that their rates of investment are the same. The countries' investments would differ in form but not in amount. Note that we are appealing here to the concept of investment as consumption forgone. Research would only contribute to wealth if a discovery were made, and it would not contribute to capital at all because the quantity of capital is assessed according to the capacity of the mix of capital goods within a given technology.

The journey to work

The journey to work is now classified as final rather than intermediate product because, and insofar as, it is paid for by consumers rather than by firms. A case can be made that it ought to be classified as intermediate product because travelling to work does not in itself contribute to the welfare of the consumer. It is, on this argument, just as much an intermediate product as the purchase by an automobile manufacturer of a battery to be installed in a car which is sold as a unit to the final consumer. Suppose Mr A and Mr B work in the same establishment, for the same number of hours each day, and for the same pay; but Mr A's contract stipulates that the employer bears the cost of transporting him to work while Mr B must bear that cost himself. We would say that Mr A is the better off, that his income is in some sense higher than Mr B's income. We might also be inclined to say that economic growth occurs if a community of people in circumstances like those of Mr B transforms itself into a community of people in circum-stances like those of Mr A. The only way to insure that our statistics give us this result is to remove transport to work from the category of final products. Under present conventions a country is recorded as becoming better off, other things being equal, if there is an increase in the cost of transport to work because the mean distance between home and work place increases, and if there is a general rise in site rents in cities due to urbanization or crowding. We should recognize, on the other hand, that the principal cost of travelling to work is the loss of leisure time, that people today have considerably more, not less leisure than did their parents or grandparents, and that the difference in leisure time is not imputed for in our measure of real income. As a general rule, we would not want to impute for a change in a part of any category of welfare if we had reason to believe that the part and the whole were changing in different directions in the course of time.

Government consumption

Current expenditure on defence and public administration might be reclassified from final to intermediate product because their benefit consists in the maintenance of the economy rather than in the production of goods and services which are useful in their own right. The analogy of the battery and the car is as relevant here as for the journey to work. No one gets direct benefit from the activity of the Ministry of Internal Revenue, notwithstanding the fact that the activity of the Ministry is a prerequisite to the operation of the economy as a whole.

Imputations associated with depreciation

The adjustments to depreciation discussed in the preceding chapter may be classified as types of imputations. It should be mentioned in passing that the cost of education and child-rearing have on occasion been reclassified as investment rather than consumption.

An interesting collection of imputations for the United States is shown here as Table 7.1. The official imputations in the table include rents on owner-occupied houses, services of banks on chequing accounts, value for food and fuel consumed on the farm, and payment in kind to the military. Of the other imputations, 'business investment charged to current expense' includes the estimate of the value of on-the-job training and expenditure on exploration, research and development, 'student compensation' is the value of students' forgone earnings, and 'frictional unemployment cost' embodies a view of the labour market in which the alternative cost of the normal period of unemployment while changing jobs is a kind of investment in the acquisition of knowledge. The combined affect of these imputations is to increase gross national product by a full 32%.

Table 7.1 Imputations to the gross national product of the US, 1966

	billions of dollars	percentage of official GNP
Market GNP	695.9	92.8
Plus: official imputations	54.0	7.2
Official GNP	749.9	100.0
Plus: additional imputations for consistency with total investments, of which:	240.6	32.1
Business investments charged to current expense	28.9	3.9
Student compensation	70.5	9.4
Frictional unemployment cost	13.7	1.8
Rentals on capital additional to components in official GNP	127.5	17.0
Consumer durables and inventories	75.1	10.1
Institutional plant and equipment	3.2	0.4
Government structures, equipment, and inventories	49.2	6.6
GNP inclusive of additional imputations	990.5	132.1

Source: J. W. Kendrick, *Economic Accounts and their Uses*, McGraw-Hill, 1972, table 8–1, p. 129.

Now with this list of possible imputations in mind, we shall take up the question posed at the outset of this chapter of how to decide which imputations are warranted and which are not. The answer will of course depend fundamentally on the purpose of the time series of income. It is doubtful whether any of the imputations are warranted—even those already in the national accounts—when the purpose of income statistics is to facilitate the preparation of the budget of the government or to chart the course of the business cycle. The case for imputations becomes much stronger when, as in this book, real income is intended to show the progress of the economy over time. Our assessment of the suitability of the different imputations is with respect to that purpose alone.

The main criterion is of course one's sense of the meaning of the word income in a comparison between people at any given time and place. I think it is a reasonable extension of the normal meaning of the word to include the value of goods and services acquired outside of the market sector but that might have been purchased with money under a different but plausible form of economic organization. We might impute for rents of owner-occupied houses because we can imagine an economy in which all houses are rented. We might impute for income in kind because we can imagine an economy in which the soldier pays for his meals at the mess hall, in which the farmer is obliged to sell the whole of his crop, and which no one is allowed to, or no one wants to, work his own vegetable garden. We might impute for the services of public capital because we can imagine an economy in which governments rent public capital from private firms. Though the borderline between what is or what is not a 'different but plausible' form of economic organization is less exact than we would like it to be, it may be adequate for many of the choices we have to make in defining income for the purpose of measuring economic growth, especially, as will be discussed in the next section, as we can impute for environmental changes outside of the range of goods and services included in income itself.

Two subsidiary criteria might also be taken into account. The national accountant must balance the desirability of imputing for everything that might conceivably be bought and sold against the requirement that the measures of real income and economic growth be composed of primary data generally recognized as correct. The imputation for housework is a case in point. The imputation is tricky because it is difficult to draw the line between housework and other activities and because there is no obviously right way to account for the increase over time in the productivity of housewives. In computing the number of hours of housework, one can count the number of housewives and can discover from sample surveys how many hours of housework are put in per day. Presumably one would also want to add the activity of the husband in fixing the plumbing or the roof. One might also include work done in the vegetable garden and, if so, a case can be made for including work done in the flower garden as well. But now it is only a small step to add time spent reading or sailing, for reading, sailing and gardening are in a sense economically equivalent ways of spending one's leisure time. Clearly, an arbitrary line has to be drawn. That is not in itself reason for excluding housework for there are a great many arbitrary lines in the national accounts, but this line is somewhat more arbitrary than most. The more intractable problem is the determination of the rate of productivity change. Housewives are better educated than they used to be and this must increase productivity per hour to some extent. The question is whether the difference between the productivity of a lady

with a college education and a lady with a high school education is
as large at housework as the difference in their average wages in
the market world suggests. This problem is similar to the problem,
to be discussed in the next chapter, of evaluating the change over
time in the output of doctors, lawyers and civil servants. Nonetheless,
the imputation for housework would involve some very arbitrary
assignments on the part of the national accountant, and it might be
considered to be insufficiently grounded in hard data to justify its inclusion as part of real income for the purpose of measuring economic
growth. One can, of course, prepare several measures of real income
under alternative assumptions about the growth of productivity of
housework.

There is also a question of what might be called congruence. However
income is defined, we would want the same kinds of things to be
included in each year of the comparison. One's decision to impute for a
particular good or service may depend on whether the boundary
between market and non-market sectors is shifting over time. There
would be a weaker case for imputing for housework in a society where
women are forbidden by law or custom to take jobs outside the home
and in which the scope of housework is rigidly prescribed, than there
would be in a society where the proportion of women who work is
changing over time.

B. IMPUTATIONS FOR CHANGES IN THE ENVIRONMENT

For the remainder of this chapter, we return to the assumption
employed in Chapter 2 that all income is consumed in the current year,
so that the terms 'real income' and 'real consumption' may be used
interchangeably to designate the aggregate of what is consumed. We
shall once again use the term real income, except at the end of the
chapter where we construct an imputation for leisure to the measure of
real consumption in Canada for the years 1926 to 1974. We emphasize
real consumption at that point because the time series we construct will
be combined with time series of investment in real terms later on in the
book. In Chapter 2, it was assumed that utility is a function of quantities
$q_1, \ldots, q_n$ designated collectively by the vector q,

$$U = U(q) \tag{1}$$

Now, instead, let it be assumed that utility is a function of two sorts of arguments, commodities q and environmental conditions $x_1, \ldots, x_m$ designated collectively by the vector x:

$$U = U(q, x) \qquad (2)$$

The distinction between commodities and environmental conditions in the pure case we are imagining is that commodities are purchased with money so that rich people may consume more than poor people at any time, while environmental conditions are not purchasable and affect everyone alike in any given year though they may change from year to year so that people may enjoy more or less of each x_1 in 1974 than in 1926. In practice, there are very few pure environmental conditions, but there are sufficiently close approximations to make the theory interesting and useful. We shall enumerate types of environmental conditions presently, but for the moment let us use as an example the average number of hours of sunshine per day looked upon as a good rather than as a bad.

The representative consumer when he goes from the base year, 1961, to the year being investigated, t, observes average income Y^t, the prices p^t, and the environmental conditions x^t, and he compares these features of the year t with the corresponding features of the base year. Real income in year t, the income that makes him as well off in the year 1961 as he was with the average income in the year t is Y^{wt} defined implicitly in the equation

$$U(Y^{wt}, p^{61}, x^{61}) = U(Y^t, p^t, x^t) \qquad (3)$$

It is the amount of money he needs at 1961 prices and at 1961 environmental conditions to be as well off as he would be in the year t with the average income, the actual prices and the actual environmental conditions in that year. This definition is identical to the definition of real income in Chapter 2 except for the inclusion of the terms x^{61} and x^t. The significance of the inclusion of these terms is that the representative consumer takes account of the change in the average hours of sunlight. He needs less income in 1961 to be as well off as he is in the year t if there is more sunlight in 1961 than there is in the year t.

Expanding equation (3) in a Taylor series we see at once that[1]

$$\hat{Y}^{wt} = \sum_{i=1}^{n} p_i^{61} q_i^t + \sum_{j=1}^{m} s_j^{61} (x_j^t - x_j^{61}) \qquad (4)$$

where $\hat{Y}^{wt}$ is a first approximation to Y^{wt} in equation (3). The meaning of equation (4) is that real income in the year t with respect to 1961 as the base year is approximately equal to the value at 1961 prices of *total* commodities consumed in the year t plus the *change* in environmental conditions from 1961 to the year t evaluated at the shadow price s_j^{61} in the year 1961.

The imputation to real income in equations (3) and (4) is illustrated in Figure 7.1 for a representative consumer whose utility function consists of two arguments, an ordinary quantity called bread and an environmental variable called sunshine. Two indifference curves are shown, one containing amounts of bread and sunshine in the year 1961 and the other containing amounts of bread and sunshine in the year t. As we are supposing that bread is part of income but sunshine it not, there is no harm in treating bread as the numeraire, in which case income may be expressed in loaves of bread. The real income in year t is the quantity of bread consumed in the year t plus the extra quantity of bread required in the year 1961 to compensate for the change in the sunshine index from the year 1961 to the year t. The true measure of real income assessed in accordance with equation (3) is Y^{wt}, the height of the intersection of the indifference curve attained in the year t with a vertical line at the value

---

[1] Expand both sides of equation (3) around the point $U(Y^{61}, p^{61}, x^{61})$. Ignoring all but first-order terms, we see that

$$U(Y^{wt}, p^{61}, x^{61}) - U(Y^{61}, p^{61}, x^{61}) \simeq (Y^{wt} - Y^{61}) \frac{\partial U}{\partial Y}$$

and

$$U(Y^t, p^t, x^t) - U(Y^{61}, p^{61}, x^{61})$$
$$\simeq (Y^t - Y^{61}) \frac{\partial U}{\partial Y} + \sum_{i=1}^{n} (p_i^t - p_i^{61}) \frac{\partial U}{\partial p_i} + \sum_{j=1}^{m} (x_j^t - x_j^{61}) \frac{\partial U}{\partial x_j}$$

where all derivatives are taken at the point $U(Y^{61}, p^{61}, x^{61})$. Combining terms and making use of equation (3), we have

$$Y^{wt} \simeq Y^t + \sum_{i=1}^{n} (p_i^t - p_i^{61}) \left(\frac{\partial U/\partial p_i}{\partial U/\partial Y} \right) + \sum_{j=1}^{m} (x_j^t - x_j^{61}) \left(\frac{\partial U/\partial x_j}{\partial U/\partial Y} \right)$$

where the term $[(\partial U/\partial p_i)/(\partial U/\partial Y)]$ is equal to $-q_i^{61}$ the term $[(\partial U/\partial x_j)/(\partial U/\partial Y)]$, called s_j^{61} in equation (4), is the shadow prices of x_j in 1961, and the first two expressions on the right-hand side of the equation differ to a second order of approximation ($\sum_{i=1}^{n} (p_i^t - p_i^{61})(q_i^t - q_i^{61})$ to be exact) from the term $\sum_{i=1}^{n} p_i^{61} q_i$ in equation (4).

of the sunshine index in the year 1961. The approximation to real income assessed in accordance with equation (4) is $\hat{Y}^{wt}$, obtained by evaluating the change in sunshine from the year 1961 to the year t at the shadow price of sunshine in 1961.

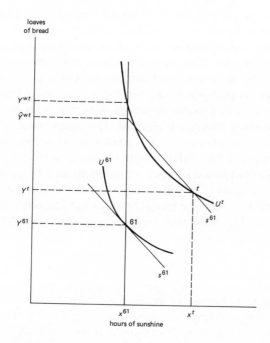

Figure 7.1 An imputation to real income for a change in the environment

The most interesting feature of imputations for changes in environmental conditions is that, unlike imputations of goods and services, they inevitably cause the rate of economic growth to increase whenever environmental conditions improve, even if the rate of improvement is slower than the growth rate of consumption of ordinary goods and services. To see this we need only divide both sides of equation (4) by Y^{61}. The first term on the right-hand side of the equation is now an ordinary Laspeyres index and the second term is positive whenever the values of x_j^t are greater on average than the values of x_j^{61}. By contrast, had we treated sunshine as the ordinary commodity and if hours of sunshine had increased very little, the effect of the imputation for sunshine would have been to reduce the rate of economic growth. When sunshine is treated as an environmental condition, the fact, if it be so, that hours of sunshine have not increased over the years, that $x_j^t = x_j^{61}$ where j is sunshine, has no effect whatsoever on our measure of the rate of economic growth. If sunshine were imputed as an ordinary commodity, we would have to say that the failure of the number of hours of sunshine to increase means that the true rate of economic growth is lower than a computation that did not take sunshine into account would show it to be.

Before we list candidates for imputations for changes in the environment, it should be noted that our pure case of environmental conditions that are: (a) the same for everyone in any given year; and (b) not counted as part of personal income in the normal usage of the term, is rarely encountered in practice. Even sunshine can be bought indirectly by going somewhere where it is plentiful. Our emphasis in the list below will be on the second condition. We shall argue that there is a case for treating something as an x variable rather than a q variable if it contributes to welfare, is not counted directly or indirectly as part of income, and if the average amount enjoyed is changing over time, even if it is possible for people to affect the amounts they enjoy through the purchase of other things. The following are candidates for environmental variables.

Air and water pollution

Time series of air pollution, amounts of mercury in fish, quality of water or other genuinely environmental conditions could be looked upon as x variables and their shadow prices could in principle be estimated by means of questionnaires. Though pollution is not part of income as normally defined, we would want to say that true economic growth is less than our statistics show it to be if pollution is becoming worse over time. But it is, in fact, doubtful whether this is the case. By all accounts, pioneer life or life in the slums of large cities in the nineteenth century was more lonely, dangerous and unsanitary than any conditions we can observe today, and there is evidence that standards of health are improving steadily.

Crime

Crime could also be treated as an x variable if quantities and shadow prices could be obtained. Quantities should be easy; we know more or less how many of each type of crime takes place each year, though underreporting may present a problem. The real difficulty is in estimating shadow prices. What is it worth to the community to reduce the number of robberies by one? We could impute to the measure of economic growth for changes in crime rates if we could answer that question for robbery and all other crimes.

Positional goods

Positional goods are defined as the benefits from status, the advantage of being boss rather than worker, of being high up in hierarchy, of being seen to enjoy what others cannot afford to enjoy. It may be that what seems to be a desire of all men to acquire income in order to consume more goods and services is really a drive for position or status. If so, it follows that what each man hopes to gain by increasing his own income cannot be obtained for the community as a whole through economic growth. Average status cannot change through economic growth because the rise of one man necessarily entails the fall of someone else. An imputation to the measure of economic growth might, in principle, be warranted if it could be shown that the burden of status to the lower classes exceeds the advantages to the upper classes and that the overall burden of status is diminishing over time as society becomes more egalitarian in tone. I know of no evidence that this is actually taking place, and no imputation is warranted unless the relevant x_j is changing over time.

Life expectancy

Though the life expectancy of the rich is somewhat greater than the life expectancy of the poor, the decline over time in age specific mortality rates is much greater than can be accounted for by the rise in income alone. There is therefore a case for treating mortality rates as an environmental variable. The imputation is discussed in detail in Chapter 11.

Leisure

Leisure might be treated as a q variable or as an x variable. This is the subject of the next section of this chapter.

C. IMPUTING FOR LEISURE AS A COMMODITY AND AS AN ASPECT OF THE ENVIRONMENT

Attempts to impute for leisure in the estimation of American economic growth have been based on the assumption that leisure is a commodity like bread or cheese. The first attempt was that of Sametz[2] who converted leisure to a commodity by assuming:

(i) that the number of hours of leisure is the difference between the maximum feasible number of hours of work per week and the average number of hours of work per week during the year.

(ii) that the efficiency per hour of input to leisure increases over time in proportion to the real wage of labour.

When income is measured with respect to ordinary goods and services as the numeraire, Sametz' estimate of income inclusive of the imputation for leisure becomes

$$\hat{Y}^t = Y^t + 52(78 - h^t)w^t \qquad (5)$$

where Y^t is real income per head in the year t as measured in the national accounts, h^t is average number of hours worked per week, w^t is real wage per hour in the year t, $\hat{Y}^t$ is the real income inclusive of the imputation for leisure, and the numbers 78 and 52 are the assumed maximum number of hours one can work per week and the number of weeks per year.

Over the period 1874 to 1966, average hours of work fell from 67 to 40, hours of leisure increased from 11 to 38, and the imputation for leisure, being the product of the increase in hours of leisure per year and the increase in the real wage, grew faster than the original measure of income causing the rate of growth of real income per head over that period to rise from 2.56% to 3.05% per year.

Another attempt to impute for leisure is that of Nordhaus and Tobin.[3] Their imputation is similar in broad outline to that of Sametz but they refine his assumptions to some extent.

(i) Instead of supposing that leisure is a homogeneous stuff, Nordhaus and Tobin employ evidence from a time-budget study to divide the 24 hours of the day into six categories of activity—work, sleep, cost of work, personal care, leisure and non-market activity. They then treat leisure and non-market activity as extra commodities, the former including entertainment, sports, reading and conversation, and the latter consisting of housework and do-it-yourself activities. 'Cost of work' (such as time spent in transport to and from work), 'personal care' and 'sleep' are treated as intermediate products, like work itself, which are

[2] A. W. Sametz, 'The Measurement of Economic Growth', Chapter 3, Indicators of Social Change, E. B. Sheldon and W. E. Moore (eds), Russell Sage Foundation, 1968.
[3] W. Nordhaus and J. Tobin, 'Is Growth Obsolete', Economic Growth, Fiftieth Anniversary Colloquium, National Bureau of Economic Research, 1972.

required to procure goods and services but are not arguments in the utility function. It is assumed that 'personal care' and 'sleep' use 7 hours a day, leaving 17 hours for all other activities.

(ii) Input to leisure and non-market activity consists of hours devoted to these activities. Output of leisure is estimated by adjusting input to reflect labour productivity in the current year. The formula for real income in the year t inclusive of an imputation for leisure and measured with regard to ordinary goods and services as the numeraire is

$$\hat{Y}^t = Y^t + N^t w^0 Z_N^t + L^t w^0 Z_L^t \tag{6}$$

where $\hat{Y}^t$ and Y^t are as defined in the explanation of equation (5), N^t is hours per head of non-market activity, L^t is hours of leisure per head, w^0 is real wage per hour in the base year, and Z_N^t and Z_L^t are productivity factors for non-market activity and leisure.[4]

Having no evidence whatsoever on the growth rate of productivity per hour of leisure and non-market activity, Nordhaus and Tobin resort to three alternative assumptions:

(A) that the productivity in both activities remains unchanged over time:

$$Z_L^t = Z_N^t = 1 \quad \text{for all } t \tag{7a}$$

(B) that the productivity of hours of leisure remains constant, but that the productivity of hours of non-market activity grows at the same rate as the real wage:

$$Z_L^t = 1 \quad \text{for all t;} \qquad Z_N^t = w^t/w^0 \tag{7b}$$

(C) that the productivity of hours of leisure and of non-market activity grow at the same rate as the real wage:

$$Z_L^t = Z_N^t = w^t/w^0 \tag{7c}$$

The effect of the imputation for leisure on the measure of American economic growth depends very much on one's choice among these three assumptions. Without the imputation for leisure, the index of personal consumption grows from 100 to 180.3 over the period 1929 to 1965. With imputation (A), it grows from 100 to 117.8, with imputation (B) it grows from 100 to 141.8, and with imputation (C), it grows from 100 to

---

[4] Equation (6) is a simplification of the procedure of Nordhaus and Tobin. They take account of wage differentials among men, women, students, and people over 65 years of age and of the leisure and non-market activities of the unemployed.

223.6. Notice that the imputation (A) reduces the rate of economic growth because the overall rate is an average of the growth rate of the consumption of ordinary goods and services and the growth rate of leisure including non-market activity, and because the growth rate of hours of leisure is the smaller of the two. Imputation (C), like Sametz' original calculation, increases the overall rate of economic growth because the sum of the growth rate of hours of leisure and the growth rate of the real wage exceeds the growth rate of consumption of ordinary goods and services.

The common feature of these imputations, in contrast to the alternative imputation discussed below, is the concept of income to which they appeal. Economic growth is always defined with reference to an analogy between comparison of incomes of the representative consumer at different periods of time and comparison of incomes among people in the chosen base year. Thus, any imputation that takes the form of adding a commodity to income in a comparison of real income over time appeals to an expanded definition of personal income as well. For instance, to impute for income in kind is to make economic growth analogous to a comparison among people, not of money income, but of money income augmented by income in kind. Nordhaus and Tobin's imputation for leisure makes economic growth analogous to a comparison among people of income assessed as follows. The standard work day consists of 17 hours, a man's money income is compensation for 17 hours of work, but a man need not actually work a 17 hour day, for he may use part of his income to buy hours of leisure from his employer at a price that varies according to assumptions A, B and C.

Several aspects of the concept of personal income implicit in the work of Sametz, Nordhaus and Tobin are worth mentioning. First, their definition of income is far from the common meaning of the term. As was evident in the discussion of the scope of income, it is hard to decide where the boundary of income ought to be drawn. Nevertheless, if we tell a man with a low cash income that his actual income is really larger than his cash income because he enjoys substantial income in kind such as home-grown food or wood gathered from the forest, he would understand what we are saying and might agree. If we tell a man with a low cash income that the differential between his income and the income of a rich man is less than appears at first sight because he and the rich man enjoy the same number of hours of leisure, he would accuse us of appealing to a definition of income which does not correspond to his understanding of the term. By the same token, Sametz, Nordhaus and Tobin's concept of economic growth is of the growth of something other than what we normally think of as real income and the analogy between incomes of different people at a moment of time and incomes of the representative consumer at different periods of time is forced.

Second, as will be discussed in some detail in connection with life expectancy in Chapter 11, the prices of leisure and non-market activities are not entirely comparable to the prices of bread and cheese, for the prices of bread and cheese are the same for everyone in a competitive market while the prices of leisure and non-market activities differ from one man to the next, each man's price of leisure being equal to his wage per hour of work. This problem is not in any way circumvented by the alternative method of imputation discussed below.

Third, the concept of a man's productivity per hour of leisure is a tricky one and there is no way of discriminating between alternative assumptions as to what the growth of productivity might be. The assertion that productivity per hour of leisure is increasing over time is not just that we have more fun per hour than we used to do, for that could be a consequence of our larger stock of entertainment goods. Our TV sets, motor boats, and golf regalia may make leisure time more pleasurable than it used to be without any increase in the productivity of hours of leisure time *per se*. For Z_N^t and Z_L^t in Nordhaus and Tobin's equation (6) to increase over time it is necessary that, as a consequence of our higher intelligence, accumulated knowledge or greater stock of human capital, we get more benefit per hour of leisure or non-market activity than our grandparents would have done if they had access to the same flows of goods and services and the same stocks of consumer durables that we have at our disposal. The assumption is

$$U = U(Y, LZ(t)) \quad Z'(t) > 0 \tag{8}$$

that utility is a function of ordinary goods and leisure, and that the benefit per hour of leisure would increase over time even if the flow of ordinary goods and the numbers of hours of leisure remained constant.

The alternative to treating leisure as a commodity is to suppose that leisure is an aspect of welfare that is not part of income, and to impute for leisure in the measure of economic growth by defining real consumption to include a premium for increases or decreases in leisure since the base year. As in equation (3), we can define real income inclusive of the imputation for leisure by the equation

$$U(\hat{Y}^t, L^0) = U(Y^t, L^t) \tag{9}$$

where Y^t is real income without the imputation for leisure, (one can think of Y as a quantity of bread.) L^t is hours of leisure in the year t, L^0 is hours of leisure in the base year, and $\hat{Y}^t$ is real consumption inclusive of the imputation for leisure.

Equation (9), approximated by the first terms of its Taylor series around the point (Y^t, L^t), is transformed into

$$\hat{Y}^t = Y^t + w^t(L^t - L^0) \tag{10}$$

where w^t is the real wage in the year t.

This alternative imputation could incorporate the assumption that productivity of leisure increases over time. The term L^t in equation (9) would be replaced by the product L^tZ^t, where $Z^0 = 1$ by definition, and the real wage w^t in equation (10) would have to be redefined as the rate of trade-off between goods and efficiency units of leisure time rather than between goods and hours of leisure. Or if we continue to define w^t as the rate of trade-off between goods and hours of labour, equation (10) would become

$$\hat{Y}^t = Y^t + \frac{w^t}{Z^t}(L^tZ^t - L^0Z^0) \tag{11}$$

In either case $\hat{Y}^t$ is an increasing function of Z^t. Partly because of the arbitrariness of assumptions about the productivity of hours of leisure, but mainly because I believe that the progress of our economy consists in our capacity to make things rather than in our capacity to enjoy them, I shall assume in the calculations to follow that $Z^t = 1$ for all t, that the productivity per hour of leisure remains constant over time. Our marginal valuation of an hour of leisure in terms of goods must necessarily rise together with the real wage rate, but that is an entirely different matter.

The imputation for leisure proposed in equation (9) makes the measurement of economic growth analogous to a comparison of incomes among people living at the same time in which incomes need only be adjusted if people are unequal in the number of hours of leisure they enjoy. No adjustment need be made to money incomes in a comparison between two men who work the same number of hours per day. If two men earn the same wage per hour and if one man chooses to work twice as many hours as the other, their money incomes would be in the ratio of two to one, but their incomes inclusive of the imputation for leisure would be the same. Even this concept of personal income is somewhat at variance with the common understanding of the term, but I think it would be generally accepted as reasonable in the context of an attempt to discover who is better off than whom.

The desirability of leisure is not in itself justification for treating leisure as a commodity as Nordhaus and Tobin have done. If we treated all desirable things as commodities, we should have to impute for enjoyment of nature, friendship, love, law and order, and the love of God; and economic growth would be reduced more and more as we add commodity after commodity for which the quantity does not appear to be increasing over time. Somewhere a line must be drawn between desirable things that are commodities and desirable things that are not, with things in the latter class precluded from affecting the rate of economic growth unless there is reason to believe, and numerical evidence to support the belief, that amounts per head of these things are increasing over time. The principle for drawing such a line would seem to be that a commodity may be identified if a form of market organization can be devised in which the commodity might be purchased with money, and if that form of market organization is enough like our own that the revised definition of income would be considered reasonable in an income comparison among people at one moment of time.

The contrast between the proposed imputations for leisure is illustrated in Figure 7.2 which is a development of Figure 7.1 with leisure replacing sunshine as the extra good, and the alternative measures of real income are presented in Table 7.2. It is assumed that 17 hours a day is to be allocated between work and leisure and that labour is the only source of income. It is convenient to measure the wage in a somewhat peculiar way. The wage is measured as an amount of money per year for each hour worked in the day. Thus a wage of $500 per year per hour of work means that annual income would be $500 if a man worked only one hour per day, $4000 if he worked eight hours, and so on. In the year 0 when the wage is $500 per year per hour of work, the representative consumer chooses to work 8 hours a day; he earns $4000 in total and enjoys 9 hours of leisure per day as indicated by the point A. In the year 1 when the wage has risen to $1000 per year per hour, the representative consumer chooses to work 7 hours a day; he earns $7000 in total and enjoys 10 hours of leisure per day as indicated by the point B. For convenience we are assuming that prices of goods are the same in both years so that real income may be measured in current dollars. Without imputation for leisure, the ratio of income in year 1 and year 0 is 1.75. In variant (A) of Nordhaus and Tobin's imputation where the productivity of leisure hours is assumed to be the same in year 0 and year 1 and where real income consists of goods and leisure valued at base year prices, the real income in the year 0 consists of $4000 worth of goods plus $4500 worth of leisure, the real income in year 1 consists of $7000 worth of goods plus $5000 worth of leisure (10 hours evaluated at $500 per hour) and the ratio of incomes in year 1 and year 0 is reduced to

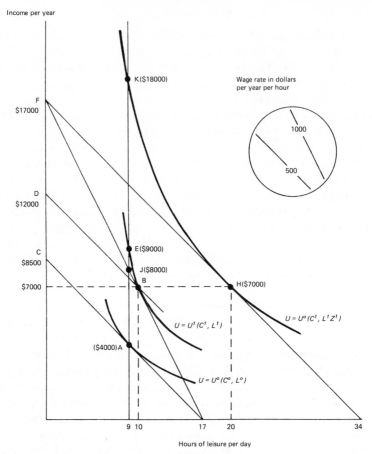

Figure 7.2 A set of indifference curves appropriate for comparing alternative imputations for leisure

Table 7.2 Alternative comparisons of real incomes inclusive of an imputation for leisure based on data in Figure 7.2

	without imputation for leisure	Nordhaus and Tobin variant (A) $Z^1 = 1$	Sametz (Nordhaus and Tobin variant (C)) $Z^1 = w(1) = 2$	alternative $(Z^1 = 1)$ ideal	alternative $(Z^1 = 1)$ approximate	alternative $Z = \frac{w(1)}{w(0)} = 2$ ideal	alternative $Z = \frac{w(1)}{w(0)} = 2$ approximate
income in year 0	4000	8500	8500	4000	4000	4000	4000
income in year 1	7000	12000	17000	9000	8000	18000	12500
their ratio	1.75	1.41	2.00	2.25	2.00	4.50	3.13

1.41. The imputation proposed by Sametz, which is the same as Nordhaus and Tobin's variant (C), is based on the assumption that the productivity per hour of leisure increases from the year 0 to the year 1 in proportion to the increase in the real wage. As the real wage has doubled, we assumed that the productivity per hour of leisure has doubled too. It is as though the representative consumer found himself in year 1, not with 17 hours to be bartered for goods at a wage of $1000 per hour, but with 34 hours to be bartered for goods at the old wage of $500 per hour, for each hour of leisure in year 1 yields the same satisfaction as two hours of leisure in year 0. On this assumption the money income and hours of work represented by the point B in the year 1 convey the same utility to the representative consumer as he would enjoy with the money income and hours of work represented by the point H in the year 0. The relative price of goods and efficiency units of leisure is the same in the two years, real incomes inclusive of the imputation for leisure are $8500 in the year 0 and $17,000 in the year 1, and the ratio of incomes in year 1 and year 0 is 2.00, precisely the ratio of the real wages per hour of work.

The alternative method of imputing for leisure leaves the income in the base year intact and adds or subtracts a sum of money to income in every other year sufficient to compensate the representative consumer for working the same number of hours as he worked in the base year. If we assume that the productivity per hour of leisure is the same in year 1 and year 0, the real income in year 1 inclusive of the imputation for leisure is indicated by the height of the point E. It is the amount of money that would make the representative consumer as well off as he was in the year 1 if he had to work as many hours as he did in the year 0. We suppose this sum to be $9000 per year, in which case the ratio of real income in year 1 and year 0 is 2.25. The approximation to real income in year 1 based on equation (10) is the sum of money income assessed in the ordinary way plus the value at the real wage in year 1 of the extra leisure consumed. This sum is $8000, indicated by the height of the point J.

If we suppose that the productivity per hour of leisure doubles between year 0 and year 1, then the indifference curve U^1 through B is no longer comparable to the indifference curve U^0 through A because a given value of L represents more leisure in U^1 than in U^0. The curve comparable to $U = U^0(Y^0, L^0)$ through A is $U = U^0(Y^1, L^1Z^1)$ through the point H where $Z^1 = 2$ by assumption. When leisure is treated as an environmental condition and $Z^1 = 2$, real income in the year 1 is the height of the point K where $U = U^0(Y^1, L^1Z^1)$ intersects the vertical line corresponding to 8 hours of work. The true value of real income in year 1 inclusive of the imputation for leisure is $18,000, the approximation according to equation (10) is $12,500, and the corresponding ratios of real incomes in year 1 and year 0 are 4.50 and 3.13.

The ratios of real incomes according to Sametz' imputation and according to the alternative imputation when the efficiency of hours of leisure is assumed constant are both equal to 2, but they acquire this value for very different reasons. Sametz' imputation is based on the assumption that the efficiency of leisure hours increases, while the alternative is based on the assumption that the valuation of leisure hours in terms of goods as the numeraire is tied to real wage. When the alternative imputation is combined with the assumption that the efficiency of leisure hours is higher in year 1 than in year 2, the ratio of real incomes becomes substantially higher than the ratio that emerges from Sametz' imputation.[5]

To see how the imputation works out in practice, we have constructed an imputation for leisure to real consumption per head in Canada from 1926 to 1974 with 1961 as the base year. Leisure is treated as an environmental condition so that the rate of growth increases because hours of leisure increase and despite the fact that the rate of increase in hours of leisure is far less than the rate of increase of real consumption per head as ordinarily defined. The results are shown in Table 7.3 for every fifth year, and indices of the whole series of real consumption per head, with and without the imputation, are shown on the accompanying graph. The imputation is computed in accordance with equation (10) and the following supplementary assumptions:

(a) that the increase or decrease in the number of hours of leisure as compared with the base year is correctly reflected by the decrease in the

---

[5] Note that the dates of the shadow prices of the imputed items differ between equations (4) and (10). In equation (4) the shadow price s_j^{61} of sunshine is for the base year, while in equation (10) the shadow price w^t of leisure is for the current year. The difference lies not in the theory of imputations but in the origin of the Taylor series expansion used to construct a measurable approximation to the true value of real income we seek. In general, it is probably best to adopt the procedure followed in the bread-sunshine example: to take the Taylor series around the values of the variables in the base year so that the shadow prices of the imputed items are for the base year as well and need not be changed with each year in the time series. The reason for not adopting this procedure with the imputation for leisure is that the alternative supplies a correction for the bias arising from the fact that the productivity of labour and the marginal valuation of leisure are, by definition, one and the same. We see at once from figure 7.2 that the true value of income inclusive of the imputation for leisure (the height of E) is underestimated by its approximation in equation (10) (the height of J) and would be underestimated still more by the approximation we would have if w^t were replaced by w^0 in equation (10) (the height at 9 hours of leisure of the intersection of the vertical with the line from B to D). There is no comparable relation in the bread-sunshine example.

Table 7.3   An imputation for leisure: Canada 1926–1974

year	(1) real consumption per head without imputation for leisure (1961 dollars)	(2) average hours worked per year	(3) wage per hour (current dollars)	(4) employed labour force (000)	(5) imputation for leisure (000,000) current dollars	(6) real consumption per head with imputation for leisure (1961 dollars)
1926	674	2756	0.41	3550	−966	488
1930	777	2659	0.47	3689	−993	599
1935	686	2519	0.41	3777	−672	547
1940	791	2629	0.50	4184	−1140	589
1945	992	2427	0.68	4447	−1039	844
1950	1143	2247	1.38	4976	−917	1059
1955	1294	2182	1.55	5364	−804	1238
1961	1422	2085	1.99	6055	0	1422
1965	1626	2037	2.40	6892	795	1665
1970	1858	1940	3.52	7879	4022	2006
1974	2227	1903	4.93	9137	8191	2455

(1) Real consumption per head is the national accounts category 'personal expenditure on consumer goods and services' divided by population and converted to $1961 by appropriate deflator, *National Income and Expenditure Accounts 1926–1974*. Statistics Canada 13–531, Volume 1.

(2) The time series of average hours worked per year for the years 1946–1974 was provided by Input–Output Division–Productivity of Statistics Canada. The series for the years 1926 to 1945 is from T. M. Brown, *Canadian Economic Growth*, Royal Commission on Health Services, Government of Canada, 1965, table A1. A 4% discrepancy between these series for the year 1946 was dealt with by adjusting the whole of the latter series.

(3) Wage per hour is computed by dividing the national accounts category (i) wages, salaries and supplementary labour income by the product of (ii) average hours of work per year from column 2, and (iii) the number of paid workers employed. This last item (iii) for the years 1946 to 1947 is from *The Labour Force*, Statistics Canada, 71–001, table 31, and for the years 1926 to 1974 is from T. M. Brown, cited above, table A1.

(4) Employed labour force and population are both from *National Income and Expenditure Accounts*, cited above.

(5) The imputation for leisure is the product of (i) the wage rate, (ii) the employed labour force, and (iii) the extra hours of leisure over and above what was enjoyed in 1961. Thus for the year 1974, the imputation for leisure was the product of $4.95 (column 3), 9.137 thousand (column 4), and 182 (2085–1903, column 2), equal to $8191 million after correction for rounding errors.

(6) Real consumption per head with the imputation for leisure is the sum of (i) total personal consumption in current dollars from the national accounts, and (ii) the imputation for leisure from column (5) all divided by the product of (iii) the population of Canada, and (iv) the price index of personal consumption from the national accounts, scaled to equal 1.0 in 1961.

number of hours of work. This assumption would be false if there has been a change in the number of hours required for what Nordhaus and Tobin called 'cost of work', principally time spent travelling to and from work. We have no evidence on this matter. I would expect that people tend to live farther away from their place of work but that transport is faster too.

(b) that the marginal valuation of an hour of leisure each year is equal to the average wage per hour in the labour force as a whole.

(c) that there is no change in the number of hours of leisure of people who are not classified as being at work, that housewives, students, the unemployed and the sick all worked as many hours in 1974 as they did in 1926.

Sources of data and details of how they are processed are presented in the notes to Table 7.3.

The table itself is largely self-explanatory. As the base year is 1961 and as the number of hours of work declines over the whole period, the imputation is at first negative, then zero in 1961, and positive thereafter, increasing year by year. The overall effect of the imputation is to increase the rate of growth of real consumption per head over the whole

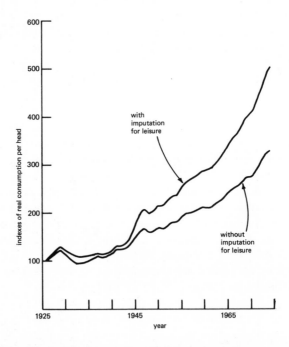

Figure 7.3 The effect of the imputation for leisure on real consumption per head in Canada

forty-eight year period by almost a full per cent per year from 2.49% to 3.37%.

NOTES FOR FURTHER READING

There is an excellent though now somewhat dated discussion of the scope of income in Part II of P. Studenski, *The Income of Nations*, New York University Press, 1958. The old debate on whether government output is final or intermediate product is thoroughly reviewed; see also S. Kuznets, 'Government Product and National Income', International Association for Research in Income and Wealth, *Income and Wealth Series I* (Bowes and Bowes, 1951), and 'National Income and Industrial Structures', *Econometrica*, 1949, supplement. Attempts to compute for housework are reviewed in O. Hawrylyshyn, 'The Value of Household Services: A Survey of Empirical Estimates', *Review of Income and Wealth*, 1976, pp. 101–32. On the imputation for the services of consumer durables see F. T. Juster, *Household Capital Formation and Financing, 1897–1962*, National Bureau of Economic Research, 1966.

The concept of positional goods is analysed in detail in F. Hirsch, *Social Limits to Growth*, Harvard University Press, 1976. Some evidence that one's position on the scale of rich and poor makes one happy but one's absolute income does not is presented in R. A. Easterlin, 'Does Economic Growth Improve the Human Lot', in P. A. David and M. W. Reder (eds), *Nations and Households in Economic Growth: Essays in Honour of Moses Abramovitz*, Stanford University Press, 1972.

On the imputation for leisure, see A. W. Sametz, 'The Measurement of Economic Growth', Chapter 3 of E. B. Sheldon and W. E. Moore (eds), *Indicators of Social Change*, Russell Sage Foundation, 1968; and W. Nordhaus and J. Tobin, 'Is Growth Obsolete', *Economic Growth*, National Bureau of Economic Research, 1971. My imputation for leisure in this chapter is similar in some respects to Pencavel's attempt to measure the real wage with the aid of a utility function encompassing goods and leisure. J. H. Pencavel, 'Constant Utility Index Numbers of Real Wages', *American Economic Review*, 1977, pp. 91–100. Alternative imputations for leisure are compared in W. Beckerman, *Measures of leisure, Equality and Welfare*, OECD, 1978.

8

Quantity and Quality

Commodities do not exist except as statistical artifacts that we ourselves impose upon the data. In defining real income in Chapter 2, we took it as a starting point that there are n distinct commodities, that income consists of amounts $q_1, \ldots, q_n$ of these commodities, that economic growth consists in having ever larger amounts of most commodities as time goes on, and that the number and nature of commodities remain invariant forever. The reader who does not already know how the national accounts are put together might well suppose that the task of the national accountant is simply to observe time series of prices and quantities and to compute real income in accordance with a Laspeyres index or some more accurate substitute. The reality is not like that at all. The flow of income consists for all practical purposes of an infinitely diverse collection of goods and services, and the composition of the flow is constantly changing, sometimes slightly as when a new grill is added to an automobile or a new material is used in the manufacture of clothing, and sometimes abruptly and dramatically as when a new wonder drug or a new product like television or the mini-computer first appears on the market. The main task of the national accountant, the task to which most of his time and energy is devoted and on which the validity of the time series of real income will largely depend, is to decompose the flow of income into a collection of supposedly homogeneous commodities and to decide how much of each commodity is consumed each year. Once these matters have been settled, the choice of a formula for recombining quantities into a measure of real income is relatively unimportant, as it is unlikely to have a comparable impact on the measure of economic growth.

It is our object in this chapter to say something about how the flow of income is, as it were, channeled into flows of n artificially constructed commodities. We begin with a discussion of the procedure in the official national accounts, with special emphasis on the fact statisticians measure quantities indirectly by deflating values by price indexes. Next we look at quality change. There would seem to be three important models of quality change—the repackaging model, the hidden commodities model, and the new commodity model—none of which completely captures the essence of the phenomenon. In the course of examining these models, I shall make a case for the proposition that the rate of economic growth as it would be assessed by a representative consumer in the conceptual experiment set out in Chapter 2 tends to be underestimated because the benefits from new types of products are inadequately accounted for in our statistical procedures. There will then be a brief discussion of the measurement of output by input for those commodities—notably, public administration, medicine, education, and legal services—to which we can attach neither prices nor quantities to the outputs. And, finally, there will be an enumeration of circumstances where prices of identical goods and services differ among people in the same country. Price differences are important because the ratio of value to price cannot (except by accident) be an accurate indicator of quantity unless the price of each unit purchased is the same.

A. THE MEASUREMENT OF REAL INCOME IN THE NATIONAL ACCOUNTS

Suppose for the moment that there really are n distinct commodities and that we have time series of prices and quantities of each. We could observe the quantities directly, or we could observe them indirectly as the ratio of value and price. For the commodity i, the direct measure of quantity is q_i and the indirect measure is v_i/p_i where p_i is its price and v_i is its value. For a group of commodities, the direct measure is the quantity index Q^t, $(\sum_{i=1}^{n} p_i^0 q_i^t)/(\sum_{i=1}^{n} p_i^0 q_i^0)$

where 0 is the base year and t is the current year, and the indirect measure is the ratio of a value index V^t, defined as

$$\left(\sum_{i=1}^{n} p_i^t q_i^t\right)\bigg/\left(\sum_{i=1}^{n} p_i^0 q_i^0\right)$$

and a price index P^t, defined as

$$\left(\sum_{i=1}^{n} p_i^t q_i^t\right)\bigg/\left(\sum_{i=1}^{n} p_i^0 q_i^t\right)$$

That the direct and indirect measures are the same follows immediately from the definitions of the indexes.

$$Q^t = \frac{\sum_{i=1}^n p_i^0 q_i^t}{\sum_{i=1}^n p_i^0 q_i^0} = \frac{\sum_{i=1}^n p_i^t q_i^t}{\sum_{i=1}^n p_i^0 q_i^0}\left(\frac{\sum_{i=1}^n p_i^t q_i^t}{\sum_{i=1}^n p_i^0 q_i^t}\right)^{-1} = \frac{V^t}{P^t} \tag{1}$$

The analogy between commodity and index is not perfect because the form of the price index is different from that of the original quantity index. The price index is what is called a Paasche index in which the weights (quantity weights in this case) are for the current year and are, therefore, variable from year to year. With this qualification, it makes no difference whatsoever if real income is measured in the first instance by revaluation of quantities in a (Laspeyres) quantity index or by deflating value by a (Paasche) price index. The result is exactly the same.

The practice in the official national accounts is to measure real income indirectly by deflating values by price indexes rather than by revaluing quantities each year at a single invariant set of prices. There are two main reasons for this choice, both having to do with aspects of the flow of income that are abstracted from when we postulate the existence of n invariant commodities.

The first has to do with the multiplicity of commodities, with the fact that there are more distinct types of goods and services than the national accountant can conveniently enumerate. Take clothing as an example. It is obviously impossible for the national accountant to take cognizance of every size, shape, colour and style of clothing individually. What he can observe is the value in current dollars of clothing purchased each year and the prices of some but not all items sold. This is sufficient to construct a quantity index of clothing if it can be assumed: (a) that arbitrage keeps prices of all items of each type of clothing the same at any given time; and (b) that the percentage change each year of the price index for the type of clothing in the sample is the same as that for the unknown index of prices of all types of clothing purchased. In fact, it is not unreasonable to suppose that prices of most types of clothing rise or fall over time to about the same extent because change in prices of inputs in the clothing industry may be expected to have more or less the same effect upon the cost of production of different types of clothing. In the extreme case, where all clothing prices rise or fall exactly in unison, a Laspeyres quantity index could be got indirectly by deflating values of clothing by the price of any type of clothing as long as the exact same item was priced year after year.[1] In the more realistic case where percentage price changes of different types of clothing are similar but not identical, the mean of the sample of price changes should be close enough to the mean of all price changes to keep the measure of real consumption of clothing tolerably accurate despite the fact that the types of clothing are not completely enumerated in the national accounts.

The other advantage of deflation has to do with quality change. One

---

[1] If all prices rise by a factor a between the year 0 and the year t, that is, if $p_i^t = a p_i^0$ for every i, then the Laspeyres price index is $(\Sigma_{i=1}^n q_i^t p_i^t)/(\Sigma_{i=1}^n q_i^t p_i^0) = a = p_j^t / p_j^0$ for any commodity j whatsoever. In that case, any single price change is as good as the whole index.

may think of value as being decomposable into three rather than two elements: $v = qmp$ where q is quantity, m is quality and p is price standardized for quality. To continue with our clothing example, q may be the number of garments, m may be an indicator of average workmanship and quality of cloth, p may be the price of a standard garment, and the average price tag per garment, the unit value, is pm rather than p. In these circumstances, one would want to include m rather than just q in the measure of real income because increases in both q and m make the representative consumer better off; qm now plays the role that q alone formerly played in the Laspeyres quantity index. We could try to obtain the time series of the product qm by observing the number of garments sold and the average quality of garments each year, but that would prove to be a formidable task if only because we have no simple rule which tells us whether on balance the quality of one garment is better than the quality of another. The advantage of deflation is that we can get at qm indirectly by the simple expedient of excluding quality altogether from the price index. All we need to do is to construct a time series of prices of garments of uniform quality to serve as the measure of p in the ratio v/p. In this way we can construct an index of quantity and quality combined without having to measure quality directly and without knowing what quality consists of.

Its a neat trick if we can do it. In the course of this chapter we shall discuss certain biases in the deflation procedure, and in Chapter 10 we shall argue that there is additional information to be gained from an alternative measure of real income based on the revaluation of quantity data. For the moment it is sufficient to note that deflation is the procedure used to obtain the initial time series of 'quantity' in the national accounts and to appreciate the reasons for that choice.

The deflation procedure in the national accounts differs slightly from the simple method just described because of the way the data present themselves and as a means of correcting to some extent for the bias in the Laspeyres quantity index. The procedure for constructing the price index is to obtain a set of weights from a family expenditure survey conducted once a decade, to maintain these weights throughout the decade until the next survey, but, of course, to measure prices every year and to splice the ten year series together into a consistent price index over a long period of time. This procedure supplies a Laspeyres price index rather than a Paasche price index which is what would be required for the resulting quantity index to be of the Laspeyres form.[2] Prices of new types of goods are added to the index from time to time to

---

[2] The expenditure survey conducted in the year 0 yields a set of weights $w_i^0, \ldots, w_n^0$ such that w_i^0 is the share of the good i in total expenditure

keep its composition representative of the composition of consumption within each broad category of goods. The discussion of possible bias in the index is best postponed to the next chapter where that subject is treated extensively. The categories themselves are quite broad. Food for instance is treated as a single commodity without any finer subdivision because the most important component of the value of food consumed is sales of grocery stores which are not always broken down into sales of the different food products. Real personal consumption in Canada is subdivided into less than fifty commodities of which food consumption is the largest.

B. QUALITY CHANGE

The problem of quality change is to express 'better' and 'different' as 'more'. Quality change presented no particular problem in the conceptual experiment where real income was defined in Chapter 2, for the representative consumer can tell us how much income he would need in the base year to be as well off as he would be with the average income in some other year, even if the commodities consumed in the two years are not identical. The problem emerges when the statistician attempts to construct a parallel to this conceptual experiment with actual time series of prices and quantities. Quality change must then be reflected in an increase in quantities of one or more commodities, where the commodities themselves are treated as though they remained the same over time; for without such an equivalence we could not construct time series of prices and quantities and real income could not be measured at all.

Three distinct models of quality change are useful in the design and analysis of statistics of real income: the repackaging model, the hidden commodities model, and the new commodities model. The first two models rationalize techniques for the design of price indexes, while the third is useful for identifying bias in our measures. The proof in the last section that the deflation procedure contains an automatic and com-

---

$$w^0 = \frac{p_i^0 q_i^0}{\sum_{j=1}^n p_j^0 q_j^0}$$

For each year t, the price index is constructed as

$$P^t = \sum_{i=1}^n w_i^0 \frac{p_i^t}{p_i^0} = \sum_{i=1}^n \frac{p_i^0 q_i^0}{\sum_{j=1}^n p_j^0 q_j^0} \cdot \frac{p_i^t}{p_i^0} = \frac{\sum_{i=1}^n p_i^t q_i^0}{\sum_{i=1}^n p_i^0 q_i^0}$$

The right-hand term is the usual definition of the Laspeyres price index.

pletely accurate correction for quality change was based on the 'repackaging' model of quality change. Utility is thought of as dependent on arguments $z_1, \ldots, z_n$ where the z variables are themselves the products of quantity q and quality m. This is called the repackaging model because it is a perfect fit to the case where z is pounds of sugar, q is the number of bags of sugar, and m is the average size of the bag. Quality change in the repackaging model is looked upon as analogous to the packaging of sugar in bigger bags.

The hidden commodities model can be looked upon as a generalization of the repackaging model. Again we suppose that utility is a function of amounts of hidden or unobservable commodities $z_1, \ldots, z_n$, that is $U = U(z)$, but we no longer constrain the z variables to be associated, one for one, with normal commodities. Instead of supposing that $z = qm$, we allow for the possibilities that a given hidden commodity may be contained in many types of ordinary goods and services and that a given good or service may be the purveyor of several different hidden commodities. Thus, for example, sweetness looked upon as a hidden commodity may be contained in candy, cake or oranges, and automobiles may be decomposed into the hidden commodities, speed, safety, volume and so on. What this means analytically is that each z_i is the sum, $\Sigma_{j=1}^r z_{ij}$, of the amounts of the i hidden commodity provided by the j good or service, and the $z_{ij} = q_j a_{ij}$ where q_j is the quantity of the j good or service and a_{ij} is the amount of i provided by each unit of j. The coefficients a_{ij} may be functions of q_j and they may change over time as, for instance, when cars get faster and safer, or oranges get sweeter. One can say that the hidden commodities model is a generalization of the repackaging model because the former collapses into the latter if each i is identified with one and only one value of j.

The new commodities model is just what the term implies. The utility function prior to the quality change was $U = U(q_1, \ldots, q_n)$, the change itself is the appearance of the $n + 1$ commodity, and the new utility function is $U = U(q_1, \ldots, q_n, q_{n+1})$. The new and old utility functions have to be comparable if the representative consumer is to compare incomes before and after the appearance of the new commodity. We therefore identify $U(q_1, \ldots, q_n)$ with $U(q_1, \ldots, q_n, 0)$ which implies, for instance, that the representative consumer can tell us how much money he needs today when TV sets are available to be as well off as he would be with the average income in 1926 when they were not.

We introduce these models simultaneously so that any two models can be used as a vantage point for examining and evaluating the third, and as a way of emphasizing that none of these models captures the whole of what we think of as quality change. A new gadget is produced that permits you to adjust the station on your TV set without getting out of your chair. This is not exactly an increase in m in the repackaging model because the gadget is not in any sense like an increase in the number of TV sets. Nor is it an increase in the amount of any hidden commodity already embedded in TV sets, for the gadget provides a service that was not available at all before it was put on the market. The gadget could be treated as a new commodity, but this would violate the assumption that there are n distinct commodities in the economy at all times, and would oblige the national accountant to estimate the demand curve for the new commodity and to include the corresponding consumer's surplus as part of real income in each year after its appearance on the market. The national accountant could perhaps allow for the appearance of a few new commodities in a long time series, but the attempt to account for the wide range of new commodities appearing on the market each year would soon lead to a situation where the measure of real income depends more on the skill and ingenuity of the national accountant as econometrician than on trends in the economy itself. There is at present no completely satisfactory way to represent quality change, and we have to make the best of the situation with whatever analytical tools are available. In this context, the demonstration that a method of accounting for quality change is biased in some direction does not necessarily mean that it should not be employed, for the alternatives may be worse. With this caveat in mind, we now turn to the consideration of the implications of the three models of quality change in the measurement of real income.

The central question is whether and to what extent the repackaging model provides a justification for the deflation procedure in the national accounts. In the absence of quality change, the true measure of real income in the year t assessed at prices in the base year 0 is $C(U^t, p^0)$ which, as we have shown, may be approximated as $\Sigma_{i=1}^{n} p_i^0 q_i^t$. By the same token, if utility depends on the z variables, that is, if $U = U(z)$ where $z = qm$ and p is the price of z rather than q, we can approximate real income at base year prices by the expression $\Sigma_{i=1}^{n} p_i^0 z_i^t$ where z_i^t is correctly measured by the ratio v_i^t/p_i^t. The repackaging model enables us to deal with quality change by, as it were, dispensing with it altogether, for there is no quality change in z. The assumption in the repackaging model that makes quality change so easy to accommodate, an assumption which is only strictly true in some rather uninteresting cases, is that q and m enter multiplicatively into the utility function so that percentage changes in m and q are additive in their overall impact on welfare. If this assumption is violated as it would be when quality change in one good affects the utility of other goods or when quality change is not fully reflected in the prices of new and old types of goods, then the terms v_i/p_i in the Laspeyres quantity index can no longer be identified with arguments in the utility function and it is no longer clear what significance to attach to a change in the value of the index.

An example will illustrate the difficulty. Suppose a government research agency invents a new variety of aspirin that costs the same to produce as the present variety, that does just as well, but no better, in relieving headaches, but which has the added property that, taken once a year, it gives complete immunity to some serious disease such as cancer. Some but not all producers of aspirin switch over to the new variety which sells at exactly the same price as the old variety because the cost of production is the same and because the marginal valuation of the new pill (which governs its price) is as a pain-killer rather than as a cancer preventative. Surely this is an example of what one would want to call quality change, but the deflation procedure fails completely to pick it up because neither v nor p are affected by the introduction of the pill. The Laspeyres approximation to the measure of real income is unchanged by the introduction of the new variety of pill. It may even decline as equipment designed to treat cancer goes obsolete and as cancer specialists switch to lower paying occupations. In this example we can look upon q as the quantity of pain-killer in aspirin and we can let m be the cancer-curing property. If m and q were multiplicative in the utility function, the value of a new pill containing both m and q would exceed the value of an old one containing q alone, and the cancer-curing property of the new pill would be reflected in the expression v/p in the Laspeyres quantity index where p is the price of the old variety of aspirin. That does not happen in this case. In the original aspirin $m = 0$. In the new aspirin m exceeds $\bar{m}$, where $\bar{m}$ is a value of m high enough that cancer is eliminated altogether. Obviously, utility is a function of q, m and other variables, but q and m cannot enter multiplicatively, for no amount of q could substitute for m or vice versa. And since by assumption the amount of m in the new pill is greater than $\bar{m}$, the marginal value of m is zero regardless of the quantity of q as long as q exceeds some very small amount. That is why new and old varieties of the pill sell at the same price.

Figure 8.1 illustrates the contrast between the aspirin example where quality change is not reflected in the price index and the sugar example mentioned at the beginning of this section where quantity is the number of bags of sugar, quality is the average size of the bag, and the deflation procedure provides a full and accurate adjustment for quality change. Both parts of the figure are ordinary demand curves, one for aspirin and the other for sugar. Prior to the invention of the new type of aspirin, the demand for aspirin as a pain-killer is indicated by the curve DD', the supply curve is the flat line at the height p^0, and the equilibrium output

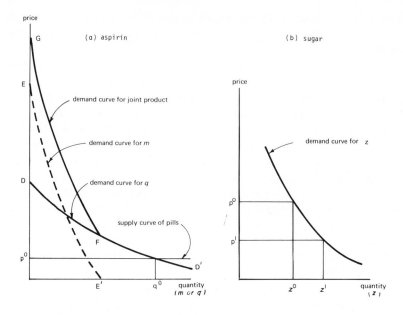

Figure 8.1 Two examples of quality change. In (a) m is the cancer curing property, q is the pain-killing property and p is the price per pill. In (b) m is the average number of pounds per bag, q is the number of bags, and p is the price per pound

of aspirin is at q^0 where the two curves cross. The invention of the new pill makes aspirin a joint product; it is a pain-killer as before but in addition it cures cancer. The demand for the latter characteristic is the broken curve EE′, the combined demand curve for the joint product is the vertical sum of the individual demand curves, GFD′, but the equilibrium output of aspirin is q^0 as before because the marginal valuation of the new aspirin is the same as that of the old. The benefit of the new aspirin is the extra surplus GFD which may well be enormous despite the absence of any effect upon price, quantity or the usual measures of real income and economic growth. Any increase, on the other hand, in the average size of a bag of sugar must result in a fall in the price of sugar if the demand curve for sugar is stable and if the number of bags does not decline accordingly. Price depends on z rather than q because mq is the appropriate term in the utility function, and the ratio of the value of sugar and the price of a pound bag is the true quantity index.

In the aspirin example, the new good has no effect on the measure of real income because it emerges as a joint product with an established good and is so plentiful right from the beginning that its marginal utility is zero despite the usefulness of the intramarginal units. This is an extreme case of a much more general phenomenon; the values of the intramarginal units of a new product escape notice in the national accounts. As long as the producer of the new good is not a discriminating monopolist, its price has to be less—perhaps very much less—than the value of the first unit of the good to each buyer or, if the good is like an electric razor where one unit per buyer is enough, to all but the least enthusiastic buyer. In a comparison of real income between two years, where for convenience in exposition we may suppose that more of each good is consumed in the second year, the consumer's surplus associated with the amount of any good consumed in the first year can be thought of as analogous to an environmental condition that has no effect on the comparison, and only the addition to surplus associated with the extra consumption in the second year need be considered at all; the matter is treated briefly in Chapter 2 and at greater length in Chapter 9. But where a new product is introduced at a time between the two years over which real income is compared, and where the first observed price is quite far down the demand curve, then a surplus which ought to be included as part of real income in the second year is overlooked.

The situation need not be quite as bad as the aspirin example would suggest because new products which cannot reasonably be looked upon as large packages of old products may sometimes be analysed as new combinations of invariant characteristics. The commodities themselves may change from year to year, but utility is a stable function of hidden commodities that can be discovered by the appropriate statistical technique. Foods of all kinds may be looked upon as purveyors of nutrients, calories, proteins, vitamins, etc. Financial instruments—shares of stock, corporate bonds, government bonds, bank deposits with different terms of maturity and rates of return—may be looked upon as combinations of two elements: capital as title to a riskless income stream, and risk. Automobiles of all shapes and sizes can be looked upon as purveyors of characteristics such as speed, roominess, safety, etc. Whenever new goods may be treated as new combinations of old characteristics, a price index, called a hedonic price index, may be estimated for the purpose of deflating values of good when amounts of characteristics are changing over time. For instance, a hedonic price index of automobiles may be estimated as the antilogarithm of v^t in the equation

$$\log p_i^t = a + \sum_{k=1}^{m} b_k m_{ki}^t + v^t + e_i \qquad (2)$$

where the parameters a, b_k, e_i and v^t are estimated in a regression of $\log p_i^t$ on the variables m_{ki}^t together with appropriate dummy variables. The superscript t refers to the date, the subscripts k and i refer respectively to characteristics of cars and makes of cars, the variable p_i^t is the price of a car of make i in year t, and the variable m_{ki}^t is the amount of the k characteristic supplied by the i make of car in the year t. The coefficients v^t and e_i are for dummy variables of the year t and the make of car i.[3] If observed increases in prices of new cars can be explained by improvements in their characteristics, then v^t will be approximately zero and no increase will be recorded in the hedonic price index. If price increases are greater than can be explained by variations in characteristics, v^t will grow over time and there will be an increase in the hedonic price index.

In practice, a statistician attempting to account for quality change in a price index may compare prices of what he believes to be identical goods and services in successive years in the hope that the values of goods not included in the price index are a reflection of their weights in the utility function of the representative consumer; or he can try to infer the degree of superiority of new over old types of goods from evidence of second hand markets or from list prices where new and old models are both available; or he can use the hedonic technique to distinguish price increases accounted for by increases in amounts of characteristics from price increases that are not. All of these techniques rely for their validity on the assumption that the world is like the repackaging model or the hidden commodities model. Now we know that these models are not so much a·solution to the problem of quality change as a denial of its existence. The models say, as it were, that what we think of as commodities may change but the real, underlying commodities remain the same all along. The hidden commodities model and the repackaging model are ways of converting better into more; new goods are old goods in bigger packages or different combinations, but the goods themselves are what they have always been and always will be. We know that is not true; new types of commodities are invented from time to time, and no set of characteristics has been devised that can account fully for the variability of prices of even a group of items as homogeneous as automobiles or refrigerators. However we must not make too much of this discrepancy, for we must recognize, on the one hand, that quality change has to be denied if real income is to be measured with the available techniques and, on the other hand, that the denial of quality

---

[3] Equation (2) is taken from Z. Griliches, 'Hedonic Price Indexes Revisited', *Price Indexes and Quality Change*, Z. Griliches (ed.), p. 7. In his study of automobiles reproduced in that volume, Griliches chose horsepower, weight and length as characteristics.

change imparts an error and possibly a bias which might be rectified as techniques improve.

Special problems arise in the construction of price indexes of capital goods. Capital goods typically exhibit great diversity and variability over time. A man fifty years ago ate three meals a day, wore clothes, lived in houses with rooms, read books, and listened to music more or less as one does today, but much of the machinery available now had no counterpart at all. It is at least arguable that such quality change as there is in consumption is not so extensive as to destroy the meaning of time series of consumption in real terms, but that the biases and arbitrary elements in our techniques for measuring price indexes become intolerable when we are faced with the greater quality change on the investment side of the accounts.

Even if all capital goods can be treated as sources of hidden commodities, it may turn out that increases in quantities are so large and reductions in price so precipitous that biases in the indexes are magnified intolerably. Computers are the prime example. I do not know what the facts are, but I do not think it unreasonable to suppose that the total capacity (measured, say, in additions per year) of all the computing equipment in North America has increased a millionfold over the last fifty years and that the price per addition has fallen comparably. A simple example will illustrate what the statistical consequences of such a change might be. Suppose a comparison of real income is to be made between 1926 and 1974, where food is the only consumption good, computers the only investment good, value shares of computers are the same in both years, and prices and quantities are as shown in Table 8.1.

In this example, the number of computers is being assessed not as the number of machines but as the adding capacity of the machines produced, and the value shares of food and machines are 100/101 and 1/101 in both years. When the year 1974 is the base year, the ratio of real income in 1976 and 1926 is $(\Sigma_{i=1}^2 p_i^{74} q_i^{74})/(\Sigma_{i=1}^2 p_i^{74} q_i^{26})$ which is approximately equal to 2 because the marginal valuation of adding capacity is low and food dominates the quantity index. But when 1926 is the base year, the ratio of real income in 1974 and 1926 is

Table 8.1

	food		computers (q is adding capacity)	
	price	quantity	price	quantity
1926	1	1	10^{-2}	1
1976	1	2	10^{-8}	10^6

$(\Sigma_{i=1}^{2} p_i^{26} q_i^{74})/(\Sigma_{i=1}^{2} p_i^{26} q_i^{26})$ which turns out to be equal to 10,000. The ratio of real incomes in 1974 and 1926 can be either 2 or 10,000 depending on the choice of the base year! Of course, it is unreasonable to suppose that the value share of computing equipment in 1926 was as large as that in 1974; adding machines and cash registers which were the only computing equipment available at that time did not play as large a role in the economy as computers do today. But we can reduce the value share of computers in 1926 by one-hundredfold without destroying the force of the example.[4]

Quantities and prices of computers in this example are illustrated in Figure 8.2 which is not drawn to scale so that very large and very small numbers can be shown. Price is measured with respect to food as the numeraire good so that the dimension of areas on the figure is quantities of food. Quantities and prices in 1926 and 1974 are represented by the points A and B. The value of the 10^6 fold increase in computers from 1926 to 1974 is assessed at only 1/100 units of food represented by the area CGJB when quantities are weighted at 1974 prices, but it is assessed at 10,000 units of food represented by the area AGJD when quantities are weighted at 1926 prices. If computers were a consumption good, we could use the assumption that tastes are invariant to construct a demand curve passing through the points A and B and we could compute the true value—to which the areas AGJD and CGJB are extreme upper and lower limits—of the extra computers as the area AGJB under the demand curve as quantity increases from 1 to 10,000. One might suppose that in this case, where the output is an investment good, we could construct a derived demand curve as illustrated on the figure to provide exactly the same information. We cannot do so, and the curve we have drawn freehand between A and B has no economic significance because a true derived demand curve, for which areas under the curve do represent a kind of surplus, shows marginal valuations corresponding to alternative stocks of factors of production with re-

---

[4] When 1974 is the base year, the Laspeyres index of real incomes in 1974 and 1926 is

$$\frac{\Sigma_{i=1}^{2} p_i^{74} q_i^{74}}{\Sigma_{i=1}^{2} p_i^{74} q_i^{26}} = \frac{(1 \times 2) + (10^{-8} \times 10^6)}{(1 \times 1) + (10^{-8} \times 1)} \approx 2$$

When 1926 is the base year, the index becomes

$$\frac{\Sigma_{i=1}^{2} p_i^{26} q_i^{74}}{\Sigma_{i=1}^{2} p_i^{26} q_i^{26}} = \frac{(1 \times 2) + (10^{-2} \times 10^6)}{(1 \times 1) + (10^{-2} \times 1)} \approx 10^4$$

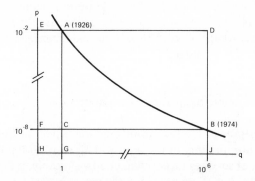

Figure 8.2 The derived demand curve for the services of computers. Quantity is measured as the capacity to do additions

spect to a given technology while what we have are prices corresponding to amounts of factors of production under enirely different technologies.

Technical change over the last fifty years may have created an economy dependent on a stock of computers with a capacity of the order of a million times what would have sufficed fifty years ago. We may have put ourselves in a position where we can never go back to the technology of a former time. Thus, though the computing capacity of machines today may be comparable to those of fifty years ago, their social and economic significance is not, and it is pointless to try to compare food, which is an argument in the utility function, and computers, which is an intermediate input in a changing technology, within the same index of real income.

Note also that the computer example, though extreme, is not preposterous. Electrical circuitry or air travel (treated as an intermediate product) might have done just as well. The point is simply that new and old types of machines are not comparable either because their uses are entirely different or because their economic consequences are different even in those cases where invariant hidden commodities can be discovered. Thus, from a different starting point and by a different route, we have arrived once again at the conclusion already reached in the discussion of investment in Chapter 5, namely, that for long time series of real income it is inappropriate to try to measure the output of capital goods in their own units, and that the best one can do is to define a concept of real income as the sum of real consumption and real saving, defined as consumption forgone in creating new capital goods regardless of nature or composition of the capital goods themselves. In our simple example of food and computers, the ratio of real incomes defined in this way in 1974 and 1926 would be exactly 2.0 because the output of food in 1974 is twice what it is in 1926 and the shares of real income devoted to investment are the same.

C. THE MEASUREMENT OF OUTPUT BY INPUT

There are portions of the flow of income for which we know values but neither price nor quantity of the output. This is so for final products that take the form of services rather than goods—notably, public administration, education, law, finance and medicine—and for a few products, of which novelties is the prime example, where there is no acceptable way of identifying outputs each year as amounts of a supposedly homogeneous stuff. There would seem to be two possible ways of dealing with these items. (i) It might be assumed that the price of the commodity in question increases in proportion to prices of other goods and services in the national accounts. The quantity index could then be computed as the ratio of the value index of the item in question and the price index of another class of goods. (ii) Hours of service may be treated as though they were outputs, so that, for instance, the output of education might be measured as the number of teacher-hours over the year. There are instances where the outputs of services can be measured directly but in such cases it is no longer true that price and quantity are unknown.

The second of these expedients—the measurement of output by input—may well result in a substantial downward bias in the measure of economic growth for the force of technical change which has increased the productivity of labour in the production of goods may have increased the productivity of labour in the production of services as well. One might argue that to measure the output of education by the number of teachers, the output of public administration by the number of civil servants and the output of medicine by the number of doctors is like measuring the output of automobiles by the number of auto workers or the output of food by the number of farmers. On the other hand, there is some presumption that technical change affects the output of goods more than the output of services. It is not obvious that university professors at Queen's in the 1970s are more proficient at transmitting knowledge to students than were their counterparts in the University of Oxford in the fifteenth century, though the knowledge itself may have advanced in some departments. In practice, where one has no idea of the size of productivity change in services and no direct measure of the output, it may be better to measure output by input rather than for the national accountant to impose a wholly arbitrary assignment of productivity onto the data.

D. PRICE VARIATION AMONG CONSUMERS

The justification for measuring real income by deflation, namely that $q = v/p$ for each commodity, rests on the presumption that prices are more or less the same for all consumers and tends to break down if this turns out not to be so. Prices are expected to be the same because of the combined effect of competition and arbitrage. A seller of butter, for instance, who charges a price significantly higher than other sellers are charging will soon find himself without customers and will have to lower his price or go out of business. A seller who charges a significantly lower price will soon take over the whole market. There are, however, several circumstances, to be enumerated below, in which prices of identical goods can differ among consumers. Whether or not this biases the rate of economic growth depends entirely on how these prices are averaged. They might be averaged in such a way that q continues to equal v/p where p is understood to be the average price rather than a unique price in the market.[5] They might be averaged so that q is measured with a random error but no predictable bias in the measure of the rate of economic growth. Or the averaging procedure may give rise to a systematic bias, up or down, in the measure of the rate of economic growth.

(i) *Regional variation in prices and the cost of living*

Transport cost makes a product cheaper in regions where it is produced than in regions where it has to be imported. One might suppose that the cost of living as a whole would be more or less the same, and would change at more or less the same rate, throughout the country because prices differentials on imports and exports cancel out in each region. This could fail to occur in a variety of ways. A region would be expected

---

[5] Suppose butter sells at m different prices $p_1, \ldots, p_m$ and that the quantity of butter selling at p_j is q_j. Total quantity of butter is $Q = \sum_{j=1}^{m} q_j$, total value is $V = \sum_{j=1}^{m} p_j q_j$, and the only price index P such that $P = V/Q$ is $P = \sum_{j=1}^{m} (q_j/Q) p_j$. The true quantity is correctly assessed by the deflation procedure if and only if the different prices of butter p_j are weighted in the index by factors (q_j/Q). Note that the measure of the rate of growth would be biased if all p_j changed proportionally over time, but there was a change in the shares of output purchased at the different prices, and this change was not accounted for in the price index.

to have a high cost of living if its output consisted of capital goods or unfinished products and most consumption goods were imported. A region would be expected to have a low cost of living in the opposite case where it exports goods that enter in an important way into the cost of living or are very close substitutes in production or in use for other goods that do. The measure of the rate of economic growth of a region within a country could be biased if its economy changed from one pattern to the other over the period in which growth is measured. The measure of economic growth in the economy as a whole could be biased if, for instance, prices were observed in one region only and the rate of price change in that region were different than the rate for the economy as a whole. I doubt that this bias is important.

(ii) *Rural–urban price differentials*

This case is similar but not quite identical to geographical price differentials. It is possible that the cost of living was at one time lower on the farm than in the city but that the differential has disappeared as farmers specialize more and more in cash crops and tend to devote an ever larger share of their expenditure to products produced in or distributed from the city. Such a change occurring over the period when economic growth is observed would lead to an upward bias in the measure of economic growth if, as is often the case, the expenditure in the country as a whole is deflated by a price index in which urban prices predominate.

Site rents present a special problem. The rent of a house may be high because the house itself is attractive (it is large, or comfortable, or has a large garden) or because it is conveniently located. The practice in the national accounts is to treat differences in rents of houses analogously with differences in prices of items of clothing. The more expensive house is counted as a better house regardless of whether it is more expensive because of its attractiveness or because of its location. Thus, if a farmer and a city-dweller live in houses that are identical in every respect except location, and if the rent of the city house is twice that of the farm house because of high site rents on urban land, the city-dweller is shown in the measure of gross national expenditure as consuming twice the quantity of housing of the farmer. Real income in housing is computed by deflating the total value of housing services (in which the city house is counted as twice the country house) by a price index of housing from which 'quality change' is, wherever possible, removed. A gradual increase over time in the proportion of the population living in large cities can cause the measure of real consumption of housing per head to increase without any corresponding increase in the standard of housing if, as would be likely, there is a corresponding increase in the share of site rents in the value of rents as a whole. Even more peculiar is the fact that the introduction of an extremely efficient highway system in a city can lower the measure of housing services enjoyed by reducing the differential between rents in the centre of the city and rents at the periphery.

(iii) *Personal goods*

Any product that is somehow attached to an individual and cannot be traded on the market is likely to be evaluated differently by different people. Leisure is a good example. For each year the imputation for leisure in Chapter 7 was computed as the difference in hours of leisure between that year and the base year weighted by the average real wage in that year. In using average real wage, we overlooked an important difference between the price of leisure and, say, the price of cheese. The price of cheese is approximately the same for everyone because the possibility of arbitrage emerges as soon as price differentials among people become large. There is no comparable force in the market for leisure. A poor man with plenty of leisure cannot sell his leisure to a rich man at a price which is the same for both parties to the transaction because each man's price of leisure is precisely his wage and because (by assumption) the rich man is rich due to his greater marginal productivity of labour. In these circumstances, there is some question as to whether it is appropriate to treat a rich man's leisure and a poor man's leisure as amounts of the same stuff, for the marginal valuation of an hour of leisure to a rich man may be, for example, twenty pounds of cheese while the marginal valuation of an hour of leisure to a poor man is only two pounds of cheese, despite the fact that their marginal valuations of ordinary commodities are constrained by arbitrage to be the same. An analogous problem in the evaluation of personal goods in cost–benefit analyis is discussed briefly in our analysis of life expectancy in Chapter 12.

(iv) *Hidden commodities*

The problem here is similar to that just discussed in connection with personal goods. Suppose that cars are evaluated according to the characteristics weight, speed and safety. The price of any make of car is approximately the same to every buyer, but the buyers' marginal valuations of the characteristics may differ. A given make of car may be purchased by one man because the car is heavy and by a second man because it is fast. The existence of many types of cars places limits on the extent to which shadow prices of characteristics may vary among consumers, but some variability will persist as long as the options are not infinitely diverse. If shadow prices were the same for everyone, it would be reasonable to expect them to be reflected in the coefficients b_k in equation (2) above. Without this uniformity, it is not clear what the coefficients of the regression mean. They may be average shadow prices, but they could be something else altogether. It is difficult to say how this bias would affect the measure of the growth of real income computed by deflating values by a hedonic price index.

NOTES FOR FURTHER READING

For a complete discussion of quality change as the subject was understood until the end of the 1950s, see E. v. Hofsten, *Prices Indexes and Quality Change*, Bokforlaget Forum AB., Stockholm, 1952. A major shift of emphasis occurred in the early 1960s with the publication in 1961 of *The Price Statistics of the Federal Government*, by the Price Statistics Review Committee chaired by George Stigler (US Congress, Joint Economic Committee, Part I, 87th Congress, 1st Session, 24 January 1961). This document included as a staff paper Z. Griliches' study 'Hedonic Price Indexes for Automobiles: An Economic Analysis of Quality Change', in which it was demonstrated that the rate of price increase in the United States was biased up and the measure of economic growth biased down accordingly by the failure of the official price statistics to allow for improvements in the characteristics of goods and for possible differences between list prices and prices paid by purchasers. See also Z. Griliches (ed.), *Price Indexes and Quality Change: Studies in New Methods of Measurement*, Harvard University Press, 1971, and G. Stigler and J. Kindahl, *The Behaviour of Economic Research*, 1970. A review of the debate somewhat more favourable to the official price indexes is presented in J. Triplett, 'The Measurement of Inflation: A Survey of Research on the Accuracy of Price Indexes' in P. H. Earl (ed.), *Analysis of Inflation*, Lexington Books, 1977.

The ambiguity in shadow prices of characteristics in circumstances where shadow prices may differ among consumers is discussed in S. Rosen, 'Hedonic Prices and Implicit Markets: Potential Differentiation in Pure Competition', *Journal of Political Economy*, 1974, pp. 34–55. The effects of changes in technology upon the 'true' price index is discussed in F. Fisher and K. Shell, *The Economic Theory of Price Indexes: Two Essays on the Effects of Taste Quality and Technical Change*, Academic Press, 1972. Geographical variability is discussed in D. Usher, *The Price Mechanism and the Meaning of National Income Statistics*, Oxford University Press, 1968.

9

Index Numbers

In Chapter 2, we showed that the true measure of real income can be approximated by a Laspeyres measure, where the true measure for any year t is the smallest amount of money sufficient to enable the representative consumer to make himself as well off at prices in the base year as he would be with the bundle of goods consumed in the year t, and the Laspeyres measure is the value at base year prices of the bundle of goods consumed in the year t. Specifically when the year 0 is the base year

$$Y(t, 0, w) \equiv C(p^0, U(q^t)) \leq \sum_{i=1}^{n} p_i^0 q_i^t \qquad (1)$$

where the expressions to the left of the inequality sign are two entirely equivalent representations of real income as an indicator of the welfare of the representative consumer, where the right-hand expression is the Laspeyres measure,[1] and where all functions are defined exactly as in Chapter 2. It is also shown in Chapter 2 that the Laspeyres measure is necessarily an overestimate of the true measure of real income; the direction of the inequality in equation (1) is an unavoidable consequence of the normal convexity of indifference curves. In Chapter 10 and at other places in the book, we use the Laspeyres measure, notwithstanding the bias, in belief that the error introduced into the measure of economic growth is likely to be small by comparison with that arising from errors of observation of prices and values, or from inaccurate accounting of quality change. In this chapter we consider whether and to what extent the bias may be eliminated through the use of a more appropriate index number formula. The subject of this chapter is the conventional theory of index numbers, slightly reformulated to focus on the bias in the Laspeyres measure as an indicator of real income.

The essence of the problem is illustrated for a two-commodity economy in Figure 2.5. Recall the meaning of the figure. On the top

[1] The use of the terms Laspeyres measure and Laspeyres index may give rise to confusion. The former is the expression $\Sigma_{i=1}^{n} p_i^0 q_i^t$. The latter is the expression $(\Sigma_{i=1}^{n} p_i^0 q_i^t)/(\Sigma_{i=1}^{n} p_i^0 q_i^0)$. The measure is converted to the index by dividing by the value of the measure in the base year.

half, quantities consumed of bread and cheese are represented as distances on the vertical and horizontal axes. If we make the harmless assumption that the price of bread is 1.0 at all times, we can treat that good itself as the numeraire and we can measure income as distance on the vertical axis. Two indifference curves are shown, one containing the bundle of goods consumed in 1961 and the other containing the bundle of goods consumed in 1974. We let 1961 be the base year, in which case nominal income and real income for that year are one and the same. Their common value, $Y(61)$, is indicated by the height of the intersection of the 1961 budget constraint with the vertical axis. Real income in 1974, $Y(74, 61, w)$, is indicated as the height of the intersection with the vertical axis of a line parallel to the 1961 budget constraint but just high enough to be tangent to the indifference curve containing the bundle of goods consumed in 1974. The Laspeyres measure of real income in 1974 with respect to 1961 as the base year is the height of the intersection with the vertical axis of a line parallel to the 1961 budget constraint and passing through the point representing the bundle of goods consumed in 1974.

From the normal convexity of indifference curves, it follows at once that the Laspeyres approximation is an overestimate of the true measure of real income, as stated in equation (1). The simple economics of the proposition is that a representative consumer with enough money to buy the 1974 bundle of goods at 1961 prices will not do so. He will instead choose a different bundle containing more of goods that are relatively cheap at 1961 prices and less of goods that are relatively dear. The representative consumer will necessarily be better off with the latter bundle, and the improvement in his welfare expressed as real income is precisely the bias in the Laspeyres measure. It is shown on the lower graph that the magnitude of the bias is what in other contexts is known as consumer's surplus. The graph itself shows a compensated demand curve constructed from the indifference curve containing the bundle of goods consumed in 1974. The horizontal axis is the same as that on the top graph, but the vertical axis is relative price of cheese. It is proved in Chapter 2 that the bias in the Laspeyres measure, $\Sigma_{i=1}^{2} p_i^{61} q_i^{74} - Y(74, 61, w)$, is just equal to an almost triangular area under the demand curve that can be interpreted as consumer's surplus. Thus the index number problem of measuring real income correctly from time series of p and q boils down in the end to one of estimating the size of consumer's surplus for each year of the time series.

Though our interest in this book is limited to measuring real income from time series of prices and quantities, it should be noted that our problem is an instance of the general problem of index numbers which may be formulated as follows. Suppose we know there to be a function

$f(x)$ where x is a vector $x_1, \ldots, x_n$ and $f(x)$ is an increasing function of each x_i. We observe time series of the vector x^t and of a second vector y^t such that each y_i^t is proportional to the first derivative of x_i^t (that is, y_i^t is equal to $\lambda(\partial f/\partial x_i)$ where the derivative is taken at time t and the scalar λ may be a function of t but not of any x_i), but that we do not know the form of the function f. The problem of index numbers to use the time series of x and y to draw inferences about the time series of f. Specifically it is to obtain a function $\varphi(x, y)$ such that $\varphi(x, y) \sim f(x)$ if f is cardinal, or φ is a monotonically increasing function of f if f is ordinal. In our problem, f is real income, x is quantity, y is price, λ is indicative of the price level and φ is the index we seek. But the logic of the problem is the same if we interpret f as the true cost of living, x as prices, y as quantities and φ as a cost of living index, or if we interpret f as the height of an isoquant, x as inputs of factors of production, y as factor prices, and φ as an index of total factor input. We have shown that one candidate for φ, namely the Laspeyres measure, is biased, though we do not yet know how important the bias is.

In this chapter we shall consider in turn four approaches to the index number problem—four ways of dealing with the bias in the Laspeyres approximation. These are the theory of limits, the development of a better index number, the estimation of shapes of indifference curves, and the use of the Divisia index. The theory of limits is about how to bracket the true index from below as well as from above. The Laspeyres index is always an overestimate. The job is done if we can find a second index guaranteed to be an underestimate, for then we can say that the true index has increased since the base year if both limits exceed the value of the index in the base year. The second approach makes use of the assumed curvature of indifference curves. The bias in the Laspeyres measure occurs because the loci of constant values of the Laspeyres measure are straight lines while the loci of constant values of utility are curved. In that case, the bias may be reduced or even eliminated altogether by the development of a new and better index that is itself curved and that makes use of relative prices in the current year to determine how curved it ought to be. The third approach is based on the fact that the size of consumer's surplus can be estimated if we know the price elasticity of demand. Since the bias in the Laspeyres measure is nothing more than consumer's surplus, we can correct for that bias by estimating demand curves, calculating price elasticities and computing the areas of appropriate triangles. A difficulty arises from the non-additivity of consumer's surplus when there are many goods, but this can be circumvented because the estimate of a complete set of demand functions is virtually the same as the estimation of the shapes of indifference curves from which the true measure of real income can be derived. The rationale for the Divisia, or chain-link, index is that the bias in the Laspeyres index is minute, even as a proportion to the size of the change in the index from one year to the next, if the change itself is very small. Thus, so the argument goes, the true index in the year t with regard to base year 0 can be constructed with little or no error as a compound of the indexes of changes from year 0 to 1, from year 1 to year 2 and so on, if the base of the index is changed accordingly.

Let the reader be warned that this chapter on index numbers is deliberately sketchy and that he will not be able to make use of the methods of index numbers described here without first mastering some of the literature cited at the end of the chapter. I do not feel it necessary to discuss index numbers thoroughly because the reader can find an adequate exposition elsewhere, because there is more material than I can cope with in a chapter, and because I do not have occasion to use sophisticated index number formulae in this book. My purpose in dealing with index numbers at all is to give the reader a vantage point from which to assess my own use of the Laspeyres measure in the next chapter and the index number conventions in the national accounts. For this purpose, a sketch is enough. We shall limit our discussion to a few simple cases of each of the four variants of index number theory to show how the theory pertains to the issues that are important in this book. However, the Divisia index will be discussed more fully than other parts of index number theory to develop results we shall need when we come to discuss technical change in Chapter 12. We shall conclude this chapter with a brief reassessment of the Laspeyres measure.

A. THE THEORY OF LIMITS

As we already have an upper limit to the true measure of real income, the problem boils down to finding a lower one. A procedure for doing so is illustrated in Figure 9.1 which is an extension of the top half of Figure 2.5 with the commodities numbered rather than named to conform to the formulae we discuss. The main addition to the figure is the expansion path at 1961 prices; this shows how consumption of both goods would increase if income increased but prices remained constant. The expansion path cuts the indifference curves containing the points 61 and 74 at the points 61 itself and at a point labelled 74*. Now project the 1974 budget constraint (the tangent to the point 74) until it cuts the expansion path at a point labelled 74**, and project the point 74** onto the vertical axis by a line parallel to the 1961 budget constraint. The intersection of this line with the vertical axis is the point labelled $K(74, 61)$ where K is mnemonic for Konus who is generally credited with the invention of this construction. The 'Konus limit' constructed in this way has to be a lower limit such as we are seeking because the convexity of indifference curves ensures that the point 74** will be lower on the expansion path than the point 74*. The expansion path itself can be estimated from cross-section data on expenditure patterns of people with different incomes but the same set of relative prices.

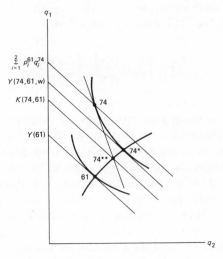

Figure 9.1 Upper and lower limits to the true measure of real income as welfare

There are several difficulties with this procedure. First, a pair of limits to real income might be an acceptable substitute for a point estimate in a comparison between two countries where the object is simply to determine the country which is better off, but it would be a great nuisance to have to compute or to use upper and lower limits for each year in a time series, especially as limits in adjacent years would tend to overlap making comparison indeterminate in many cases where it may be obvious on other grounds—quantities in year $t + 1$ may all be slightly greater than quantities in year t—that people are better off in one year than the other. Second, since the expansion path can only be estimated within a margin of error, one cannot always be sure that the lower limit is correct. And third, if one is going to use econometric techniques to estimate the expansion path, one might push the process a stage further to estimate a complete set of demand curves, in the manner to be discussed in Section C, from which a point estimate of real income can be derived.

B. ALTERNATIVE INDEX NUMBER FORMULAE

The Laspeyres index of real income could be replaced by another type of index that conforms better to the curvature of indifference curves. The most popular such index, used primarily in comparisons between pairs of years, is called Fisher's ideal index. It is defined as the square root of the Paasche and Laspeyres indexes; specifically, for any pair of years 0 and t, the ideal quantity index F is

$$F = \left(\frac{\sum_{i=1}^n p_i^0 q_i^t}{\sum_{i=1}^n p_i^0 q_i^0} \cdot \frac{\sum_{i=1}^n p_i^t q_i^t}{\sum_{i=1}^n p_i^t q_i^0} \right)^{1/2} \tag{2}$$

The index has many nice properties. A proportional increase in all quantities increases the index accordingly. The product of a Fisher quantity index and the corresponding Fisher price index equals the value of output in the year t as a multiple of the value of output in year 0. The Fisher index for the year t when the year 0 is the base year is the inverse of the index for the year 0 when the year t is the base year. These properties are known respectively in the index number literature as proportionality, factor reversal and circularity. It is easy to verify from the definition of F that it does indeed possess these properties.

The most important property of the Fisher index from our point of view is that it is dead accurate as an indicator of the height of the utility function whenever the utility function is quadratic. If the utility function is of the form

$$U = \sum_{i=1}^n \sum_{j=1}^n a_{ij} q_i q_j \tag{3}$$

where $a_{ij} \geq 0$ for every i and j, then the Fisher index is exactly[2]

---

[2] First, let $b_{ij} = \frac{1}{2}(a_{ij} + a_{ji})$ and note that $U = \sum_{i=1}^n \sum_{j=1}^n b_{ij} q_i q_j$ where $b_{ij} = b_{ji}$ for all i and j. Next write U in matrix form as $U = q'Bq$ where B is the matrix of all b_{ij}. Differentiating U with respect to q, we see that the vector of prices is $p' = \lambda Bq$ where λ is an unknown variable which is the same for every value of i but which changes from year to year. Substituting for the value of p in Fisher's ideal quantity index of equation (2), we have

$$F = \left(\frac{\lambda^0 q'Bq^0}{\lambda^0 q^0 Bq^0} \cdot \frac{\lambda^t q'Bq^t}{\lambda^t q^0 Bq^t} \right)^{1/2} = \left(\frac{U^t}{U^0} \right)^{1/2}$$

$$F = \frac{C(p^0, U^t)}{C(p^0, U^0)} \tag{4}$$

for any time series of prices and quantities mutually consistent with equation (3). If we know that the utility function is of the form (3), then we know that F is the perfect index.

It is hard to say how much importance to attach to these desirable properties of the Fisher quantity index. The index would really be ideal if we knew in advance that the utility function was quadratic. What we know, on the other hand, is that it is not, for it is not even homothetic unless all income elasticities happen to equal 1.0. If we have learned anything at all from studies of elasticities of demand it is that a man, as his income increases, consumes relatively more of some goods and less of others, so that income elasticities cannot all be 1.0 and the quadratic form cannot be representative of indifference curves. If the utility function is not homothetic, the Fisher ideal quantity index is a biased indicator of real income, though the magnitude and direction of the bias may be difficult to assess.

Other indexes have been put forward with various advantages and disadvantages. Theil's 'best linear' index is designed to come as close as possible to the factor reversal property for all possible combinations of price indexes and quantity indexes in an n-period or n-country comparison. Specifically, let $W(\tau, t)$ be the value of goods consumed in the year τ at prices in the year t:

$$W(\tau, t) \equiv \sum_{i=1}^{n} q_i^{\tau} p_i^t \tag{5}$$

---

because the λ^0 and λ^t cancel out and the northwest expression is equal, by symmetry, to the southeast expression in the square root. The utility function is homothetic, because an increase in all q_i by a uniform factor a leaves all relative prices the same, and all expansion paths are straight lines through the origin. Now real income in the year t, $C(p^0, U^t)$, is the value of the expression $\sum_{i=1}^{n} p_i^0 \bar{q}_i^t$ where $U(\bar{q}^t) = U(q^t)$ and $\bar{q}^t$ is a point on the expansion path at prices p^0. From the fact that expansion paths are straight lines through the origin, it follows that there is some a for which $\bar{q}_i^t = a q_i^0$ for all goods i. From this, it follows: (a) that $C(p^0, U(q^t)) = aY^0$; and (b) that $a = (U^t/U^0)^{1/2}$. Combining (a) and (b), we see finally that

$$C(p^0, U(q^t)) = Y^0 (U^t/U^0)^{1/2}$$

from which equation (4) follows at once.

A pair of price and quantity indices $P(t)$ and $Q(\tau)$, where $t = 1, \ldots, T$, possess the generalized factor reversal property if

$$W(\tau, t) \equiv Q(\tau)P(t) \tag{6}$$

for every pair of years. No index possesses this property exactly, but indexes can be designed to approach it as closely as possible according to a least squares criterion. For any pair of price and quantity indexes $P(t)$ and $Q(\tau)$, let

$$E(\tau, t) \equiv W(\tau, t) - Q(\tau)P(t) \tag{7}$$

be the deviation from the generalized factor reversal property. The best linear index is defined to minimize the value of

$$\sum_{\tau=1}^{T} \sum_{t=1}^{T} E(\tau, t)^2$$

Theil shows how to design prices and quantity indexes to minimize the value of this expression. Stuvel has constructed an index to apportion the increase in the value of a series into price and quantity components so that it may be said that a given increase in value is $x\%$ due to price change and $(100 - x)\%$ due to quantity change. Diewert has identified a class of indexes which he calls superlative, all members of which are accurate representations of second degree approximations to the true function that the index is intended to reflect.

C. THE ESTIMATION OF INDIFFERENCE CURVES

As shown in Chapter 2, we could dispense with index numbers altogether if we knew the shapes of indifference curves. The essence of the index number problem is that we do not have this information and must make do with time series of prices and quantities instead. But developments in the theory of demand and econometric technique have enabled us to estimate shapes of indifference curves with an accuracy that may at times be sufficient for our purpose. The procedure is to postulate a general form for a utility function with unknown parameters, and to estimate the parameters from evidence of time series of prices and quantities. The procedure was originally designed to compute elasticities of demand, but it can be used equally well for the measurement of real income.

The first such function to be estimated and the one that is easiest to work with is the Stone–Geary utility function

$$U^t = \sum_{i=1}^{n} \beta_i \ln (q_i^t - \gamma_i) \tag{8}$$

where, by assumption, $\Sigma_{i=1}^{n}\beta_i = 1$, where the parameters γ_i can be interpreted as minimal subsistence requirements, and where the parameters β_i can be interpreted as elasticities of demand for commodities over and above subsistence requirements. The set of β_i and γ_i can all be estimated from time series of quantities q_i^t and the corresponding prices. Once these are known, real income $C(p^0, U(q^t))$ can be computed as follows. First observe that the Stone–Geary utility function gives rise to the demand curves[3]

$$q_i = \gamma_i + \frac{\beta_i}{p_i}\left(Y - \sum_{j=1}^{n} p_j\gamma_j\right) \tag{9}$$

in which the term $(Y - \Sigma_{j=1}^{n}p_j\gamma_j)$, often referred to as supernumerary income, is the difference between actual income Y and the cost, $\Sigma_{j=1}^{n}p_j\gamma_j$, of subsistence requirements. Then substitute the demand curves back into the utility function to obtain the indirect utility function in which U is expressed as a function p^t and Y rather than as a function of q^t. The indirect utility function is

$$U^t = \sum_{i=1}^{n} \beta_i \ln \left[\frac{\beta_i}{p_i^t}\left(Y^t - \sum_{j=1}^{n} p_j^t\gamma_j\right)\right]$$

$$= \sum_{i=1}^{n} \ln [\beta_i^{\beta_i}] - \sum_{i=1}^{n} \ln [(p_i^t)^{\beta_i}] + \ln \left(Y^t - \sum_{j=1}^{n} p_j^t\gamma_j\right) \tag{10}$$

[3] Form the Lagrangian

$$L = \sum_i \beta_i \ln (q_i - \gamma_i) - \lambda\left(\sum_i p_iq_i - Y\right) \tag{i}$$

The first-order conditions are

$$\frac{\partial L}{\partial q_i} = \frac{\beta_i}{q_i - \gamma_i} - \lambda p_i = 0 \tag{ii}$$

To determine λ, add up numerators and denominators of the expressions for λ in each of the first-order conditions:

$$\lambda = \frac{\beta_i}{p_i(q_i - \gamma_i)} = \frac{\Sigma_i \beta_i}{\Sigma_i p_i(q_i - \gamma_i)} = \frac{1}{Y - \Sigma_i p_i\gamma_i} \tag{iii}$$

because, by assumption, $\Sigma_i \beta_i = 1$. The demand curves are obtained by substituting for λ into first-order conditions.

Since any monotonically increasing function of a utility function is a utility function itself, we can represent the indirect utility function equally well as

$$\hat{U}^t = \exp\left(U^t - U^0\right) = \left[\prod_{i=1}^{n}\left(\frac{p_i^0}{p_i^t}\right)^{\beta_i}\right] \frac{Y^t - \sum_{j=1}^{n} p_j^t \gamma_j}{Y^0 - \sum_{j=1}^{n} p_j^0 \gamma_j} \qquad (11)$$

Then by inverting the indirect utility function $\hat{U}^t$, we obtain the cost function with respect to the representation of utility given by $\hat{U}^t$ rather than U^t itself.

$$C(p^t, U(q^t)) = \sum_{j=1}^{n} p_j^t \gamma_j + \hat{U}_t\left[\prod_{i=1}^{n}\left(\frac{p_i^t}{p_j^0}\right)^{\beta_i}\right]\left(Y^0 - \sum_{j=1}^{n} p_j^0 \gamma_j\right) \qquad (12)$$

And finally, we see that real income in the year t defined with respect to prices in the year 0—the income required at base year prices to make the representative consumer as well off as he was in the year t—is

$$C(p^0, U(q^t)) = \sum_{j=1}^{n} p_j^0 \gamma_j + \hat{U}^t\left(Y^0 - \sum_{j=1}^{n} p_j^0 \gamma_j\right) \qquad (13)$$

which is the sum of two parts: the cost of subsistence in the base year, and the base year supernumerary income scaled up by the value of the utility function in the year t. The true measure of real income $C(p^0, U(q^t))$ may therefore be computed from data on the parameters of the utility function, β and λ estimated econometrically, and from prices and incomes, p^0, p^t, y^0 and y^t, in the year 0 and the year t, where the data on β, p^t and y^t which do not appear directly in equation (13) are required to estimate $\hat{U}^t$.

As with the Fisher index, this measure of real income is dead accurate if the data of prices and quantity conform precisely to the postulated utility function, but that there are reasons for skepticism as to whether this will actually be so. The Stone–Geary utility function is a very simple function in which all goods are gross substitutes and there are no special relations of complementarity or substitutability among pairs or subgroups of good. One can see this by inspection of the utility function in equation (8); no pairs of quantities q_i and q_j are classified together in a separate subfunction. The demand for butter is not more sensitive to the price of margarine than to the price of books, and there is no particular relation between right and left shoes. Actually, the failure of the Stone–Geary utility function to account for substitutability and complementarity matters less than these examples would suggest because the use of the function is typically limited to the estimation of demand elasticities of between four and ten aggregate commodities into which total personal consumption is subdivided prior to the estimation process. For instance, the commodities might be food, clothing, shelter and miscellaneous, in which case β_1, β_2, β_3, β_4, γ_1, γ_2, γ_3 and γ_4 would be the only parameters to be estimated. The main issues in evaluating this procedure for measuring real income are how closely the Stone–Geary function corresponds to the shapes of the true indifference surfaces, whether the estimates of the parameters are accurate, and whether it is worth making a fuss about combining four to ten aggregate commodities into a measure of real income when the real biases are those in the procedures by which the quantities of the aggregate commodities are built up from the primary data.

The great merit of this technique is that it improves together with the progress in the econometrics of the estimation of demand curves. More complex and interesting functional forms can be investigated—in particular, utility functions can be nested so that quantities of butter and margarine are combined in a special function the value of which enters as a single commodity in the larger utility function—and more and more commodities can be accounted for.

D. THE DIVISIA INDEX

In introducing the Divisia index, it is best to be a bit more general than we have been so far. Suppose our object is to track a function $X(q_1, \ldots, q_n)$ where X might be but is not necessarily a utility function and where all the evidence we have about the function X consists of a time series of q_i for each i and a complementary time series of p_i defined by the property

$$p_i = \lambda \frac{\partial X}{\partial q_i} \tag{14}$$

where λ is independent of i but may vary in any way whatsoever with time. Suppose also that q_i vary continuously over time so that $q_i = q_i(t)$ and, by substituting for all q_i in the function X, $X = X(t)$ as well.

The Divisia index, $D(t)$, is got by adding up the effects of small changes in the time series $q_i(t)$. First, the rate of change of D is defined by the relation

$$\frac{d(\ln D(t))}{dt} = \sum_{i=1}^{n} v_i \frac{d(\ln q_i)}{dt} \tag{15}$$

where v_i is the value share defined as $p_i(t)q_i(t)/(\Sigma_{j=1}^n p_j(t)q_j(t))$. Then the value of D itself is computed by integration:

$$D(t) = D(0) \exp \left(\int_0^t \frac{d(\ln D(t))}{dt} \, dt \right) \tag{16}$$

where $D(0)$, the value of the index in the year 0, may be assigned arbitrarily or may be set equal to $\Sigma_{i=1}^n p_i(0)q_i(0)$.

We can establish three positions about the accuracy of the Divisia index:

(a) The Divisia index is constant if and only if X is constant and the direction of change of the Divisia index at any time is the same as the direction of change of X.

(b) If X is homogeneous in degree 1, and if we set $D(0) = X(0)$, then $D(t) = X(t)$ for all t and for all continuous functions $q_i(t)$.

(c) If X is homothetic, the Divisia index is a perfect ordinal indicator of X; the value of $D(t)$ depends only on the initial and terminal quantities, $q_i(0)$ and $q_i(t)$, and is independent of the path between.

Proposition (a) is derived by expressing the derivative of $\ln X$ as a function of derivatives of all $\ln q_i$. For any function X, it is necessarily the case that

$$\frac{d}{dt} (\ln X) = \sum_{i=1}^n \left(\frac{(\partial X/\partial q_i)q_i}{X} \right) \frac{d}{dt} (\ln q_i) \tag{17}$$

On substituting equations (14) and (15) into equation (17), we see that

$$\frac{d}{dt} (\ln X) = \left(\frac{\Sigma_j p_j q_j}{\lambda X} \right) \sum_{i=1}^n \left(\frac{p_i q_i}{\Sigma_j p_j q_j} \right) \frac{d}{dt} (\ln q_i)$$
$$= \frac{\Sigma_j p_j q_j}{\lambda X} \frac{d}{dt} (\ln D) \tag{18}$$

which establishes that X is an increasing function of D.

Proposition (b) is a consequence of the fact that

$$X = \sum_{i=1}^n \frac{\partial X}{\partial q_i} q_i = \lambda \sum_{i=1}^n p_i q_i \tag{19}$$

whenever X is homogeneous in degree 1. From equations (17) and (19) it follows that

$$\ln X(t) - \ln X(0) = \int_0^t \sum_{i=1}^n \frac{\partial(\ln X)}{\partial q_i} \frac{dq_i}{dt} dt$$

$$= \int_0^t \sum_{i=1}^n \frac{1}{X} \frac{\partial X}{\partial q_i} \frac{dq_i}{dt} dt$$

$$= \int_0^t \sum_{i=1}^n \frac{1}{\lambda \sum_{i=1}^n p_i q_i} \lambda p_i q_i \frac{d(\ln q_i)}{dt} dt$$

$$= \int_0^t \sum_{i=1}^n v_i \frac{d(\ln q_i)}{dt} dt$$

$$= \int_0^t \frac{d}{dt} (\ln D(t)) dt$$

$$= \ln D(t) - \ln D(0) \qquad (20)$$

so that

$$\frac{X(t)}{X(0)} = \frac{D(t)}{D(0)} \qquad (21)$$

for all t, in which case growth rates of X and D are exactly the same.

Proposition (c) is established in a similar way. As indicated in Chapter 2, a function $X(q)$ is said to be homothetic if X is a monotically increasing transformation of a function Y that is homogeneous in degree 1 in the arguments $q_1, \ldots, q_n$, that is, if $X = f(Y)$ and $Y = Y(q)$ where Y is a function such that $Y(aq) = aY(q)$ for any positive scalar a, and $f' > 0$. By analogy with the argument leading to equation (23), it immediately follows that

$$\frac{Y(t)}{Y(0)} = \frac{D(t)}{D(0)} \qquad (22)$$

in which case

$$\frac{X(t)}{X(0)} = \frac{f^{-1}(D(t))}{f^{-1}(D(0))} \qquad (23)$$

proving that the Divisia index is a monotonically increasing function of $X(t)$.

An immediate implication of proposition (c) is that the Divisia index possesses the 'proportionality property' with regard to homothetic functions. From the definition of the Divisia index it follows that

$D(t) = a(t)D(0)$ whenever changes in the q_i lie on a line from the origin such that $q_i(t) = a(t)q_i(0)$. This is true no matter what the form of the price-generating function X. If the unknown function X is homothetic, then the ratio $D(t)/D(0)$ depends only on the initial and final values of q_i (on $q_i(0)$ and $q_i(t)$). So if $q_i(t) = aq_i(0)$ for every i, then $D(t) = aD(0)$ regardless of the path of $q(\tau)$ between $q(0)$ and $q(t)$ because the expansion of q_i on a straight line from the $q(0)$ to $q(t)$ is a possible path of integration.

If we interpret X as real income, so that $X(t) = C(p(0), U(q(t)))$, it follows at once that the Divisia index is an accurate representation of real income, that

$$D(t) = \frac{C(p(0), U(q(t)))}{C(p(0), U(q(0)))} \qquad (24)$$

whenever the utility function itself is homothetic. For the function $C(p(0), U(q(t)))$ is simply that transformation of U for which the value of the transformed function is $\Sigma_{i=1}^{n} p_i^0 q_i^0$ in the year 0 and the scale of the transformed function is such that a proportionate increase in all q_i increases the measure of utility accordingly.

Though the Divisia index possesses some excellent properties, it is not robust and can perform very badly if the assumptions under which it is constructed are violated by the data to which it is applied. The major problem with the Divisia index, and the reason why national accountants tend to be uneasy about it, is that all of the nice properties we have attributed to the Divisia index break down if the unknown function X is not homothetic. This happens because the Divisia index is a line integral and because the change in the value of a line integral between any two points is as a rule dependent on the path of integration. The case where $n = 2$ is illustrated in Figure 9.2; a line integral such as the Divisia index

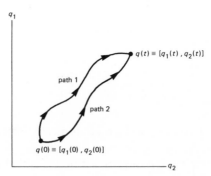

Figure 9.2 Two paths along which the Divisia index may have different values

of equation (16) commencing at the point $q(0)$ and continuing to $q(t)$ along path 1 need not have the same value as the line integral commencing at $q(0)$ and continuing to $q(t)$ along path 2. On each path in Figure 9.2 the Divisia index rises or falls whenever $X(q_1, q_2)$ rises or falls, but the overall rise or fall of the Divisia index need not be the same. Thus if real income is estimated by means of a Divisia index, an economy commencing in year 0 with a bundle of goods consumed represented by the point $q(0)$ and changing year by year along the path 1 until it consumes the bundle of goods represented by the point $q(t)$ would appear to have a different rate of economic growth between the year 0 and the year t than an economy which advanced from the same initial consumption $q(0)$ in the year 0 to the same final bundle $q(t)$ in the year t by way of path 2 instead of path 1. This possibility is ruled out by proposition (c) if the unknown function X is homothetic, but not otherwise. This possibility is important in practice because, as already mentioned, everything we know about utility functions leads us to believe that they are not homothetic.

A striking example of the dependence of the Divisia index on the history of the vector $q(t)$ when the price-generating function X is not homothetic is illustrated in Figure 9.3. Think of X as utility and let X depend on amounts consumed of two commodities, q_1 and q_2. A pair of non-homothetic indifference curves are designated as U^0 and U^1. The

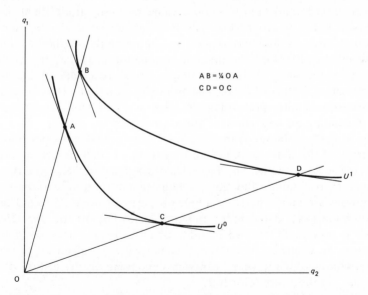

Figure 9.3 A simple example of the dependence of the Divisia index on the path of integration when the price-generating function is not homothetic

lines OAB and OCD are rays through the origin cutting U^0 at A and C and cutting U^1 and B and D. Because (and only because) indifference curves are not homothetic, we can suppose that $AB = \frac{1}{4}OA$ and $CD = OC$. Set the value of the Divisia index at 1 for the point A, and consider its value at the point B. It follows from the proportionality property of the Divisia index along rays from the origin that the value of the index at B assessed along the line AB is 1.25 because $AB = \frac{1}{4}OA$. However, the value of the Divisia index at B rises to 2 when assessed along the indirect route ACDB. By proposition (a), the Divisia index is constant along the paths AC and DB because both of these paths lie on indifference curves, and the value of the Divisia index doubles between C and D because $CD = OC$. Thus, the value of the Divisia index at B could be 1.25 or 2 depending on which path is followed between A and B.

A disturbing implication of the dependence of the Divisia index on the path of integration is that the Divisia index need not possess the 'circularity property'; an economy commencing at $q(0)$, proceeding to $q(1)$ by path 1, and returning to $q(0)$ by path 2 could experience a net change in its Divisia index. The Divisia index could increase, or decrease as the case may be, with each journey around the closed path and could be made as large or as small as we please without any net change in quantities consumed.

It should also be recognized that the Divisia index as defined by equations (15) and (16) is unobservable because infinitesimal increments in q_i are unobservable. The best we can do is to construct an approximation to the Divisia index by combining the smallest available finite increments of q_i; the integral in equation (16) may be approximated by the sum of annual changes or, if available, of quarterly changes in the values of the q_i. The approximation to the Divisia index is not necessarily value preserving, though it may be almost value preserving depending on how good an approximation it is.

Once again, as in our examination of Fisher's ideal index, we find the accuracy of the index to depend critically on whether or not the utility function is homothetic. The Divisia index is a case of extreme dependence. If the utility function is homothetic (and if certain other conditions are met), the Divisia index is perfectly accurate as indicated in equation (24). If the utility function is not homothetic, the Divisia index is potentially the worst index of all those we have considered because the value of the index associated with any given set of prices and quantities for the year t can vary depending on the history of the economy in the years prior to t.

E. THE LASPEYRES INDEX ONCE AGAIN

Having looked briefly at other types of indexes, we can now assess the Laspeyres index from a broader perspective. In fact, the index has quite a bit to recommend it. It is simple, and makes few demands on data, for almost alone among the indexes we have considered it does not require a time series of prices as well as quantities. The direction of the bias is known with certainty, even in the case—which is after all the only important one—where the function it is to represent is not homothetic; the same cannot be said for the Fisher index or the Divisia index despite their virtues when the function is homothetic.

But I think the main virtue of the Laspeyres index, which is the other side of its minimal requirement of data, is that it is robust. The nice properties of the Fisher index and the Divisia index depend on the assumption that there is a stable function X generating time series of prices and quantities and that all prices are proportionate to first derivatives of X in accordance with equation (14). The assumption might prove false for a variety of reasons. If we think of X as utility, the violation of equation (14) means that indifference curves are unstable over time because taste is intrinsically unstable or perhaps because of habit formation. A sudden fall in the relative price of good A and good B may not have its full effect on consumption of good A all at once; consumption may increase gradually as people learn how to incorporate more of good A into their consumption patterns. Should this be the case, the relative price of good A and good B is not uniquely determined by quantities consumed and equation (14) is violated even though taste may still be considered invariant in some broad sense of the term. Under these circumstances the Fisher index would be biased in an unpredictable direction and to an unpredictable extent, and the Divisia index could yield bizarre results, but the Laspeyres index would still be an overestimate of the true quantity index assessed according to the utility function that was in force in the base year.

The main fault of the Laspeyres index is that its deviation from the true index could be substantial. In fact the evidence, though somewhat mixed, suggests on balance that the deviation is not particularly large in those circumstances where there is a real choice among indexes. A number of studies based on time series of prices and quantities of a few aggregate commodities—the flow of income might, for instance, be divided into as few as four aggregate commodities, such as food, clothing, housing and miscellaneous—have shown the measure of economic growth to be almost impervious to the choice of index number formula. On the other hand, there is reason to believe that the observed bias in the Laspeyres index might have been greater if income had been broken down into a larger number of commodities because the elasticity of substitution in use is greater among commodities within the broad categories than among the categories themselves.

NOTES FOR FURTHER READING

For a simple introduction to index numbers see R. G. D. Allen, *Index Numbers in Theory and Practice*, Macmillan, 1975. Though now over forty years old, R. Frisch's paper 'Annual Survey of Economic Theory: The Problem of Index Numbers', *Econometrica*, 1936, pp. 1–38, is still useful as an overview of the subject. For more advanced treatments of the subject, see S. Afriat, *The Price Index*, Princeton University Press, 1978, and P. A. Samuelson and S. Swamy, 'Invariant Index Numbers and Canonical Duality: Survey and Synthesis', *American Economic Review*, 1974, pp. 566–93; both contain extensive bibliographies.

On the theory of limits, see A. A. Konus, 'The Problem of the True Index of the Cost of Living', *Econometrica*, 1939, pp. 10–29; H. Staehle, 'A Development in the Economic Theory of Price Index Numbers', *Review of Economic Studies*, 1935, pp. 163–8; and Y. Toda, 'An Index Number Approach to the International Comparison of Consumption: Western Europe and the United States', *Review of Income and Wealth*, 1971, pp. 353–62.

For a more complete account of the alternative index number formulae discussed in this chapter, see I. Fisher, *The Making of Index Numbers*, 1922; H. Theil, 'Best Linear Index Numbers of Prices and Quantities', *Econometrica*, 1957, pp. 123–31; G. A. Stuvel, 'A New Index Number Formula', *Econometrica*, 1957, pp. 123–31; E. Diewert, 'Exact and Superlative Index Numbers', *Journal of Econometrics*, 1976, pp. 115–45; and K. S. Banerjee, *Cost of Living Index Numbers*, 1975, which reviews much of the literature.

There is an introduction to the Stone–Geary utility function in H. A. J. Green, *Consumer Theory* (revised edition), Macmillan, 1976. For an example of how it is used in measuring real income and the cost of living, see A. S. Goldberger and T. Gameletsos, 'A Cross-Country Comparison of Consumer Expenditure Patterns', *European Economic Review*, 1970, pp. 357099. Indifference surfaces for more sophisticated utility functions have been estimated in M. Brown and D. Heien, 'The S Branch Utility Tree: A Generalization of the Linear Expenditure System', *Econometrica*, 1972, pp. 737–47, and L. R. Christensen and M. E. Manser, 'Cost of Living Indexes and Price Indexes for U.S. Meat and Product 1947–1971', in N. Terleckyj (ed.), *Household Behaviour and Consumption*, National Bureau of Economic Research, 1976.

Opinions differ on the value of the Divisia index, with professional national accountants tending on the whole to mistrust it and theorists tending on the whole to recommend it. The national accountants have tended to emphasize the 'drift' of the Divisia index, the tendency for errors to cumulate. The theorists have tended to emphasize its accuracy when the underlying function is homothetic. For a generally negative view, see the section entitled 'Authorities Pro and Con the Chain Index', in Bruce Mudget, *Index Numbers*, 1951, p. 76, and for a discussion of drift see J. M. Keynes, *A Treatise on Money*, Vol. 1, p. 118. The properties of the index are investigated in M. K. Richter, 'Invariance Axioms and Economic Indices', *Econometrica*, 1966, pp. 739–55. The use of the Divisia index is vigorously advocated for productivity measurement in Z. Griliches and D. Jorgensen, 'The Explanation of Productivity Change', *Review of Economic Studies*, 1967, pp. 249–83; this paper is discussed in Chapter 12 of this book. The subject of how best to approximate a Divisia index with data referring to discrete time periods is discussed in S. Star and R. E. Hall, 'An Approximate Divisia Index of Total Factor Productivity', *Econometrica*, 1976, pp. 257–63.

On the size of the bias in the Laspeyres index see P. J. Lloyd, 'Substitution Effects and Biases in Non-True Price Indices', *American Economic Review*, 1975, pp. 301–13; N. Noe and G. von Furstenberg, 'The Upward Bias in the Consumer Price Index Due to Substitution', *Journal of Political Economy*, 1972, pp. 1280–6; and other literature cited in J. Triplett, 'The Measurement of Inflation: A Survey of Research on The Accuracy of Price Indexes', in P. H. Earl (ed.), *Analysis of Inflation*, D. C. Heath and Company, 1977.

10

Measuring Real Consumption from Quantity Data

This chapter is the report of an attempt to measure real consumption by revaluation of quantity data rather than by deflation as is the practice in the national accounts. As already shown in Chapter 8, the two methods of converting money income to real income would be identical if the full time series of prices and quantities were known because, just as the quantity q of a single good can be represented as the ratio v/p of its value and its price, so too is the quantity index $(\Sigma_{i=1}^{n}p_i^0q_i^t)/(\Sigma_{i=1}^{n}p_i^0q_i^0)$ equal to the ratio of a value index $(\Sigma_{i=1}^{n}p_i^tq_i^t)/(\Sigma_{i=1}^{n}p_i^0q_i^0)$ and an appropriately chosen price index $(\Sigma_{i=1}^{n}q_i^tp_i^t)/(\Sigma_{i=1}^{n}q_i^tp_i^0)$. The two methods differ in practice because of quality change and because the statistics of q and v/p are from related but not identical bodies of data. Deflation is the preferred method in the official national accounts. I hope to show in this chapter that the time series of real consumption assessed by revaluation is complementary to the time series assessed by deflation, that it contains valuable information not contained in the other series at all, and that the comparison of the two series gives rise to, admittedly imperfect, time series of quality change that could not be got in any other way.

A comparison of time series based on deflation and revaluation at 1961 prices for Canada from 1935 to 1974 is presented in two tables at the end of the chapter. Table 10.1 is a brief summary of growth rates of real consumption and its major components. Table 10.2 is a presentation of the 225 time series of quantity data together with prices and subindexes, leading up to the overall index in Table 10.1. There is also a set of graphs (Graphs 10.1–10.9) showing the time series of real consumption assessed by deflation, the corresponding time series assessed by revaluation, and their ratios which may be interpreted as time series of quality change implicit in the official national accounts. Before discussing the tables themselves we shall review the advantage of deflation, set out the reasons why it may be useful to have a second time series of real consumption based directly on quantity data, and discuss some of the statistical problems encountered in constructing the series.

A. THE ADVANTAGES OF DEFLATION

From the discussion of deflation and quality change in Chapter 8, we can identify three strong reasons why deflation might be the preferred method for measuring real consumption:

(i) The data on value and prices required for measuring real consumption by deflation are more readily available than the quantity data required for measuring real consumption by revaluation. Data required for deflation are consumption in current dollars, which can be got from financial statements of firms, and a sample of prices. We need not have a complete enumeration of prices because competition can be trusted to keep price differentials among firms within a narrow range. By contrast quantity data can only be obtained from a complete enumeration of firms or from a very large and detailed sample of households, and there are many items of consumption for which we have no quantity data at all.

(ii) Quantity data can never reflect the full diversity of goods and services in the economy. In measuring real consumption by deflation, one can get by with a price index composed of a few representative goods in each category of expenditure, in the hope that prices of goods in the index change at about the same rate as the average of prices of all goods in the category. In measuring real consumption by revaluation of quantity data, we must somehow come to grips with the fact that there is an infinite variety of goods and services, and that no two goods are really identical in every respect. Some goods, such as pounds of flour bought at different times, are similar enough that we are content to treat them as amounts of the same commodity. However, novelties, such as hula hoops, clackers, and yoyos, are so different from one another that one has little option but to assume that prices of novelties rise at about the same rate as prices of some other class of goods. One deflates the value of novelties by, for instance, the consumer price index to obtain a time series of the real output of novelties on the assumption that, whatever novelties may be, the efficiency of labour and capital in producing them is rising at about the same rate as the efficiency of labour and capital in producing other things. Since one cannot construct a genuine time series of the quantity of novelties, the validity of the assumption cannot be checked, and we can never know whether the estimate of the quantity of novelties is accurate or not. As an alternative, we could derive a quantity series for novelties by assuming that consumption of novelties increases at the same rate as consumption of some other class of commodities. This assumption is probably less satisfactory than the assumption that the relative price of novelties and some other class of commodities remains constant over time.

(iii) Devaluation entails an automatic correction for quality change. Think of value, v, as the product of price, p, and quantity, q, and quality, m. We would like the time series of real consumption to reflect changes in quantity and quality but not price. We get this result if we deflate value by a price index, as long as the price index represents the value each year of a bundle of goods of a given quality and design; the price index would be a true reflection of p, and the deflated series would be $v/p = qm$ which is exactly what we require. If consumers consider one good suit to be the equivalent of two poor suits no matter how many good suits and how many poor suits are put onto the market, the dollar value of expenditure on suits deflated by the price of one kind of suit or by a price index with fixed weights is an ideal measure of real consumption of suits while a quantity index of the number of suits purchased would be inappropriate. We have discussed other examples, notably the aspirin and cancer example, in which deflation does not do so well. However, the time series of real income assessed by deflation is almost always more sensitive to quality change than the time series of real consumption assessed by revaluation, and, with a few exceptions to be discussed below, any quality change that escapes the former series can be expected to escape the latter as well.

B. USES FOR A TIME SERIES OF REAL CONSUMPTION ASSESSED BY REVALUATION

The advantages of deflation over revaluation—the availability of data, the ease of accounting for the diversity of goods and services, and the automatic correction for quality change—provide justification enough for choosing the deflated series of real consumption if one must choose between the two. But no such choice is imposed upon us. A great deal of quantity data are collected and published, and we can evaluate these quantities at the prices of a chosen base year to form a new index of real consumption as a supplement to the index of real consumption in the national accounts. The additional series can be useful in the following ways:

(i) The principal reason for wanting a time series of real consumption derived from quantity data is to connect our measure of aggregate consumption with information about particular goods and services we enjoy. One can think of national income statistics as constituting the last chapter and summation of an imaginary statistical abstract. Each preceding chapter shows change, improvement or deterioration of some aspect of the economy—food, clothing, transport and communication, health, education. The final chapter combines changes in all aspects of the economy into one measure of the progress of the economy as a whole. The accounts as they are now set up do not serve that purpose because one cannot link time series of real consumption to more detailed and specific information about the economy. Measures of real consumption based directly on quantity data forge the link automatically.

For example, the Canadian national accounts show that the increase in food consumption per head from 1935 to 1974 has been at a rate of 1.6% per annum, amounting to a total increase of 86% over the whole 39-year period. What information does this time series convey about food consumption in Canada? Can we infer from the data whether the average Canadian diet was adequate in 1935, whether the expenditure on food in 1935 was sufficient to purchase an adequate diet at food prices in that year, whether the 86% increase in food consumption represents an improvement in standards of nutrition, or whether food intake in 1974 is in excess of what is generally considered appropriate for good health? To all of these questions the answer is the same: we can draw no inferences whatsoever about average food consumption in Canada even by examining the primary data that enter into the construction of the national accounts.

Food consumption as measured in the national accounts may have increased for a number of reasons: Canadians may be consuming more food of all kinds, more bread, cheese, fish, milk, etc. Canadians may be switching from less nutritious to more nutritious food—from bread to meat, fruit and fresh vegetables. The increase in food consumption may reflect a change in the seasonality of our eating habits; we may be paying a premium for fresh fruits and vegetables out of season. The quality of food may have improved. Bread may be richer in vitamins, apples less likely to be rotten or wormy, flour less likely to be dirty or to contain impurities. Increased food consumption has many dimensions, but nothing in the national accounts as they are now constructed permits us to apportion the total increase among the contributing factors or even to say with confidence which factors are accounted for and which are not. Worse still, the measured increase in food consumption may reflect factors quite apart from the amount and quality of the food we eat. Part of the measured increase in food consumption is factory preparation of TV dinners, cloth for tea bags, tin for cans, ice for freezing, paper for packaging, or labour cost of washing, peeling, grinding or mashing food before it enters the home. Factory preparation of food may improve its quality as food, or it may be a convenience for housewives, in effect, a labour-saving device comparable to home freezers or mixmasters. Food and packaging are both goods, and increases in both have a place in the national accounts, but one would like to know which is which. One would like to know what proportion of the 1.6% increase is food and what proportion is paper and tin. On this matter the accounts are silent. The increase might be food, packaging, or any mixture of the two.

The argument for connecting aggregate consumption with the detail of quantities consumed is reinforced by the growing interest in social indicators because social indicators are themselves quantity data in the sense that they could serve as arguments in the utility function. Crime rates, hours of leisure, proportions of eligible age groups attending school, age-specific mortality rates, pollution indices, or Gini ratios of the income distribution can be arranged in time series; and, wherever prices can be found or imputed, social indicators can be incorporated into the body of the accounts in the manner discussed in Chapter 7. These imputations can be introduced more easily and naturally when real consumption is initially developed from quantity data than when real consumption is measured as a value deflated by a price index.

A case can be made that the increase over time in urban site rents should be looked upon as a cost of progress and should not be included in the measure of real consumption. To exclude site rents is to limit consideration of housing to the physical characteristics of the house—number of rooms, floor space per room, area of the lot, facilities, etc.—and to ignore advantages of location. This correction comes automatically when real consumption is measured by revaluing quantity data.

(ii) An index of quality change in consumption goods can be obtained as the ratio of real consumption assessed by deflation and real consumption assessed by revaluation because the former includes quality change while the latter does not. This measure of implicit quality change is a crude one, for the two time series of real consumption may diverge for a variety of reasons, not the least of which is that the index number formula employed in measuring real consumption from quantity data differs substantially from the formula employed in the construction of the national accounts. Nevertheless, this measure of quality change is the only such measure we possess, and it is possible on occasion to bring general knowledge to bear on the question of whether the rate of implicit quality change is reasonable or not. For instance, it is shown in Table 10.1 that of the 1.6% annual increase in real food consumption per head in the national accounts, 0.8% can be accounted for by the increase in quantity, leaving 0.8% that must be explained by quality change. That seems to me to be a very high rate of quality change in food and suggests that the sources of quality change ought to be examined closely. The work on hedonic price indexes has tended to suggest that quality change has been imperfectly removed from the price indexes used in the national accounts so that the growth rate of real income is underestimated. By contrast, the growth rate of our quality series seems unreasonably large for some categories of expenditure, suggesting that the overall bias in the growth rate of real consumption may go in either direction.

(iii) All commodities, even those we call goods as opposed to services, are really bundles of goods and services. A pound of cheese purchased at the grocery is more than just cheese; it is the convenience and aesthetic appeal of the shop where it is sold, the length of time one has to wait at the cash register, the delivery from the shop to the purchaser's home, the extent to which it is processed, cooked or cut to save the purchaser time in preparation at home. These services, ancillary to the purchase of a piece of cheese, are included in real consumption measured by deflation but excluded from real consumption measured by revaluation, and any increase over time in services provided per unit of goods is reflected as part of the growth rate of one series but not the other. A strong case can be made that an increase in services per unit of goods ought to be counted as part of economic growth, but enough exceptions can be found to this general rule to justify the creation of a supplementary series of goods exclusive of their service component. A large part of the improvement in the service component of goods consists either of a substitute for housework or of some other labour-saving arrangement. Since housework is excluded from the national income, substitutes for housework might be excluded as well. On the other hand, it would be double counting to include labour-saving increases in services as part of growth if extra leisure is imputed for directly.

(iv) Time series of quality might have some interesting uses in the theory of demand. In every attempt that has come to my attention to compute a set of demand elasticities for all commodities simultaneously, the author has used real expenditures by commodity group in the national accounts as if these series were quantity data. It may be that the different quality series implicit in national accounts have more in common with one another than with the series of quantities to which they are attached. 'Quality of food' and 'quality of clothing' may be more like one commodity in their response to changes in income or to changes in prices of other goods than 'quality of food' is like 'quantity of food' or 'quality of clothing' is like 'quantity of clothing'. I have not attempted to test this conjecture. In view of the biases and approximations that enter into the construction of the two series of real consumption and of the fact that the quality series is a residual, it is doubtful whether this conjecture could be tested with the available data.

C. STATISTICAL PROBLEMS

In theory, it is simple enough to measure real consumption by revaluation; one collects time series of quantities and evaluates them at prices of the chosen base year. In practice, there are many statistical problems, the series cannot be constructed at all without a considerable input of judgement and plain guesswork on the part of the statistician, and the results are far less dependable than one would like. The main problems are these:

(i) Missing data. The data are incomplete in two respects. There are whole categories of expenditures for which we have no quantity data or so little that it is not worth attempting to construct a quantity index, and there are some items missing from every category of expenditure. For the categories of 'recreation' and 'miscellaneous' where we have virtually no quantity data at all, I have treated the time series of real consumption in the national accounts as though they were quantity data, and have included these series with genuine time series of quantities in computing the overall rate of real consumption as assessed by revaluation. For all other categories of expenditure, I have adopted a procedure equivalent to assuming that the rate of growth of the missing series is equal to the rate of growth of the series included in Table 10.2. The procedure is to weight growth rates of the principal categories of real consumption, not by the 1961 values derived from the prices and quantities in Table 10.2, but by the corresponding values in the official national accounts. Consider, for instance, the growth rate of food consumption of 0.8% in the far right-hand column of Table 10.1. This figure is the growth rate of the value at 1961 prices of all items of food consumption included in Table 10.2. However, the list of foods in Table 10.2 is not quite complete. It excludes salt, spices and I do not know how much else. To compensate for the missing items in Table 10.2, I have assessed the share of food in the growth rate of total consumption in the last row of the right-hand column of Table 10.1 by weighting the estimated growth rate of food consumption by the value share of food consumption in 1961 in the national accounts rather than by the corresponding value share derivable from Table 10.2.

A more important instance of missing data is in the category of clothing. From 1961, we can measure domestic consumption of clothing as shipments of domestic producers plus imports minus exports. For the years prior to 1961, there are no quantity data in the trade statistics and we have to make do with shipments alone, scaling the whole time series up or down by the ratio of consumption to production in 1961 which is the first year for which statistics on both are available. This weighting procedure compensates for the missing data on exports and imports if and only if the proportion between shipments and consumption of clothing has remained constant over time. As we have no quantity data on fuel and furniture, I assume the growth rates of consumption of fuel and furniture to be the same as the growth rates of consumption of the services of houses; the value of housing in Table 10.1 includes fuel and furniture, but the quantity data pertain to housing alone. Missing data for particular years within a time series were interpolated or extrapolated; interpolated or extrapolated data are put in brackets to distinguish them from genuine quantity data.

(ii) The choice of the base year. The choice of 1961 as the base year was arbitrary, but it is helpful to have a base year that is (i) recent enough for new goods like television to be priced, and (ii) used as a base year in the official national accounts so that a good deal of price data are available. It would be interesting to compare my measure of real consumption with one constructed from prices of an earlier year, but I have not done so because prices have proved difficult to obtain. An attempt to measure the rate of growth of food consumption using 1935 prices, obtained for the most part from advertisements in newspapers, showed that the change of base year had no appreciable effect. The choice of the base year has a significant effect on the measure of the growth rate of the quantity of purchased transport because there has been a substantial shift over time from trains and buses to airplanes, and a gradual fall in the relative price of air transport and surface transport.

(iii) Public and private consumption. The attempt to specify outputs of health and education gives rise to two interesting problems in pure accounting. The first problem is one which is latent in the measurement of real consumption by deflation but which is brought into the open when one measures consumption from quantity data. The issue is simply that health and education are provided partly in the public sector and partly in the private sector. Expenditure on health is not treated as unity in the national accounts because the first and fundamental division of expenditure in the accounts is between the public and private sectors. In the Canadian accounts, private expenditure on health and education is included in personal consumption, while public expenditure is included in total government consumption but not presented separately. One can discover from the accounts how much private individuals spent on health and education in current dollars or in 1961 dollars, but one cannot find out how much was spent in total or whether society's total real consumption of these items is increasing or not. For growth accounting, one needs statistics of gross national expenditure subdivided in the first instance by commodities, objects or purposes, rather than by agents, so that public and private expenditure on the same or closely connected objects might be combined. The need is especially acute when the dividing line between the public and private sectors is changing over time. The quantity data for health and education in Table 10.2, though far from adequate, do refer to these categories as a whole regardless of whether services are provided in the public or the private sectors. The value weights in Table 10.1, by which growth rates in the different categories of consumption are aggregated, are adjusted to appear as they would do if total expenditure in these categories were in the private sector.

The other accounting problem is to apportion expenditure on health and education among consumption, investment and intermediate products. It is the convention in the national accounts that, with certain exceptions which need not concern us here, all public expenditure is counted as final product and any public expenditure that does not lead to the creation of tangible capital is counted as public consumption. This convention evolved at a time when the main purpose of the accounts was to serve as a tool of stabilization policy, and the convention is reasonable in that context. The convention is less reasonable in the context of measuring economic growth, for as has often been observed, a large part of what the national accounts classify as government consumption might be classified instead as public cost of production. Parliament is not primarily entertainment and its main output is not such as may be consumed. It is intermediate, and its contribution is as a prerequisite to the production of goods and services already included in the accounts. And of 'public consumption' not classifiable as intermediate product, a good share might be classified as investment rather than consumption. It is often claimed that current expenditure on education is really investment in human capital. The same might be said of health and (with more justification) of research. I have been conservative in adjusting values of consumption in Tables 10.1 and 10.2 because I wished to emphasize the contrast between deflation and revaluation and not accounting problems *per se*. No private expenditure was shifted from consumption to cost of production, but private consumption was enlarged to include current public expenditure on health and education, for the quantity series pertain to health and education as a whole.

(iv) Quality and quantity. This distinction is by no means absolute, for the rate of quality change depends on what aspects of a good or service one is able to, or chooses to, record as quantity data. The shift over time from cereal consumption to meat consumption is quality change if the quantity of food is measured in calorific equivalents but not if cereals and meats are treated as separate goods. In Table 10.2, the shift from cereals to meats is recorded as an increase in the quantity of food consumed, but any improvement over time in the processing of food is unaccounted for in the quantity data and thereby assessed as part of quality change.

The data on education would seem to allow us to measure the quantity of education either as numbers of students or as numbers of teachers and other inputs to the educational process. In conformity with its general procedure for expressing services in real terms, the national accounts deflate the value of education by a price index of inputs. We have chosen instead to measure the quantity of education by the number of students subdivided into primary, secondary, undergraduate and graduate, and evaluated at the cost per student in 1961 dollars inclusive of earnings forgone. Numbers of students has the advantage as a quantity indicator that it is an aspect of output rather than input, but it has the disadvantage that it fails to account for improvements in the quality of education resulting from changes in student–teacher ratios. Neither measure of the quantity of education captures the really important quality change manifest in the expansion of knowledge over time.

Since we have no data on the output of health comparable to numbers of students as measures of the output of education, we follow the accounts in assessing output by input. The quantity index of health contains four items: numbers of doctors, numbers of dentists, numbers of graduate nurses in hospitals, and numbers of hospital beds. Services of doctors and dentists are evaluated at their gross incomes. Graduate nurses in hospitals and numbers of hospital beds are together considered as surrogates for all other aspects of medicine including drugs and services of medical equipment. Nurses' services are evaluated in Table 10.2 at a price substantially higher than the nurse's wage, and the value of the services of hospital beds is measured as the difference between total expenditure on medicine and estimated expenditure on doctors, dentists and nurses. This measure of real consumption of medicine has little to recommend it other than the availability of data. But it is important to recognize that the problem of choosing measures of real output of health and education is not circumvented when real consumption is measured by deflation, for difficulties inherent in the choice of quantities are also inherent in the choice of a price index, and a true price index cannot be constructed unless one can specify exactly what is being priced. The quantity indexes of health and education in Table 10.2 may not be much worse than corresponding quantity indexes implicit in the official national accounts.

Housing is the one category for which I have adjusted original quantity data for what might be called quality change. The original data are numbers of dwellings subdivided according to numbers of rooms and evaluated according to the purchase price of dwellings in 1961 on the assumption that house rents are proportional to house prices. This time series of the quantity of housing is then adjusted for the percentage of dwellings with running water, flush toilets, baths and showers to obtain the series used in measuring real consumption in Table 10.1. It is significant that the rate of quality change, the difference between real consumption assessed by deflation and real consumption assessed by revaluation, is much higher for housing than for any other category. This may be genuine quality change or it may be the outcome of errors of measurement in one or both of the time series.

(v) Stock and flows. Ideally, real consumption should be a flow of services, and the increase over the year in the stock of consumer durables should be counted as investment. Housing is treated in this way in the national accounts, for rent is counted as part of real consumption and the purchase of new houses is counted as investment. Purchases of durables like automobiles, furniture and appliances are counted as consumption rather than as investment and no attempt is made to impute values of the services of these items. In measuring the quantity of services of automobiles, we assume that the flow is proportional to the stock, but we follow the national accounts in treating purchases of appliances as consumption, and in not imputing for services of the stock.

D. THE RESULTS OF THE RECOMPUTATION

The main comparison between growth rates of the two time series of real consumption is presented in Table 10.1. Each row pertains to a major component of real consumption—food, alcohol, tobacco, clothing, housing, appliances, health, transport, automobiles, communication, education, and a residual category called miscellaneous—except the bottom row which pertains to real consumption as a whole. The columns contain growth rates from the official national accounts and from the time series of quantity data together with the appropriate 1961 values to serve as weights in aggregating growth rates of individual items to growth rates of real consumption as a whole. The growth rates recomputed from quantity data are themselves aggregates of growth rates of the more detailed list of quantities in Table 10.2. The central fact to emerge from the table is that, as shown on the bottom line, the growth rate of real consumption per head is a full percentage point less when measured by revaluation of quantity data than when measured by deflation, 2.0% per year against 3.0% per year in the national accounts. Part of the 1.0% difference is undoubtedly a genuine improvement in the quality of goods, part is due to conceptual differences between the series, and part is due to errors of measurement. Though we cannot apportion the 1.0% among these factors, some insight can be obtained from the time series in Table 10.2 and the accompanying charts.

The numbers in Table 10.2 are quantities consumed in physical units per head—pounds of foods, number of garments purchased, letters posted and so on. Though the data were collected for each year from 1935 to 1974, only every fifth year is shown because that is sufficient to indicate the long-term trend, and because the year to year changes are uninteresting. The last figure in each row is the best estimate I could get of the 1961 price. These prices are used as weights in all the subindexes, but the subindexes themselves are aggregated, as already mentioned, by the weights in the national accounts. With minor exceptions, the quantity data are from publications of Statistics Canada. The price data are in part from Statistics Canada and in part collected from newspapers. Time series of quality change can be constructed for the main aggregates of personal consumption, but not for the 225 primary time series of quantity in Table 10.2, because the values in the national accounts are not sufficiently disaggregated. Each time series of quality in Table 10.2(j) and in the accompanying graphs is the ratio of the index of real consumption assessed by deflation and the corresponding index assessed by revaluation when all indexes are set at 100 for the year 1961.

It is interesting to glance over the data in Table 10.2 to see how consumption patterns have changed over the years. The gradual switch in food consumption from cereals to meat and vegetables, the extraordinary rise in the consumption of poultry and alcohol, the slower but still substantial increase in consumption of tobacco with no indication of any slackening off with the identification of tobacco as carcinogenic, the much more modest increase in quantity of housing which may be a reflection of the fact that the real improvement has been in the form of square feet per room or other aspects of housing not accounted for in the quantity data, the growth of university education, the replacement of trains and buses by cars and airplanes, the increasing usage of the telephone, the enormous rise in the usage of appliances of all kinds, and the appearance of television—all of these features of economic growth as we know it in our daily lives are quantified here, and their contributions to economic growth are displayed.

A substantial improvement in the quality of food has been concentrated in the period prior to the end of the Second World War. Quality change ceased abruptly in 1947, and since then the deflated and revalued time series of real consumption have grown at about the same rate. I would be inclined to speculate that the apparent quality change before and during the Second World War is spurious, and that the revalued series is a fair representation of what should have been measured in the deflated series. The food series is the best of the quantity series, the coverage is detailed and comprehensive, and the choice of 1961 as a base year does not seem to make much difference to the growth of the series. There may have been some improvement in the processing of food prior to the Second World War, but it is hard to see why the improvement should have been greater before the War than afterwards, considering that the introduction of frozen food occurred in the latter period. The rapid rise from 1940 to 1945 in the quality of tobacco and alcohol may also be due to errors of measurement in the deflated series. On the other hand, the obviously spurious zig-zags in the alcohol quality series prior to the War are transmitted from the quantity series where they probably reflect my failure to adjust for changes in inventory. The rate of growth of quality of housing seems high, but it may be that there was a steady improvement over and above the quality already incorporated into the quantity index. Part of the growth of the quality of housing is a consequence of the gradual movement of people from farms and small towns where housing is cheap to cities where housing is dear. This shift is counted as an increase in real consumption of housing in the deflated series but not in the revalued series. One can have little confidence in the quality index of clothing because the coverage of the revalued series is incomplete. The reader should be warned that the quality indexes for health and education in Table 10.2(j) are virtually meaningless because the quantity series in the national accounts is for personal consumption while the quantity series assessed by revaluation is for the public and private sectors combined.

The rapid increase in the quality of purchased transport prior to 1961 and the decline thereafter may be primarily an index number phenomenon. Over the whole of the period 1935 to 1974, the quantity of air travel increased rapidly, quantities of other forms of purchased transport increased slowly or declined, and the relative price of air travel declined. Now it is a consequence of the use of the Laspeyres index that the rate of growth prior to the base year, 1961, is biased up while the rate of growth after the base year is biased down; this is the standard bias discussed in Chapters 2 and 9. It is probably present in all categories of consumption but it is most evident in purchased transport because changes in relative prices are particularly large within that category. Except for the war years, the deflated series and revalued series of automobile services grew at about the same rate, so that the overall growth of the quality series is negligible. The apparent decline in quality of automobile services during the war is a consequence of our decision to measure the flow of automobile services by the stock of cars. The corresponding series in the national accounts includes purchases of new cars as well as operating expenses. During the war the flow of new cars was cut off and gasoline consumption was reduced sharply, but the decline in the stock of cars was only moderate by comparison. The surprising feature of the automobile chart is that improvements commonly believed to have taken place in the quality of auto-mobiles—improvements such as automatic clutch, larger engines and safety features—are not reflected in the quality series. It should perhaps be stressed that the quality series in automobiles, as in every other category of expenditures, is strictly a relation between the two quantity series. A genuine quality change not reflected in the time series of real consumption assessed by deflation would be excluded from our quality series as well.

Table 10.1 A comparison of growth rates of consumption per head: Canada, 1935–1974

	from the national accounts		recomputation from quantity data	
	values in dollars per head in 1961	growth rates (%)	values in dollars per head in 1961	growth rates (%)
Food	263.79	1.6	263.79	0.8
Alcohol	52.64	4.4	52.64	3.6
Tobacco	43.32	3.1	43.32	1.6
Clothing	123.64	2.6	123.64	1.4
Housing	{ 409.80	3.3	{ 335.53	0.8
Appliances			74.27	6.4
Health services	62.01	1.9	87.05	2.1
Purchased transport	34.27	2.7	34.27	0.8
Automobiles	126.38	4.5	126.38	3.7
Communication	19.08	4.6	19.08	3.1
Education	16.23	5.4	151.25	2.2
Miscellaneous	250.36	2.9	250.36	2.9
Total real consumption	1401.52	3.0	1561.58	2.0

Note to Table 10.1
Columns 1 and 2 are from Tables 54 and 54A of *National Income and Expenditure Accounts*, volume 1, Statistics Canada, 13–531. The values in column 1, originally in 1971 dollars, are converted to 1961 dollars by the deflator for consumption goods. The growth rates in column 4 are from Table 10.2(i), except for the category miscellaneous which is carried over from column 2. The values in column 3 are the same as those in column 1 except for health services where the value is 'total expenditure on personal health care' from Part III, Section 2 of the *Canada Yearbook*, 1972, and education where the value is the sum of 'expenditure on education for all levels for Canada' (Table 9, *Financial Statistics of Education 1975, Statistics Canada*, 81–208) and forgone earnings of students as estimated in the construction of Table 10.2. The growth rates for total consumption in columns 2 and 4 are computed as

$$G = \frac{\sum_i v_i G_i}{\sum_i v_i}$$

where G is the growth rate of total real consumption, v_i is the value in the i row of column 1 or 3, and G_i is the growth rate in the i row of column 2 or 4.

Table 10.2 Quantity data: Canada, 1935–1974

(a) Food: domestic disappearance, pounds per capita, calendar year or crop year commencing:

	1935	1940	1945	1950	1955	1960	1965	1970	1974	1961 price (¢ per lb)
Meat (carcass weight)										
Beef	53.6	54.5	67.0	50.6	71.5	69.2	81.7	85.9	94.7	81.7
Veal	9.8	10.8	12.5	9.4	8.7	7.6	8.4	4.4	3.5	90.0
Mutton and lamb	6.0	4.5	4.3	2.2	2.8	3.2	2.8	3.8	2.5	71.2
Pork	39.3	44.7	52.7	54.9	57.6	55.3	49.2	57.2	59.9	79.3
Offal	5.5	5.5	5.7	4.9	5.7	4.9	3.6	3.8	3.7	10.0
Canned meat	1.3	1.1	3.4	4.0	4.5	6.4	4.3	0.0	0.6	47.2
Total meat	115.5	121.1	145.6	126.0	150.8	146.6	150.0	154.7	164.9	
Eggs	34.6	30.8	33.0	30.1	36.4	36.7	32.0	32.8	28.5	26.4
Poultry (edible weight)										
Chicken	8.6	9.0	11.5	9.2	12.6	15.1	19.2	24.4	24.3	70.5
Other	1.8	2.6	2.7	2.3	4.1	5.6	8.0	8.4	8.9	70.9
Total poultry	10.4	11.6	14.2	11.5	16.7	20.7	27.2	32.8	33.2	
Pulses and nuts										
Dry beans	4.3	3.8	3.8	4.8	3.7	2.9	2.4	3.1	4.8	11.1
Dry peas	6.3	5.1	2.9	1.8	0.9	1.4	1.6	1.3	2.7	11.1
Nuts	3.0	3.2	4.4	3.6	3.9	4.2	4.9	6.4	7.8	49.2
Cocoa	2.6	4.4	3.3	2.9	2.7	1.5	3.5	3.4	3.2	122.6
Total pulses and nuts	16.2	15.5	14.4	13.1	11.2	10.0	12.4	14.2	18.5	
Oil and fats										
Butter	30.6	30.4	21.1	22.3	20.5	13.8	15.1	12.8	10.8	69.9
Lard	3.9	7.0	11.3	9.5	8.6	7.2	7.4	6.7	6.5	23.1
Margarine	0.0	0.0	0.0	6.8	8.0	7.6	7.0	7.5	8.7	31.0
Shortening	9.8	7.6	9.8	9.6	9.8	9.4	9.9	15.3	17.0	34.3
Other	(3.0)	(3.0)	(3.0)	3.0	2.4	4.1	4.7	5.8	7.6	42.1
Total oils and fats	47.3	48.0	45.2	51.2	49.3	44.9	44.1	48.1	50.6	

Potatoes										
White	198.6	213.0	162.9	180.8	150.6	158.9	156.0	155.9	132.1	4.8
Sweet	0.5	0.6	0.8	0.8	0.6	0.5	0.4	0.4	0.7	16.8
Total potatoes	199.1	213.6	163.7	181.6	151.2	159.4	156.4	156.3	132.8	
Cereals										
Flour:										
Wheat	179.2	164.2	197.2	158.3	147.8	135.2	142.6	132.5	133.0	24.9 (bread)
Rye	0.4	0.4	0.2	0.3	0.9					
Total	179.6	164.6	197.4	158.6	148.7					
Oatmeal and rolled oats	8.0	7.3	9.5	6.2	5.0	4.8	5.1	4.0	3.1	9.2
Pot and pearl barley	0.3	0.3	0.8	0.3	0.2	0.2	0.1	0.1	0.1	9.2
Cornmeal and flour	1.7	0.2	0.8	0.8	0.8	1.7	3.0	4.1	5.5	9.2
Buckwheat flour	0.2	0.1	0.1	0.1	0.1	0.1	0.04	0.03	0.01	9.2
Rice	4.0	3.7	3.3	4.1	4.5	4.5	6.1	5.0	5.1	20.8
Breakfast food	5.3	5.2	8.0	6.8	7.3	7.2	7.0	6.5	9.9	31.8
Total cereals	199.1	181.4	219.9	176.9	166.6	153.7	163.9	152.2	156.7	
Sugars										
Sugar	87.5	96.5	74.3	101.0	97.1	96.6	100.5	102.2	91.3	9.6
Maple sugar, etc.	2.8	2.7	1.1	1.6	1.1	0.8	0.4	0.2	0.4	30.0
Honey	2.9	2.2	3.1	2.3	1.7	1.4	1.8	1.7	1.5	30.3
Other	(7.0)	(7.0)	(7.0)	(7.0)	(7.0)	5.5	5.7	6.2	1.4	19.1
Total sugars	100.2	108.4	85.5	111.9	106.9	104.3	108.4	110.3	94.6	
Coffee	3.2	3.5	4.5	6.0	6.6	9.0	8.7	9.2	9.2	120.0
Tea	3.2	3.6	4.2	4.0	2.7	2.4	2.4	2.2	2.5	74.0
Vegetables										
(fresh equivalent basis)										
Cabbage		13.6	18.9	14.1	12.4	10.2	9.0	9.2	11.2	8.9
Lettuce		5.2	6.2	7.2	8.2	8.4	9.7	11.3	17.2	19.0
Spinach		1.6	1.2	1.2	1.1	0.8	0.7	0.5	0.9	24.4
Carrots: fresh		9.6	12.0	15.6	13.2	16.9	14.1	18.0	15.6	13.4
canned	0.1	0.1	1.3	0.5	0.5	1.1	1.8	1.0	1.4	
Total	10.3	10.3	15.1	17.3	15.5	18.0	15.9	20.0	18.9	

Table 10.2 (continued)

	1935	1940	1945	1950	1955	1960	1965	1970	1974	1961 price (¢ per lb)
Beans: fresh		2.6	2.4	2.6	2.1	1.9	1.7	0.7	1.2	28.3
canned	0.7	1.1	2.0	1.8	2.3	2.3	2.4	2.6	2.7	
frozen							1.2	1.6	1.1	
baked canned	2.1	3.6	1.8	4.4	3.9	4.2	5.3	(5.1)	5.5	
Total beans	2.8	7.3	6.2	8.8	8.3	8.4	10.8	(10.0)	10.5	26.9
Peas: fresh		1.5	1.0	0.9	0.7		0.1	0.2	0.2	
canned		3.6	5.5	4.6	5.7	4.3	4.0	3.2	3.0	
frozen							2.2	2.5	2.6	
Total peas		4.8	6.9	6.3	7.8	4.3	6.3	6.9	5.8	12.2
Beets: fresh	0.1	5.1	5.0	5.6	4.2	3.3	1.1	1.1	0.23	
canned		0.3	1.1	0.9	1.0	0.9	1.0	1.0	0.92	
Total beets		5.4	6.3	6.3	5.4	4.2	2.1	2.1	1.2	
Cauliflower		2.3	2.9	2.6	2.4	1.6	2.0	2.2	2.0	34.4
Celery		5.2	7.1	6.6	8.2	6.6	6.4	6.4	7.4	15.5
Corn: fresh	6.4	4.0	5.1	3.1	2.0	3.9	4.0	5.1	3.91	10.1
canned		6.0	7.2	10.8	10.4	9.8	10.6	11.1	13.13	
frozen							2.4	2.5	1.83	
Total corn		12.1	14.3	18.0	16.3	13.7	17.0	18.7	18.9	
Cucumbers		(1.7)	(1.7)	(1.7)	(1.7)	(1.7)	1.4	3.0	3.4	15.0
Onions, not processed		10.5	13.2	14.2	13.0	11.8	13.0	12.4	12.9	11.5
Asparagus: fresh	0.3	0.4	0.3	0.4	0.3	0.3	0.3	0.2	0.6	33.6
canned		0.5	0.3	0.5	0.5	0.6	0.6	0.6	0.7	
frozen							0.1	0.1	0.0	
Total asparagus		0.6	0.6	0.6	0.7	0.9	0.9	0.9	1.3	
Turnips		(4.5)	(4.5)	(4.5)	(4.5)	(4.5)	7.2	5.8	5.4	7.3
Unspecified: fresh					0.7	13.9	1.8			15.0
canned				0.8	2.7	0.8	3.0			
frozen		0.3	0.4	0.8		5.5	1.3			
Total		0.3	0.4	1.6	3.4	20.2	6.1	20.0	18.9	
Total vegetables		81.8	103.8	106.6	105.1	110.6	113.9	129.4	136.5	

Fruit										
(fresh equivalent basis)										
Apples: fresh		29.4	12.8	24.7	31.6	14.7	27.4	24.8	25.1	18.4
canned		4.1	2.4	2.1	3.2	2.9	3.5	0.5	0.3	
juice		2.2	4.5	7.0	11.5	8.1	8.9	9.3	5.6	
frozen							0.6	0.7	0.2	
Total apples		37.2	25.6	37.3	45.5	25.7	40.4	38.1	36.6	
Apricots: fresh		0.3	0.4	0.4	0.7	0.4	0.1	0.2	0.2	33.6
canned		0.1	0.1	0.2	0.5	0.4	0.4	0.3	0.2	
Total apricots		1.4	0.5	1.3	1.6	0.8	0.5	0.5	0.4	
Bananas	13.2	13.0	24.0	11.5	18.2	(16.7)	16.1	17.6	21.6	18.7
Cherries: fresh		0.4	0.7	0.5	1.4	0.2	0.6	0.8	1.5	29.1
canned		0.3	0.1	0.5	0.6	0.6	0.5	0.3	0.2	
frozen						0.1	0.7	0.6	0.5	
Total cherries		0.8	1.0	1.3	2.4	0.9	1.8	1.7	2.2	
Peaches: fresh		4.4	5.6	2.2	4.6	4.8	4.2	5.4	4.8	33.6
canned		1.8	1.4	3.6	4.0	4.2	4.4	3.0	3.5	
Total peaches		6.6	7.6	6.5	9.1	9.0	8.6	8.4	8.4	
Pineapples: fresh		0.9	1.3	0.6			0.3	0.3	0.5	11.0
canned		2.6	0.2	2.2	3.1		4.0	3.5	3.6	
juice		0.5	0.3	1.4	1.7		1.3	1.7	1.6	
Total pineapples		4.0	1.8	4.2	4.8	(5.7)	5.6	5.5	5.7	
Plums, etc.: fresh		1.3	2.2	1.5	2.3	1.7	1.7	1.8	2.3	20.0
canned		0.2	0.8	0.5	0.5	0.3	0.3	0.2	0.2	
Total plums		6.1	10.7	5.2	5.1	2.0	2.0	2.0	2.5	
Raspberries: fresh		0.9	0.6	0.6	0.4	0.1				
canned		0.1		0.1	0.1	0.1	0.1		0.05	56.1
frozen						0.5	0.6	0.4	0.59	
Total raspberries		1.2	1.3	1.1	1.1	0.7	0.7	0.4	0.6	
Strawberries: fresh		2.3	1.0	1.1	1.4	1.5	0.9	1.5	2.15	56.1
canned		0.1		0.2	0.2	0.1	0.1	0.1	0.05	
frozen						1.0	1.3	1.3	1.2	
Total strawberries		3.0	1.6	2.0	2.7	2.6	2.3	2.9	3.4	

Table 10.2 (continued)

	1935	1940	1945	1950	1955	1960	1965	1970	1974	1961 price (¢ per lb)
Grapes		21.1	23.9	24.7	22.4	8.7	11.9	8.2	13.6	27.5
Pears: fresh		2.1	3.9	1.8	3.0	2.6	2.1	2.8	3.7	21.1
canned		1.0	0.9	1.9	2.2	1.8	2.4	1.5	2.2	23.2
Total pears		3.0	4.8	3.8	5.2	4.4	4.5	4.3	5.8	25.0
Unspecified: fresh				0.4	0.7		7.9	10.2	10.3	
canned							5.1	4.1	4.3	
frozen				0.3	1.1		0.4	0.2	0.3	
juice							3.9	8.7	18.3	
other		2.9	3.4	11.2	2.7				2.1	
dried	23.2	19.2	25.6	19.2	15.6		21.7	13.5	10.6	
Total	23.2	22.1	29.0	31.1	20.1	37.7	38.4	38.4	47.4	
Citrus: fresh lemons		2.7	3.4	2.1	2.0					
fresh oranges		21.9	37.8	24.0	27.1					
fresh grapefruit		4.5	9.7	6.7	8.4					
fresh total		29.1	50.9	32.8	37.5	31.7	25.0	27.1	30.3	20.0
juice		3.4	4.0	13.0	31.5	34.3	21.6	29.6	34.4	
Total citrus		32.5	54.9	45.8	69.0	66.0	46.6	56.7	64.7	
Tomato (fresh equivalent)		42.4	52.8	53.9	55.9	59.3	60.9	60.0	79.5	25.1
Total fruit		194.4	239.5	229.7	263.1	240.2	243.1	244.7	292.4	
Fish										
Fresh and frozen		6.1	6.8	6.8	7.3	7.7	9.0	7.4	7.5	48.0
smoked, salted, pickled		1.7	1.6	2.3	1.8	1.8	1.6	0.8	0.66	30.3
canned		3.8	2.6	4.6	4.5	3.1	2.9	3.8	4.41	35.9
Total fish		11.6	11.0	13.7	13.6	12.6	13.5	12.0	12.6	
Milk and cheese										
Fluid milk and cream: (retail weight)	400.7	387.6	468.8	401.1	397.7	393.2	318.5	286.9	266.3	11.7
milk solid	45.7	44.2	53.4	45.7	45.3	44.3	36.3	32.8	33.3	102.3

Cheese										
Cheddar: (retail weight)	2.7	2.2	2.4	2.3	2.8	5.9	3.4	4.1	4.5	73.0 (all cheese)
milk solid equivalent	1.8	1.5	1.6	1.5	1.9	3.8	2.2	2.7	2.9	121.7
Processed: (retail weight)	1.0	1.5	2.9	2.5	2.9		3.8	4.5	5.7	
milk solid equivalent	0.6	0.9	1.7	1.5	1.7		2.2	2.6	3.7	
Cottage: (retail weight)		0.2	0.4	0.6	0.9	1.3	1.6	2.0	2.3	121.7
milk solid equivalent		0.1	0.1	0.2	0.2	0.3	0.4	0.4	0.5	121.7
Other: (retail weight)						1.3	1.9	3.3	5.9	
milk solid equivalent						0.8	1.2	2.1	7.6	121.7
Ice cream: (retail weight)	3.0	4.9	7.2	8.6	10.4	39.1	27.4	39.0	40.1	
milk solid equivalent	0.4	0.6	0.9	1.1	1.3	4.7	3.4	4.9	8.4	237.0
Whole milk										
Evaporated: (retail weight)	4.3	8.3	11.4	17.5	18.4	17.7	16.1	12.7	9.7	16.1
milk solid equivalent	1.1	2.1	2.9	4.4	4.6	4.6	4.2	3.2	2.5	64.4
Condensed: (retail weight)	0.7	0.6	0.8	0.8	0.8	0.8	1.0	0.8	0.8	35.3
milk solid equivalent	0.2	0.2	0.2	0.2	0.2	0.2	0.3	0.2	0.2	141.2
Powdered: (retail weight)		0.1	0.5	0.4	0.2	0.3	0.2	0.1	0.08	35.5
milk solid equivalent		0.1	0.5	0.4	0.2	0.3	0.2	0.1	0.08	35.5
Skim milk										
Evaporated: (retail weight)	0.0	0.1	0.2	0.9	0.6	0.2				14.8
milk solid equivalent		0.02	0.03	0.2	0.1	0.1				87.1
Condensed: (retail weight)	0.4	0.4	0.3	0.3	0.2	0.1				17.4
milk solid equivalent	0.1	0.1	0.1	0.1	0.07	0.3				52.7
Powdered: (retail weight)		2.3	2.6	3.4	5.6	6.9	7.1	6.2	5.7	34.1
milk solid equivalent		2.2	2.5	3.3	5.4	6.6	6.9	6.0	5.5	35.5
Buttermilk										
Condensed: (retail weight)	0.0	0.0	0.2	0.2	0.1					17.4
milk solid equivalent			0.1	0.1	0.0					52.7
Powdered: retail weight						0.4	0.4	0.5	0.3	34.1
milk solid equivalent						0.4	0.4	0.5	0.3	34.1
Whey: milk solid equivalent							2.1	2.0	2.5	(100)
Miscellaneous: milk solid equivalent							0.8	9.1	8.9	(100)
Total milk equivalent	49.9	52.0	64.0	58.7	61.0	66.4	60.5	58.1	68.0	

Table 10.2 (continued)

	1935	1940	1945	1950	1955	1960	1965	1970	1974	1961 price (¢ per lb)
Soft drinks (gallons)		4.7	4.3	7.5	8.0	9.0	10.3	12.5	13.6	94 (per gallon)
Alcoholic beverages										
Spirits (proof gallons)	0.65	1.09	0.89	0.83	0.98	1.16	1.38	0.85	1.28	2017 (per proof gallon)
Beer/ale (gallons)	5.04	6.35	10.24	12.37	13.30	13.20	14.21	16.24	18.83	250 (per gallon)
Wines (gallons)	0.34	0.46	0.36	0.38	0.39	0.50	0.61	0.96	1.28	923 (per gallon)
Tobacco										
Cigarettes (number)	491	682	1422	1277	1599	1952	2223	2364	2628	2 (per cigarette)
Cigars (number)	11	15	17	15	16	19	26	18.3	9.7	15 (per cigar)
Tobacco (lbs smoking, chewing, snuff)	2.2	2.7	2.4	2.2	1.6	1.3	1.0	0.9	0.8	1000 (per lb)

Table 10.2 (continued)
(b) Food index (1961 = 100)

	1935	1940	1945	1950	1955	1960	1965	1970	1974	Value in dollars 1961
Meat	83	87	105	90	108	105	109	114	121	107.74
Eggs	102	91	97	89	107	108	94	97	84	8.95
Poultry	45	50	61	50	72	90	118	142	144	16.31
Pulses and nuts	128	174	152	132	125	96	156	170	188	4.58
Oils and fats	144	143	117	131	124	99	106	110	111	18.74
Potatoes	121	130	100	111	92	97	95	95	81	7.94
Cereals	130	119	144	116	110	101	107	99	103	37.08
Sugars	104	110	89	111	105	100	104	105	87	11.00
Vegetables	(69)	74	89	95	96	100	97	115	121	17.4
Fruit	(82)	84	89	103	116	107	107	108	131	51.61
Fish	(90)	91	107	106	107	102	111	98	102	5.28
Milk and cheese	77	78	96	87	89	102	88	90	114	67.32
Coffee	36	39	50	67	73	100	97	102	102	10.8
Tea	133	150	175	167	113	100	100	92	104	1.78
Food index	89	91	104	96	103	102	104	107	117	366.53
Soft drinks	(38)	52	47	82	88	99	113	137	150	8.55
Alcohol	41	52	77	87	95	98	108	131	167	50.82
Tobacco	59	76	98	88	90	97	104	105	110	56.38
Food index including soft drinks	88	90	103	96	103	102	104	108	118	375.08

Table 10.2 (continued)
(c) Appliances: number per 1000 people

	1935	1940	1945	1950	1955	1960	1965	1970	1974	1961 price (dollars per unit)
Stoves										
Electric	2.2	2.8	1.8	11.9	14.1	12.5	15.1	16.2	26.9	137.85
Gas	2.2	3.0	2.2	4.3	3.8	2.8	2.5	2.0	2.0	123.06
Vacuum cleaners	3.3	5.1	1.4	15.5	15.3	15.6	20.9	25.5	34.2	47.70
Refrigerators	3.1	6.9	0.3	16.6	23.8	16.7	18.0	21.3	30.6	172.72
Radio receiving sets	17.6	43.3	4.2	57.4	72.6	77.0	120.2	165.0	242.1	42.27
TV sets				2.4	51.7	20.0	26.8	40.8	60.9	164.66
Washing machines	73	11.5	4.8	21.1	19.4	17.9	21.0	18.7	29.8	120.30
Home freezers					3.9	5.6	8.6	8.4	16.6	173.92
Toasters	11.4	15.0	11.8	23.8	21.8	16.7	33.2	33.8	50.2	8.54
Electric flat irons	16.2	20.5	14.9	37.8	38.3	22.2	38.3	34.4	44.5	9.05
Clothes dryers					3.1	7.7	10.3	10.5	19.3	135.05
Th. of incandescent lights (no. per head)	2.1	2.5	3.7	5.1	5.4	5.0	5.6	6.6	8.2	0.19
Water heaters		4.8	7.6	19.9	25.6	30.8	36.5	32.3	45.0	48.00
Value per capita	3.70	6.42	2.70	13.61	25.05	19.18	24.84	29.60	44.76	
Index (1961 = 100)	19	33	14	69	128	98	127	151	228	

Table 10.2 (continued)

(d) Clothing: shipments by Canadian manufacturers (number per person)

	1935	1940	1945	1950	1955	1960	1965	1970	1974	1961 price (dollars per unit)
Aprons	0.084	0.181	0.269	0.209	0.213	0.178	0.144	0.060	0.053	0.62
Bathing suits	0.062	0.076	0.104	0.126	0.120	0.160	0.183	0.220	(0.206)	2.81
shipments + imports − exports							0.190	0.271	(0.342)	
Bathrobes	0.053	0.096	0.142	0.084	0.088	0.121	0.213	0.096	0.059	4.25
Blouses	0.092	0.116	0.512	0.559	0.673	0.682	0.765	0.754	0.960	1.87
shipments + imports − exports							1.041	1.107	1.872	
Regular model coats	0.208	0.200	0.261	0.234	0.219	0.171	0.201	0.176	0.150	21.30
shipments + imports − exports							0.222	0.180	0.182	
Fur coats	0.008	0.011	0.017	0.015	0.014	0.012	0.009	0.007	0.009	229.87
Fur-lined coats (per 10 people)	0.001	0.004	0.003	0.004	0.002	0.000	0.001	0.000	0.001	103.18
Jackets	0.008	0.006	0.057	0.007	0.077	0.073	0.102	0.113	0.183	10.59
shipments + imports − exports							0.131	0.244	0.401	
Raincoats	0.057	0.073	0.052	0.057	0.116	0.072	0.120	0.106	0.074	8.88
shipments + imports − exports							0.156	0.147	0.140	
Short coats	0.114	0.118	0.169	0.210	0.290	0.358	0.535	0.451	0.367	6.84
shipments + imports − exports							0.537			
Dresses	1.124	1.134	1.382	1.190	1.077	0.870	0.892	1.258	0.982	6.78
shipments + imports − exports							0.918	1.304	1.015	
Footwear	3.378	4.070	4.737	3.578	3.249	3.151	3.462	2.435	(2.228)	4.18
shipments + imports − exports							3.860	4.448	3.751	
Foundation garment	0.277	0.319	0.599	0.728	0.895	0.970	1.293	1.084	0.930	1.82
shipments + imports − exports							1.318	1.112	1.024	
Gloves and mittens	0.989	1.148	2.105	1.659	1.384	1.165	1.278	1.004	1.125	0.76
shipments + imports − exports							2.282	2.437	4.658	

Table 10.2 (d) Clothing (continued)

	1935	1940	1945	1950	1955	1960	1965	1970	1974	1961 price (dollars per unit)
Headwear	1.394	0.973	1.182	0.941	0.868	0.731	0.742	0.468	0.379	1.71
shipments + imports – exports							1.636	1.434	2.397	
Hosiery	6.849	8.641	8.442	8.086	7.051	9.122	10.632	10.610	8.549	0.34
shipments + imports – exports							10.533	10.333	8.986	
Nightdresses, nightshirts	0.145	0.152	0.178	0.184	0.234	0.207	0.312	0.325	0.311	1.82
Pants	0.247	0.265	0.389	0.361	0.328	0.320	0.501	0.468	0.605	4.75
shipments + imports – exports							0.835	0.934	1.242	
Playsuits	0.102	0.032	0.175	0.083	0.121	0.103	0.172	0.025	(0.019)	1.27
Pajamas	0.213	0.225	0.335	0.336	0.387	0.525	0.531	0.501	0.489	1.74
Sleepwear							0.843	0.827	0.801	1.76
shipments + imports – exports							0.984	1.012	0.948	
Scarves	0.086	0.160	0.246	0.263	0.249	0.202	0.192	0.072	0.074	0.75
shipments + imports – exports							0.284	0.205	0.215	
Shirts	1.270	1.466	1.277	1.498	1.887	1.764	1.714	1.631	2.640	1.85
shipments + imports – exports							1.168	2.385	(3.201)	
Ski suits and snowsuits	0.011	0.021	0.054	0.046	0.037	0.087	0.118	(0.030)	0.093	3.09
Skirts	0.037	0.049	0.126	0.185	0.321	0.323	0.281	0.220	0.203	3.40
shipments + imports – exports							0.283	0.237	0.213	
Slacks and jeans	0.025	0.012	0.062	0.137	0.285	0.420	0.748	0.573	0.920	2.12
shipments + imports – exports							0.868	0.680	1.014	
Sport shorts	0.013	0.013	0.131	0.138	0.144	0.150	0.208	0.253	0.164	1.32
shipments + imports – exports							0.291	0.334	0.216	
Suits	0.172	0.172	0.359	0.212	0.172	0.137	0.291	0.211	0.357	31.27
shipments + imports – exports							0.229	0.212	0.378	
Sweaters	0.366	0.692	0.833	1.109	0.812	1.013	1.227	1.113	1.233	3.10
shipments + imports – exports							1.394	1.717	2.470	
Underwear	3.268	3.796	4.133	4.242	4.716	4.666	5.005	4.952	4.503	0.67
shipments + imports – exports							5.146	5.430	5.273	
Clothing index (1961 = 1.00)	0.830	1.020	1.230	1.050	1.020	0.970	1.150	1.240	1.410	

Table 10.2 (continued) (e) Housing

	1931	1941	1951	1955	1960	1965	1970	1974	1961 price (dollars per house)
Number of dwellings									
1 room(s)	84	65	64	51	55	51	69	94	2180
2	151	151	166	143	120	119	133	168	5200
3	198	255	344	373	386	389	479	625	8250
4	312	422	669	787	858	845	999	1102	11,504
5	343	438	673	856	1060	1260	1406	1551	14,851
6	418	508	662	803	967	1097	1222	1355	17,617
7	286	310	371	408	466	531	653	773	18,685
8	213	218	239	252	263	305	388	464	21,050
9	250	209	221	199	229	259	296	361	26,591
Total	2253	2576	3409	3872	4404	4853	5646	6493	
Number of dwellings with running water									
hot and cold			1940	2530	3472	4243	5336	6219	
cold only			584	532	468	312	147	172	
total		1559	2524	3062	3940	4555	5483	6391	
Number of dwellings with flush toilets		1450	2187	2751	3469	3820	5369	6313	
Number of dwellings with installed bath or shower		1270	1938	2483	3375	4171	5186	6246	
Dwellings per thousand people									
1 room(s)	8.09	5.6	4.6	3.2	3.1	2.6	3.2	4.2	
2	14.55	13.1	11.8	9.1	6.7	6.2	6.2	7.5	
3	19.08	22.2	24.6	23.8	21.6	19.8	22.5	27.8	
4	30.07	36.7	47.8	50.1	48.0	43.0	46.8	49.0	
5	33.06	38.1	48.0	54.5	59.3	64.1	65.9	69.0	
6	40.29	44.1	47.3	51.2	54.1	55.8	57.3	60.3	
7	27.56	26.9	26.5	26.0	26.1	27.0	30.6	34.4	
8	20.53	18.9	17.1	16.1	14.7	15.5	18.2	20.6	
9	24.09	18.2	15.8	12.7	12.8	13.8	13.9	16.1	
Total	217.17	223.8	243.5	246.7	246.4	247.7	264.8	288.8	

Table 10.2 (e) Housing (continued)

	1931	1941	1951	1955	1960	1965	1970	1974	1961 price (dollars per house)
Value of dwellings in 1961 dollars per head	3385	3413	3646	3701	3743	3828	4076	4433	
Index of value of housing per head	85.8	90.3	96.3	98.8	100.0	101.2	108.4	117.9	
Quality of housing									
% running water (P_1)	0.64	0.64	0.74	0.79	0.89	0.94	0.97	0.98	
% flush toilet (P_2)		0.56	0.64	0.71	0.79	0.79	0.95	0.97	
% bath and shower (P_3)		0.49	0.57	0.64	0.77	0.86	0.92	0.96	
Quality index[a]		0.83	0.87	0.89	0.93	0.95	0.98	0.99	
Revised housing index[b]		78.2	88.2	92.5	97.9	101.3	111.8	122.9	

[a] Quality index $= 0.6 + .001P_3 + .001P_2 + .001P_1$.
[b] Revised housing index $=$ housing index $\times$ quality index (based 1961 $= 100$).

Table 10.2 (continued) (f) Health: number per 1000 people

	1935	1940	1945	1950	1955	1960	1965	1970	1974	1961 price (dollars per unit)
Physicians in active fee practice	0.718	0.743	0.746	0.745	0.769	0.810	0.838	0.89	1.110	26,000
Dentists in active fee practice	0.357	0.347	0.350	0.318	0.322	0.307	0.303	0.30	0.30	24,000
Graduate nurses in hospitals	0.642	0.710	0.809	1.276	1.532	1.893	2.191	2.72	3.90	25,000
Hospital beds	8.526	9.952	9.381	10.179	10.688	10.345	10.478	10.00	9.20	3590
Expenditure per head at 1961 price	73.80	80.26	81.74	95.51	104.45	112.73	121.53	134.16	166.66	
Index (1961=100)	68	75	75	88	96	104	112	124	154	

Table 10.2 (continued) (g) Education

	1935	1940	1945	1950	1955	1960	1965	1970	1974	cost inclusive of forgone earnings 1961 dollars
Number of students (×10³)										
primary	1877	1818	1735	1956	2184	3234	3818	4203	3834	300
secondary	277	329	307	349	387	715	1150	1558	1851	1600
undergraduate	33	36	38	69	65	95	164	258	288	3600
graduate	1.5	1.6	1.7	5.3	4.9	9.1	21.9	46.0	60.7	8000
Students per 100 people										
primary	17.31	15.97	14.39	14.26	13.91	18.43	19.44	19.71	17.06	
secondary	2.55	2.89	2.54	2.55	2.47	4.00	5.85	7.31	8.23	
undergraduate	0.30	0.32	0.31	0.50	0.41	0.53	0.83	1.21	1.28	
graduate	0.014	0.014	0.014	0.039	0.031	0.051	0.112	0.22	0.27	
Expenditure $ per head at 1961 prices	104.64	106.70	96.10	104.68	98.51	142.44	190.22	236.89	250.52	
Index (1961 = 100)	69	71	64	69	65	95	127	157	166	

Table 10.2 (continued)
(h) Transport and communication

	unit	1935	1940	1945	1950	1955	1960	1965	1970	1974	1961 price (dollars per unit)	percentage not contributable to business use	imputed price (dollars per unit)
Transport													
civil aviation	passenger miles per capita	0.732	3.617	13.184	42.577	81.622	159.318	257.865	482.09	734.77	0.0557	67	0.0371
railroad	passengers carried per capita	146.11	191.24	528.51	205.38	184.21	126.68	135.71	106.55	83.55	0.0312	75	0.0234
motor buses	per capita	5.24	5.73	8.26	9.81	5.10	3.43	2.65	2.67	1.58	0.81	100	0.81
urban transport	per capita	103.39	116.14	127.57	113.80	77.47	57.59	50.11	47.76	46.55	0.20	100	0.20
automobiles (stock)	no. per 1000 people	91.0	108.0	96.0	139.0	187.0	230.0	269.0	310.0	377.0	553.32	80	442.66
motorcycles (stock)	no. per 1000 people	1.0	1.2	1.2	3.2	2.3	1.9	3.8	7.2	14.3	92.22	80	73.78
Communication													
first-class letters	no. per capita	46.06	46.62	46.64	49.67	58.93	58.65	61.17	63.58	74.56	0.05	50	
telephones	no. per capita	0.057	0.064	0.078	0.110	0.145	0.221	0.270	0.323	0.390	75.63		
telegrams		0.882	0.989	1.305	1.351	1.139	0.768	0.587	0.324	0.167	3.90		
cablegrams		0.120	0.145	0.182	0.123	0.143	0.142	0.155	0.222	0.324	3.90		
Automobile and motorcycle													
value		40.36	47.90	45.58	61.77	82.95	101.95	119.36	137.76	167.94			
index (1961 = 100)		38	46	41	59	79	97	114	132	161			
Purchased transport													
value		28.97	32.37	45.06	37.09	26.96	23.17	25.91	32.09	39.81			
index (1961 = 100)		127	142	198	163	118	102	109	141	175			
Transport inclusive of automobiles													
value		69.32	80.26	87.65	98.86	109.91	125.12	144.27	169.85	207.74			
index (1961 = 100)		54	63	69	77	86	98	113	134	164			
Communication													
value		9.96	11.01	13.44	15.97	18.02	22.53	25.57	29.74	35.14			
index (1961 = 100)		42	47	57	68	77	96	109	124	147			
Transport and communication													
value		79.29	91.27	101.09	114.83	127.93	147.66	169.84	199.59	242.88			
index (1961 = 100)		52	60	67	76	85	98	112	132	161			

Table 10.2 (continued)

(i) Quantity indexes for the main categories of expenditure

	1931	1935	1940	1945	1950	1955	1960	1965	1970	1974	value in 1961 ($ per head)	growth rate
Food (including soft drinks)		88	90	103	96	103	102	104	108	118	263.79	0.8
Alcohol		41	52	77	87	95	98	108	131	167	52.64	3.6
Tobacco		59	76	98	88	90	97	104	105	110	43.32	1.6
Housing (no. of rooms)	86						100	101	108	118	} 335.53	0.8
Housing (with quality index)		(73)	(79)	(83)	(88)	93	98	101	112	123		
Automobiles		38	46	41	59	79	97	114	132	161	126.38	3.7
Purchased transport		127	142	198	163	118	102	109	141	175	34.27	0.8
Communication		42	47	57	68	77	96	109	124	147	19.08	3.1
Appliances		19	33	14	69	128	98	127	151	228	74.27	6.4
Education		69	71	64	69	65	95	112	157	166	151.25	2.2
Health		68	74	75	88	96	104	115	124	154	87.05	2.1
Clothing		83	102	123	105	102	97	124	124	141	123.64	1.4
Total consumption		66	73	83	87	94	99	111	125	145	1561.58	2.038

Note: All time series are from other parts of Table 10.2. The value shares used in computing total consumption on the last line are not those in this table but are, instead, taken from the national accounts and reproduced in the first column of Table 10.1. In estimating total consumption, index numbers of recreation and miscellaneous are incorporated from the national accounts because there are no quantity data on these items.

Table 10.2 (continued)
(j) Quality indexes (1961 = 100)

	1935	1940	1945	1950	1955	1960	1965	1970	1974	% growth rate
Food (including soft drinks)	79	89	98	96	95	100	100	105	108	0.8
Alcohol	79	84	84	100	99	100	106	106	107	0.7
Tobacco	60	63	82	90	94	99	104	107	110	1.6
Housing	57				83	98	108	120	116	1.8
Automobiles	83	91	29	121	114	101	121	107	117	0.8
Purchased transport	41	44	58	69	85	98	103	88	87	1.9
Communication	86	88	97	86	95	98	110	139	153	1.5
Education	56	55	55	78	98	97	114	140	—	2.2
Health	85	93	109	112	117	141	103	86	79	2.2
Clothing	71	69	85	85	89	103	94	99	116	1.3
Total consumption	75	79	86	96	98	102	103	105	107	0.9

Note: All quality indexes are ratios of 'quantity indexes implicit in the national accounts' from table 10.2k and 'quality index for the main categories of expenditure' from table 10.2c. The growth rate for education is computed for the years 1935 to 1973.

Table 10.2 (continued)
(k) Quantity indexes implicit in the national accounts (1961 = 100)

	1935	1940	1945	1950	1955	1960	1965	1970	1974	value in 1961 ($ per head)	growth rate
Food	69	80	100	92	98	102	104	113	127	263.79	1.6
Alcohol	33	43	65	87	93	98	114	139	179	52.64	4.4
Tobacco	36	48	80	79	84	96	108	112	121	43.32	3.1
Housing (inclusive of fuel, rent, furniture, appliances, household operation)	44	49	52	74	86	97	115	139	160	409.80	3.3
Automobiles	32	42	12	72	91	99	139	141	188	126.38	4.5
Purchased transport	52	63	115	112	100	100	112	123	152	34.27	2.7
Communication	38	42	57	60	75	95	120	172	224	19.08	4.6
Education	39	39	35	54	64	91	144	220	—	16.23	5.4
Health	58	70	82	99	113	147	115	107	121	62.01	1.9
Clothing	59	71	104	89	91	100	109	122	164	123.64	2.6
Miscellaneous	50	54	81	85	91	98	114	130	157	250.36	2.9
Total consumption	50	57	71	83	91	101	114	131	156	1401.52	2.970

Notes to Table 10.2
Almost all the quantity data are from Statistics Canada. The sources are described in detail in D. Usher, 'Measuring Real Consumption from Quantity Data, Canada, 1935–1968' in N. Terleckyj (ed.), *Household Production and Consumption*, Studies in Income and Wealth, Vol. 40, National Bureau of Economic Research, 1976. With one or two exceptions, the data for the years 1968 to 1974 are from updated volumes of the sources described there.

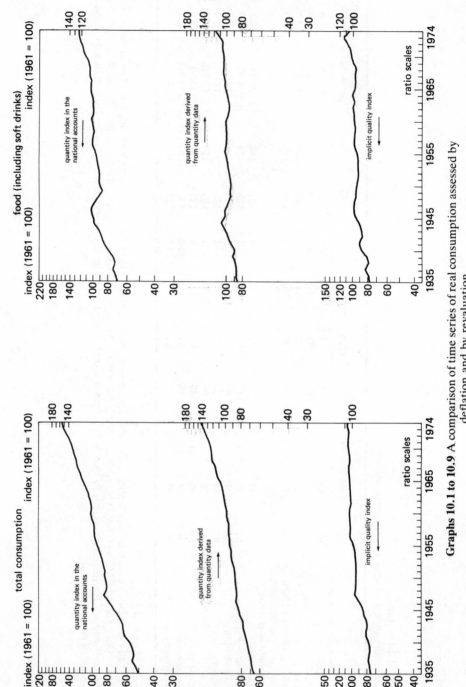

Graphs 10.1 to 10.9 A comparison of time series of real consumption assessed by deflation and by revaluation

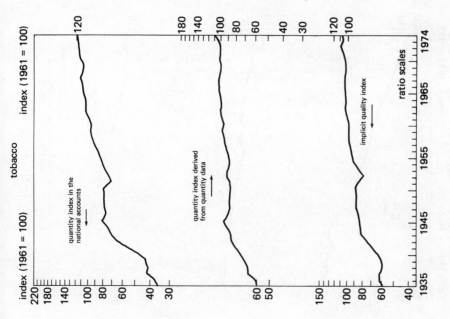

tobacco

index (1961 = 100)

index (1961 = 100)

quantity index in the national accounts

quantity index derived from quantity data

implicit quality index

ratio scales

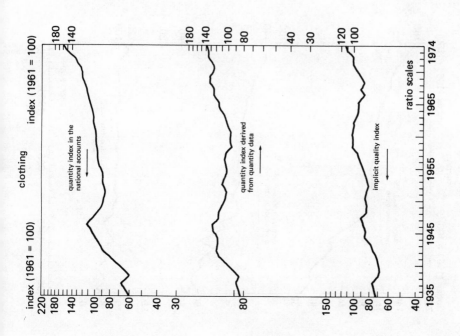

clothing

index (1961 = 100)

index (1961 = 100)

quantity index in the national accounts

quantity index derived from quantity data

implicit quality index

ratio scales

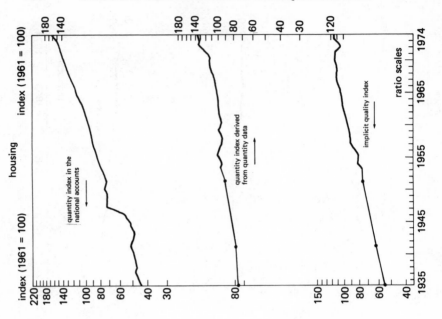

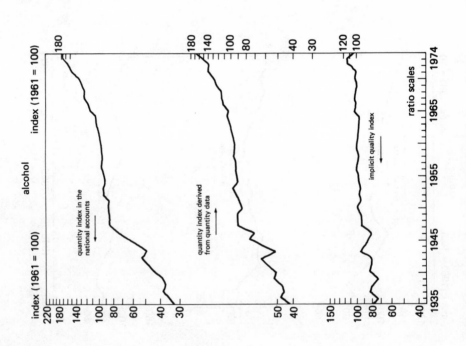

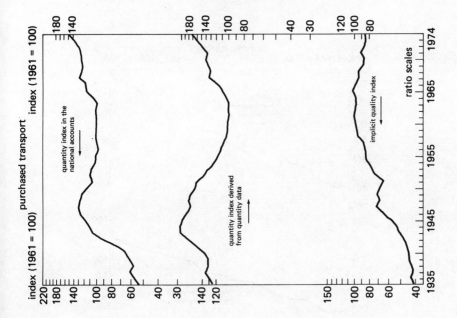

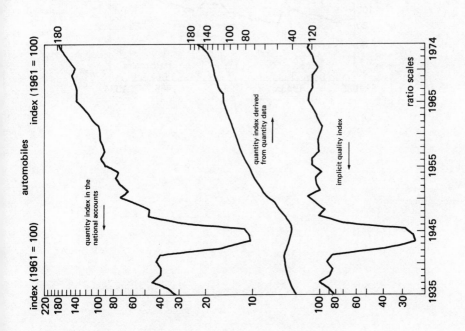

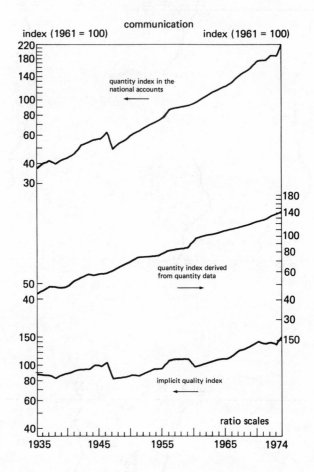

11

An Imputation for Changes in Life Expectancy

One of the ways we are becoming better off is that we live longer. Between the census years 1931 and 1971, life expectancy at birth in Canada increased by about 10 years for men and 14 years for women, the infant mortality rate fell from about 1 in 10 to about 1 in 50, and the mortality rate of children between the ages of one and four fell from about 1 in 100 to about 1 in 1000 per year. A case can be made for the proposition that the decline in mortality rates outweighs all other aspects of economic progress in the sense that a representative consumer forced to choose between a return to the mortality rates of 1926 and a return to other conditions of life would forgo our higher standard of living as conventionally measured to preserve the current mortality rates.

Whether the improvement in life expectancy should be recorded as part of the growth of real income depends to a large extent on what the measure of real income is intended to do. If it is intended as an instrument of fiscal policy and as a means of determining, for instance, what tax increase is required to balance the budget after a given increase in public expenditure, then an imputation for changes in mortality rates would not be appropriate. If, on the other hand, the measures of real income and economic growth are intended to show how rapidly the representative consumer is becoming better off, then an imputation should contain some useful information. The purpose of this chapter is to develop a method of imputing for changes in mortality rates to the measure of economic growth and to carry out the imputation for Canada and for other countries as well.

There are four main aspects of the imputation. First, it is necessary to decide whether life expectancy is a quantity comparable to bread and cheese or an environmental condition comparable to a pollution index. Though life expectancy has some features in common with ordinary goods and services and though an individual may use his income to modify his life expectancy to some extent, I feel that on balance the change over time in life expectancy is better treated as an environmental variable because it is due primarily to the gradual accumulation of knowledge of how to prevent and cure disease. We will come back to this point at the end of the chapter. Second, life expectancy must be quantified. For reasons which will become evident in the course of the discussion, I find it best to conduct the analysis in terms of the whole set of age-specific mortality rates. Third, we must develop shadow prices of age-specific mortality rates. These prices are necessarily arbitrary to some extent because arbitrage cannot be counted upon to equalize the prices of mortality rates among people in the way it can be counted upon to equalize the prices of bread or of cheese. To estimate these prices we draw on some fairly strong assumptions about utility functions and on a growing body of economic literature on the value of life; for the price required to construct an imputation for life expectancy is the same price that is appropriate in cost–benefit analysis of medical expenditure, road safety and the like. Fourth, changes in life expectancy are more like investment than consumption because a reduction in an age-specific mortality rate commencing today and continuing forever does not affect us directly until we become old enough for the age-specific mortality rate to take effect. In constructing an imputation for increased life expectancy, we have to extend the definition of real income as the sum of real consumption and real savings from Chapter 5. We define real income to be the amount of consumption which is judged equivalent at base year mortality rates to the maximum consumption that could be sustained indefinitely at current technology and at current mortality rates. This definition justifies our treating current age-specific mortality rates as the relevant environmental conditions in the current year.

A. CANADIAN MORTALITY RATES SINCE 1926

The quantities in the imputation for changes in life expectancy are age-specific mortality rates. These are readily available and tolerably accurate at least by comparison with the price data in the imputation.[1] Broadly speaking, the trends in mortality rates seem to have been as follows:

(i) There was a steady and dramatic fall in the mortality rates of infants and young children, with mortality rates of girls consistently lower than mortality rates of boys.

(ii) Until about 1956, there was a substantial decline in mortality rates of teenagers and young adults, a decline more pronounced for

---

[1] *Vital Statistics*, Statistics Canada, 84-001, various years.

women than for men. After 1956, mortality rates in these age groups are approximately constant.

(iii) There was no reduction whatsoever in mortality rates of middle-aged men but there was a substantial reduction in mortality rates of middle-aged women.[2]

(iv) There was a moderate but persistent decline in mortality rates of the very old.

The general pattern can be seen in the history of mortality decline in the four age groups, infants (children under one year), 20–24, 55–59, and 80–84, as illustrated in Figure 11.1. The constant and rapid decline in infant mortality rates and the abrupt termination of the decline for females aged 20–24 are particularly striking.

B. THE PRICING OF MORTALITY RATES

Shadow prices of mortality rates may be designed to answer one of three broad questions: The first, which might be called the *insurance question*, is 'What is my life worth to my wife and children?' The expected answer is a sum of money that would enable my wife and children to be as well off financially in the event of my death as they would be if I remained alive. The second, which might be called the *birth control question*, is 'How much better or worse off would the community at large be if I ceased to exist or if I had never been born?' The answer to the question might well be that the rest of you would be better off without me because you would acquire my assets and my title to the use of publicly owned capital such as roads and schools. The third question, which might be called the *valuation of life question*, is 'How much would I pay to avoid a small increase in the probability of my death?' If I were prepared to pay $500 to avoid a 1 in 1000 probability of death through disease or accident, then it might be said that my valuation of my life is $500,000. The valuation of life in the community would be some average of the valuations of individuals. It is important to distinguish among these questions because only the third, the value of life question, is relevant to the imputation for mortality rates and because an explicit distinction may save us from inadvertently choosing shadow prices to answer one of the other questions instead. Each of these questions has to be answered

[2] By contrast, mortality rates of adult males in the United States have risen dramatically in the late 1960s. See A. Joanklebba, *Leading Components of Upturn of Mortality for Men*, Vital and Health Statistics, Series 20, Number 11, US Department of Health, Education and Welfare.

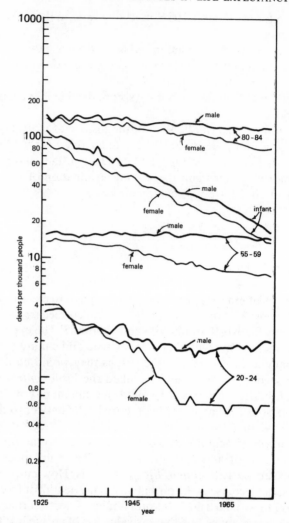

Figure 11.1 Canadian mortality rates 1926–1974 for infants and age groups 20–24, 55–59 and 80–84

by a number of dollars per death, but the questions themselves are distinct, and the answers are not the same.

Dublin and Lotka,[3] though by no means the first to examine these issues, are generally taken as the starting point for modern work. It is significant that they were employees of an insurance company. Their

[3] Louis I. Dublin and Alfred J. Lotka, *The Money Value of a Man*, Ronald Press, 1946.

purpose was to determine the amount of insurance a man ought to carry to guarantee that his wife and children would be as well off in the event of his death as they would be if he remained alive. They referred to this amount as the value of a man's life, and they computed the value of life in this sense as the difference between the present value of a man's earnings and the present value of his consumption over his whole life. Given their purpose, their procedure was correct to the best of my knowledge.

Dublin and Lotka's measure of the value of life is a straightforward computation based on readily available data, and it would certainly be convenient if we could adopt it in imputing for the historical decline in mortality rates. There is some precedent for doing so. The cost of disease has been measured as the sum of direct cost, including medical expenditure and the loss of the patients' earnings while they are alive, and indirect cost consisting of the present value of the forgone earnings of the victims of the disease.[4] Whether it is appropriate to measure the loss of life from disease as the forgone earnings of the dead depends on what we mean by the cost of disease and why we choose to measure it. The measure might be correct in the context of an attempt to determine the capacity of an economy to support a long war; in that case forgone earnings would indicate the increase in economic power that would accrue if the disease could be eradicated. On the other hand, if the cost of disease is really a euphemism for the amount of money that rational men would pay to have the disease eradicated, or that should be paid by a government concerned to enhance the welfare of its citizens, then forgone earnings of the dead is no indicator of the value of a potential decline in mortality rates. The present value of the forgone earnings of the dead is the 'right' amount of insurance for a man to carry; it is not indicative of the amount of money he would pay to avoid a small risk of losing his life, it is not indicative of the amount of money that rational men would be prepared to pay to eradicate a disease,[5]

[4] The history of attempts to compute the value of life saving in medicine and accident prevention is reviewed in J. A. Dowie, 'Valuing the Benefits of Health Improvement', *Australian Economic Papers*, June 1970, pp. 21–41, and M. W. Jones-Lee, *The Value of Life*, The University of Chicago Press, 1976.

[5] My views on this issue are very close to those of Thomas Schelling, 'The Life You Save May Be Your Own', *Problems in Public Expenditure Analysis*, S. Chase (ed.), Brookings, 1968, pp. 127–61. A more complete exposition of this approach to life saving is contained in E. J. Mishan, 'Evaluation of Life and Limb: A Theoretical Approach', *Journal of Political Economy*, July/August 1971, pp. 687–705. Mishan evaluates the saving of lives by means of the concept of consumer surplus, and formally at least, incorporates externalities into the analysis, but he makes no attempt to specify functional forms for his curves or to produce numerical estimates.

and it is not indicative of the value of the historical decline in mortality rates.

The use of discounted future income as a measure of the value of one's life is sometimes justified on the grounds that one's earnings are a measure of one's value to the rest of the community. This justification is spurious in my opinion because it involves a confusion between the valuation of life question and the birth control question. A concensus has emerged in the literature on the cost–benefit analysis of birth control that, at high birth rates, the benefits derived from preventing a birth are very great and that the eventual per capita income of the community is a decreasing function of the birth rate. The reason is the Malthusian one that an increase in the population raises the capital–labour ratio. This applies with less force to adults than to unborn children, but it applies nonetheless. Suppose a family complete with children and all heirs is destroyed in an automobile accident. Notwithstanding the loss of forgone earnings, this event makes the rest of us better off because we acquire title to all the family's assets including their rights to the use of schools and other public property. By definition, if the family is typical, any excess of its earnings over its consumption would accrue to its heirs and not to the rest of us. There is some dislocation in the economy if a departure is less orderly, but there is no reason to suppose that the costs to the survivors of having people go separately rather than in families outweighs the effect of a man's death on the capital–labour ratio. Certainly, we are concerned as a community to keep each other alive but that concern is based on something other than the maximization of GNP, in total or per head.

To equate the value of life to discounted earnings forgone is to suppose that the lives of housewives and old people are worthless. In one sense this is quite true. The calculations of Dublin and Lotka would imply that old people and wives ought not to carry insurance, and this may well be the case. It is not the case that old people and wives place no value on prolonging their lives or that society as a whole is unconcerned with the matter.

To find a value of life for converting reductions in age-specific mortality rates into an imputation in the national accounts, we need to look carefully into the question of what it is that is maximized in expenditures to reduce age-specific mortality rates and to seek evidence on what people actually pay for this purpose. In principle, one could get the information from a questionnaire. One would ask, 'Suppose there is a 1 in 1000 chance that the cup in front of you contains hemlock rather than coffee: what would you pay to avoid having to drink the contents of the cup?' The answer, multiplied by 1000, is the value the respondent places on his life, and, by questioning people of different ages and with different incomes, one could obtain some notion of how the response is affected by these variables. Of course, no statistician would pose this question because the respondent cannot be expected to answer it truthfully. I introduce it in this context to keep in mind the sort of information we would like to obtain, for there are situations where this question has to be answered. Decisions have to be made in circumstances where lives are at stake, and where valuations of changes in mortality rates are implicit in what we choose to do.

(a) We place values on life saving in our decisions to engage or not to engage in medical expenditures. If the cost per patient of a kidney transplant is $72,000, and if we decide that those who need kidney transplants will get them, and if the expected life of a person with a kidney transplant is 17 years, we are deciding that a 17-year extension of life is worth at least $72,000.

(b) Similarly, a valuation of life saving is implicit in expenditures to prevent road accidents.

(c) A valuation of changes of mortality rates reflecting private as opposed to public decision making is implicit in rates of hazard pay. If a carpenter who works at the top of a high building runs a 1 in 1000 risk per year of falling off, and if he accepts a premium of $100 for taking that risk, he values his life at $100,000.

(d) If the amount of armour on an airplane affects the chances of it being shot down, a valuation of life is implicit in decisions as to how much armour the plane should have.

Though the pricing of life is implicit in many public and private decisions, it is difficult to find prices and to extricate valuation of life from other considerations. I have only been able to find a few prices and these are shown in Table 11.1. In interpreting these prices and in using them to impute values of decreases in mortality rates, several considerations should be kept in mind.

First, by value of life, I mean nothing more than the amount one would pay per unit for a decrease in one's mortality rate in the current year. The statement that the price of life is $200,000 in this sense does not mean that a man would sacrifice his life for $200,000, any more than the statement that the price of butter is $0.25 per pound means that a man would pay $200,000 for the pleasure of consuming 400 tons of butter.

Second, the valuation of life implicit in decisions affecting mortality rates is different from the valuation society puts on saving the lives of identifiable people. Thedie and Abraham[6] have expressed this point as

[6] J. Thedie and C. Abraham, 'Economic Aspect of Road Accidents', *Traffic Engineering and Control*, **11**, 1961, p. 590.

Table 11.1   Scraps of evidence on the value of life

Implicit or explicit value of the life of a man of about 30 years old	$ (000)
(1) Hazard pay	
premium miners accept for working underground	34–159
test pilot	161
(2) Medical expenditure	
kidney transplant	72
dialysis in hospital	270
dialysis at home	99
(3) Valuation of the cost of disease	75
(4) Valuation of the cost of airplane accidents	472
(5) Traffic safety	
recommended for cost–benefit analysis by the National Safety Council	37.5
value of life in a cost–benefit study of highways	100
(6) Military decision making	
instructions to pilots on when to crash-land airplanes	270
decision to produce a special ejector seat in a jet plane	4500
(7) Valuation of risk in occupational choice	200 ± 60

Note: These estimates are for various years in the decade 1957 to 1967. The sources for this table are presented as an appendix to this chapter.

follows: 'If a miner is imprisoned at the bottom of a pit, if a mountaineer is in danger up in the mountains, if a vessel is in danger of shipwreck on the high seas, it would be criminal to reckon efforts and money according to the number of human lives to be saved. It would be vain to inquire whether the sum spent on saving these few lives if invested elsewhere (on roads for instance) might not have enabled more lives to be saved. It is impossible to weigh in the balance certain deaths and probable deaths, even if the latter are in greater number.'

Third, the price of life is different from the price of butter in that the price of butter is the same to everyone who buys butter while the price of reductions in mortality rates may vary from one man to the next within the same market. Mortality rates are private commodities, by which I mean that they are not and cannot be traded in the market because they are produced from ordinary commodities by the individual or in the household as discussed in Chapter 8. Suppose, as illustrated in Figure 11.2, that a man is confronted with a number of ways of reducing his mortality rate listed here in order of cost: wearing a safety belt in his car, visiting his doctor for an annual check-up, fire-proofing his house, having a special test for cancer, installing a radio transmitter in his yacht, reinforcing his automobile, keeping a co-pilot at all times in his private jet plane. These options constitute a supply curve to the individual of

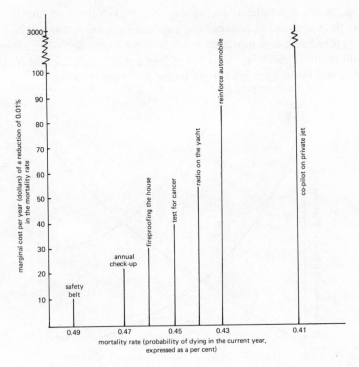

Figure 11.2 A person's supply curve of mortality rates

reductions in his mortality rate, and corresponding to this supply curve is a demand curve for reductions in mortality rates which can be derived in a manner discussed in the following section. The position of the demand curve would depend on the tastes of the individual and on his income; the more wealthy he is, the more he would pay to reduce mortality rates and the higher would his demand curve be. Each man's supply curve of reduction of mortality rates is also unique as it depends on the circumstances of his life, particularly on the nature of his work. In Figure 11.3 the supply curves facing a rich man and a poor man are presumed to be identical, but their demand curves differ, and the value of life of a rich man (in our special sense of the term 'value of life') is higher in equilibrium than the value of life of a poor man.

Evidence on shadow prices of mortality rates is of limited use in constructing an imputation to economic growth because mortality rates are private commodities. Even in perfect markets, values of reductions in mortality rates differ from one man to the next so that prices implicit in particular transactions are relevant only to people who actually engage in those transactions and not to the population as a whole. And a great many mortality-reducing expenditures convey no information about the value of life because the expenditures are intramarginal. The cost of a reduction in mortality rates implicit in the decision to have an annual medical check-up need not reflect a man's valuation of his life if his demand curve cuts his supply curve at a higher value.

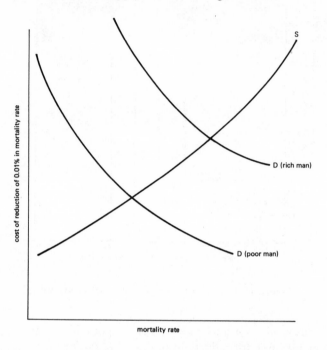

Figure 11.3 Choice of mortality rates of a rich man and a poor man of the assumption that their supply curves are the same

The issue is complicated further by the fact that reductions in mortality rates have externalities. We are prepared to sacrifice to prolong our neighbour's life, though we are relatively unconcerned about the size of our neighbour's income. Evidence of public and private behaviour in circumstances where decreases in mortality rates can be bought conveys some useful information and gives hints as to what might be a reasonable valuation of life in cost–benefit analysis and in our imputation for increased life expectancy. This evidence does not point to a unique price or to a unique range of prices depending on a man's age and mortality rates in each future year. Reductions in mortality rates differ from ordinary commodities in that unique prices do not exist.

Having said this, we shall overlook the variability among people in the shadow prices of reductions in mortality rates, and shall measure economic growth by postulating that there is a unique shadow price of changes in mortality rates for each age group in each year of the time series.

C. UTILITY AND LONGEVITY

The next step in constructing our imputation for changes in life expectancy is to specify a utility function that includes mortality rates among its arguments in a natural way. We cannot use the utility function set out in Chapter 2 because it was defined for an atemporal model in which the representative consumer need only concern himself with currently-available goods and services. The utility function in Chapter 5 does take time into account, but it is not suitable for our present purpose because it refers to a representative consumer who lives forever; the consumer in the intertemporal model in Chapter 5 is representative, not of mortal individuals, but of immortal families or of the community as a whole. We shall have to postulate a third form of the utility function referring to individuals and recognizing long life as an important aspect of welfare.

The procedure in this section and the next is as follows. We first define utility quite generally as a function of the whole set of probabilities of living for one year, for two years, for three years and so on up to an assumed maximum length of life, and of the consumption in each year of life. Next we make some strong simplifying assumptions to represent the utility function as dependent on a few observable parameters. Finally, we use the theory of imputation from Chapter 7 to construct a simple formula that enables us to compute the imputation for Canada and other countries from data on mortality rates and the value of life.

Let the utility function of the representative consumer in the year 0 be

$$U = U(U_0, P_0, U_1, P_1, \ldots, U_n, P_n) \tag{1}$$

where U is his welfare in the present circumstances, P_i is the probability of his living for exactly i years, U_i is his welfare if he lives for exactly i years and n is the postulated upper limit to the length of his life. The probabilities must sum to 1:

$$\sum_{i=0}^{n} P_i = 1 \tag{2}$$

Values of the terms U_t, P_t and n depend on a man's age. If the maximum length of life is assumed to be 90 years, the n relevant to a 50-year old man is 40. The value of P_{10} for a 50-year old man depends on mortality rates between age 50 and age 60, the value of P_{10} for a 60-year old man depends on mortality rates between age 60 and age 70, and so on. In deriving an imputation for the national accounts, values of U will have to be averaged over the age distribution of the population.

The utility function U_t corresponding to a life of t years depends on consumption in each of those years

$$U_t = U_t(C_0, C_1, C_2, \ldots, C_{t-1}) \tag{3}$$

where C_i is consumption in the year i.

The functions (1), (2), and (3) form a discrete representation of what is in reality a continuous process. It is convenient to think of consumption C_i as evenly spread out over the year i, and of death occurring if at all on the first day of the year. It is as though the whole risk of dying in a year were concentrated on one's birthday. A man alive in the year 0 is presumed safe until the first day of the year 1, and if he survives that day he is safe again until the first day of the year 2, and so on.

It should be noted that the specification of the utility function in equations (1), (2) and (3) entails a 'selfishness' assumption. Each man is supposed to be concerned with his own life expectancy exclusively. Even the concern of parents for children is abstracted away, and improvements in infant mortality are evaluated from the point of view of the representative child whose welfare is assessed by the same formula used to assess the welfare of the representative adult. The welfare of a child is given considerable weight in equation (1) because, and insofar as, the life expectancy of a child is greater than the life expectancy of an adult.

It is useful to define two additional mortality variables: D_t is the mortality rate t years hence, and S_t is the probability of surviving up to the year t. The variables P_t, D_t and S_t are related by the formulae

$$S_t = \prod_{j=0}^{t-1} (1 - D_j) \tag{4}$$

$$P_t = D_t S_t = D_t \prod_{j=0}^{t-1} (1 - D_j) \tag{5}$$

Obviously

$$0 < D_t < 1, 0 < P_t < 1, \quad \text{and} \quad 0 < S_t < 1$$

and $D_n = 1$ if n is the maximum length of life.[7]

The utility functions can be expected to have the following properties:

$$\partial U_i/\partial C_i > 0 \quad \text{for all} \quad i < t \tag{6}$$

$$\partial U/\partial U_t > 0 \tag{7}$$

$$\partial U/\partial D_t > 0 \tag{8}$$

These properties jointly imply that a man thinks himself better off if consumption in any year is increased or if his probability of dying in any given year is reduced. These properties also imply that the value of life as defined in the preceding section is positive, that $\partial C_0/\partial D_0|_U > 0$, that a man will forgo some consumption in the current year to reduce his current mortality rate.

We now introduce two strong assumptions about the form of the utility function. The first is that equation (1) takes the special form

$$U = \sum_{t=0}^{n} P_t U_t \tag{9}$$

This specification which we shall refer to as the 'expected utility' assumption fits exactly into the terms of reference of the 'states of the world' approach to the theory of choice under uncertainty. All possible lengths of life t correspond to mutually-exclusive states of the world and

---

[7] Equations (2) and (5) are consistent as long as $D_n = 1$. From equation (4) it follows that $S_t \equiv S_{t-1} - D_{t-1}S_{t-1}$ for all values of t. Consequently,

$$\sum_{t=0}^{n} P_t = \sum_{t=0}^{n} D_t S_t = D_n S_n + \sum_{t=0}^{n-1} D_t S_t$$

$$= S_{n-1} - D_{n-1}S_{n-1} + \sum_{t=0}^{n-1} D_t S_t$$

$$= S_{n-1} + \sum_{t=0}^{n-2} D_t S_t = S_{n-2} + \sum_{t=0}^{n-3} D_t S_t$$

$$= S_1 + D_0 S_0 = S_0 = 1$$

the P_t are probabilities of their occurrence.[8] It is a well known property of utility functions of this sort that they are cardinal rather than ordinal and may be defined up to a linear transformation.[9] In principle, if we are given the values of any two utility functions U_i and U_j for the years i and j and for a given time path of consumption, we could determine all values of all utility functions U_t for all years t and all time paths of consumption by a conceptual experiment of the sort used to determine the shape of an ordinary indifference curve.

In this study we make no attempt to perform experiments of that kind, but our observations of the value of life in the preceding section serve a similar function when combined with a 'separability' assumption which greatly restricts the form of equation (3). The assumption is that the utility of a stream of consumption for a fixed length of life is the sum of discounted annual utilities. Specifically, we assume that

$$U_t = \sum_{i=0}^{t-1} \frac{C_i^\beta}{(1+r)^i} \tag{10}$$

where r is a rate of discount connecting 'annual utility' accruing at different periods of time and β is the elasticity of annual utility with respect to consumption.

The separability assumption (10) is a much stronger assumption and a much less theoretically-acceptable one than the expected utility hypothesis. It is a discrete version of an assumption used widely in the theory of economic growth, and its advantages and disadvantages in that context are well known.[10] The role of the separability assumption in our analysis is to make utility dependent on only two parameters r and β, which may be determined as we shall show from 'observations' of the value of life. The separability assumption is particularly unrealistic because it places no value on longevity itself independently of the level of consumption. Instead of assuming that U_t takes the form (10), we might have assumed that

$$U_t = t^\alpha \sum_{j=0}^{t-1} \frac{C_i^\beta}{(1+r)^j} \tag{11}$$

[8] See J. Hirschleifer, 'Investment Decisions under Uncertainty', *Quarterly Journal of Economics*, November 1965 and May 1966.

[9] For a justification of this assertion see R. D. Luce and H. Raifa, *Games and Decisions*, Wiley, 1967, Chapter 2.

[10] See H. Wan, *Economic Growth*, Harcourt Brace & Jovanovich, 1971, pp. 267–85.

which would imply, if $a > 1$, that a man would accept a reduction in the present value of the time stream of C_j^β in order to prolong his life. The consequences of assumptions like (11) will not be investigated.

Combining the 'expected utility' assumption with the 'separability' assumption, that is, by substituting equation (9) and equation (10) into equation (1), we see that the overall utility function becomes

$$U = \sum_{j=0}^{n} P_j \left(\sum_{i=0}^{j-1} \frac{C_i^\beta}{(1+r)^i} \right) = \sum_{j=0}^{n-1} \frac{C_j^\beta S_{j+1}}{(1+r)^j} \qquad (12)$$

We can now differentiate the utility function with respect to C_0 and D_t to obtain formulae expressing the value of life in terms of the time series D_i and C_i and the parameters r and β. Applying the expected utility assumption without the separability assumption and taking current consumption as the numeraire, we see that the value of a reduction in the mortality rate of the year t is[11]

[11] By definition,

$$\left. \frac{\partial C_0}{\partial D_t} \right|_U = - \frac{\partial U / \partial D_t}{\partial U / \partial C_0}$$

where

$$\frac{\partial U}{\partial C_0} = \sum_{j=0}^{n} \frac{\partial U}{\partial U_j} \frac{\partial U_j}{\partial C_0} = \sum_{j=0}^{n} p_j \frac{\partial U_j}{\partial C_0}$$

and

$$\frac{\partial U}{\partial D_t} = \sum_{j=0}^{n} \frac{\partial U}{\partial P_j} \frac{\partial P_j}{\partial D_t}$$

$$= \sum_{j=t}^{n} U_j \frac{\partial P_j}{\partial D_t} \quad \text{(because} \quad \partial P_j / \partial D_t = 0 \quad \text{if} \quad j < t\text{)}$$

$$= U_t \frac{P_t}{D_t} - \sum_{j=t+1}^{n} \frac{P_j}{1 - D_t} U_j$$

$$= \sum_{j=t}^{n} \frac{P_j}{1 - D_t} (U_t - U_j)$$

The final step in this derivation follows from the fact that

$$\frac{P_t}{D_t} - \sum_{j=t+1}^{n} \frac{P_j}{1 - D_t} = S_t - S_t \left(\sum_{j=t+1}^{n} D_j \prod_{i=t+1}^{j-1} (1 - D_i) \right) = 0$$

The proof in footnote 7 can be extended to show that the expression in large parentheses is equal to 1.

$$\frac{\partial C_0}{\partial D_t} = \frac{\sum_{j=t}^{n}[P_j/(1-D_t)](U_j-U_t)}{\sum_{j=1}^{n} P_j \, \partial U_j/\partial C_0} \tag{13}$$

By adding the separability assumption, that is, by replacing values of U_j and U_t in equation (13) with their values from equation (10), we arrive at the stronger result that[12]

$$\frac{\partial C_0}{\partial D_t} = \frac{C_0}{\beta}\left(\sum_{j=t}^{n-1}\frac{(C_j/C_0)^\beta S_{j+1}}{(1+r)^j}\right)\frac{1}{(1-D_0)(1-D_t)} \tag{14}$$

The term $1/[(1 - D_0)(1 - D_t)]$ enters equation (14) as a consequence of our assumption that consumption and risk of death enter the utility function as discrete units instead of as flows over time. The term could be eliminated from equation (13) by shortening the time periods enough that the probability of dying in any period is effectively zero. Instead of graduating time in years we might graduate it in weeks, days or seconds.

The parameter r in equation (14) is different from and as a rule less than the real rate of interest on riskless assets. A lender of money faces two types of risk. The first is that the borrower does not repay the loan. The second is that the lender himself dies before the date of repayment. Normally, when we speak of a loan as being riskless we are referring to the absence of only the first type of risk whereas r is a rate of discount assumed to be riskless in both respects. An individual in a competitive market arranges his time pattern of work and consumption to equate his

---

[12] The numerator of equation (13) becomes

$$\sum_{j=t}^{n}\frac{P_j}{1-D_t}(U_j-U_t) = \sum_{j=t}^{n}\frac{P_j}{1-D_t}\left(\sum_{i=0}^{j-1}\frac{C_i^\beta}{(1+r)^i} - \sum_{i=0}^{t-1}\frac{C_i^\beta}{(1+r)^i}\right)$$

$$= \sum_{j=t}^{n}\frac{P_j}{1-D_t}\left(\sum_{i=t}^{j-1}\frac{C_i^\beta}{(1+r)^i}\right) = \frac{1}{1-D_t}\sum_{j=t}^{n-1}\left[\frac{C_i^\beta}{(1+r)^j}\left(\sum_{i=j+1}^{n} P_i\right)\right]$$

$$= \frac{1}{1-D_t}\frac{C_i^\beta S_{j+1}}{(1+r)^j}$$

The denominator becomes

$$\sum_{j=0}^{n} P_j\frac{\partial U_j}{\partial C_0} = \sum_{j=1}^{n}\beta P_j C_0^{\beta-1} = (1-D_0)\beta C_0^{\beta-1}$$

Consequently

$$\frac{\partial C_0}{\partial D_t} = \frac{1}{\beta}\,C_0\left(\sum_{j=t}^{n-1}\frac{(C_j/C_0)^\beta S_{j+1}}{(1+r)^j}\right)\frac{1}{(1-D_0)(1-D_t)}$$

rate of substitution in use between present and future consumption to the discount factor in the market. To be precise,

$$-\frac{\partial C_0}{\partial C_t}\bigg|_U = \frac{1}{(1+i_t)^t} \tag{15}$$

where i_t is the market's real rate of interest on riskless t-year loans. On the other hand, it is a consequence of equation (10) that for any $j > t$,

$$-\frac{\partial C_0}{\partial C_t}\bigg|_{U_i} = \frac{1}{(1+r)^t} \tag{16}$$

It is easily shown that

$$\frac{1}{(1+i_t)^t} = -\frac{\partial C_0}{\partial C_t}\bigg|_U = \frac{S_{t+1}}{S_1}\left(\frac{C_0}{C_t}\right)^{1/\beta}\frac{1}{(1+r)^t} \tag{17}$$

which implies that $r < i_t$ as long as $C_0 \leqslant C_t$. The term S_{t+1}/S_1 in equation (17) is like a second discount factor, for it is the product of annual components all of which are less than 1.

D. ASSUMPTIONS ABOUT TIMING AND DISTRIBUTION

We would like to measure real income inclusive of the imputation for changes in mortality in accordance with the general procedure developed in Chapter 7 for adjusting real income to compensate for changes in environmental variables since the base year. In this case, real income inclusive of the imputation would be defined implicitly by the relation

$$U(\hat{Y}(t), D(1961)) = U(Y(t), D(t)) \tag{18}$$

where $D(t)$ is a vector of mortality rates in year t, $Y(t)$ is real income without the imputation for changes in longevity, $\hat{Y}(t)$ is real income inclusive of the imputation, and 1961 is the base year.[13]

Equation (18) is illustrated in Figure 11.4 which is a variant of Figure 7.1. Imagine three representative consumers, one living in 1926, one

---

[13] We use a term of the form $X(t)$ to refer to the value of any variable X in the year t. This usage should be distinguished from X_t which refers to an event t that may or may not occur t years in the future.

living in 1961 and one living in 1974. They can live for at most two periods, they face probabilities $D(t)$ of dying at the start of the second period, their utility functions are identical, and their consumption is the same in both periods so that real income (not including the imputation) and real consumption are one and the same.

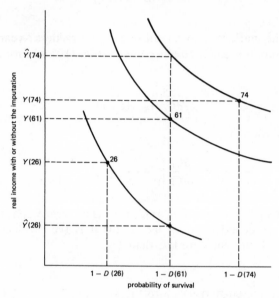

Figure 11.4 Real income inclusive of an imputation for the change in the mortality rate

Three indifference curves, one containing Y and D of 1926, another containing Y and D of 1961, and another containing Y and D of 1974, are shown on Figure 11.4. Points representing values of Y and D in the years 1926, 1961 and 1974 are labelled accordingly. Real income without the imputation for changes in mortality rates is indicated by the points $Y(26)$, $Y(61)$ and $Y(74)$ on the vertical axis, while real income inclusive of the imputation as defined in equation (18) is indicated by the points $\hat{Y}(26)$, $Y(61)$ and $\hat{Y}(74)$. By definition, there can be no imputation in the base year.

We would like to substitute the utility function in equation (12) into equation (18) so as to express $\hat{Y}(t)$ as a function of the parameters r and β together with information about mortality rates and other variables. We cannot make this substitution with equation (12) as it stands because utility in equation (12) is a function of the time stream of consumption and mortality rates as far ahead as the representative consumer can expect to live. The welfare of a man who is 40 years old today depends upon the mortality rate of 50-year old men ten years hence, upon the mortality rate of 60-year old men twenty years hence, and so on. Real income, on the other hand, is designed to reflect conditions in the economy as it is today regardless of what may happen tomorrow.

To deal with this discrepancy between the arguments in the utility function of equation (12) and the requirements for a definition of real income, we must reconsider our definition of real income as sustainable consumption in perpetuity as set out in Chapter 5. Real income in the year t was defined as the amount of consumption that could be sustained indefinitely if all population growth, net saving and technical change ceased in that year. In our imputation for life expectancy, we look upon mortality rates as analogous to technical change. We record the improvement from the base year to the year t as an aspect of real income in the year t. But we deliberately disregard the fact that people alive in the year t will experience the presumably better mortality rates in subsequent years just as we disregard the fact that they will be the beneficiaries of subsequent technical change. A measure of real income as the sum of consumption plus the change in wealth ought to take account of technical change and improvements in mortality rates occurring after the year t if people alive in the year t will be affected, but a measure of real income as the sum of real consumption and real saving ought not to do so. Thus we define real income inclusive of the imputation as an amount of consumption such that a representative consumer who enjoyed that consumption in the year t and every subsequent year together with the mortality rates of the base year would be as well off as he would be with the actual sustainable consumption and the actual mortality rates of the year t.

This line of reasoning suggests that we ought to consider real income as a surrogate for utility, defined in equation (12), as it would be if consumption today and forever more were equal to current income measured with regard to consumption goods as the numeraire, and if survival probabilities depended on current mortality rates. Thus, for each year t we suppose that

$$C_0(t) = C_1(t) = \ldots = C_n(t) = Y(t) \tag{19}$$

where $Y(t)$ is current real income in the year t, and we measure all the terms $S_j(t)$ in equation (12) with regard to observed mortality rates in the year t. With this substitution we can now rewrite the utility function of equation (12) as

$$U(t) = Y(t)^\beta L(t) \tag{20}$$

where $L(t)$, which we shall refer to as discounted life expectancy, is defined as

$$L \equiv \sum_{j=0}^{n-1} \frac{S_{j+1}}{(1+r)^j} \tag{21}$$

Substituting the simplified utility function of equation (20) into equation (18), we finally obtain an expression for real income inclusive of the imputation for longevity

$$\hat{Y}(t) = Y(t)[L(t)/L(1961)]^{1/\beta} \tag{22}$$

The significant feature of equation (22) is that the terms on the right-hand side of the equation representing income, $Y(t)$, and increased life expectancy, $[L(t)/L(1961)]^{1/\beta}$, are multiplicative so that the rates of growth of the two terms cumulate rather than average out in the formation of the final rate of economic growth:

$$G_{\hat{Y}} = G_Y + G_L/\beta \tag{23}$$

Normally imputations to the national income are additive rather than multiplicative, and the effect of an imputation is to reduce the rate of growth whenever the growth of the imputed item is less than the growth of the rest of the accounts. It follows from the assumptions we have made about the form of utility function and the concept of income that the effect of the imputation for increased life expectancy is necessarily to increase the rate of growth, and that the increase is normally greater than the rate of growth of life expectancy itself.

In assessing the value of L each year, it is important to specify whose utility we are considering. We would want to measure the average value of $\hat{Y}$ in the population as a whole, taking young and old into account. Other things being equal, the $\hat{Y}$ of a young man would be greater than the $\hat{Y}$ of an old man, and these values of $\hat{Y}$ should be averaged according to the proportions of young men and old men in the population. However, this averaging procedure must be conducted with respect to a standard age distribution (for instance, the age distribution in the base year), for we would not want our statistics to imply that people are becoming better off over time if all that is happening is that the proportion of young people in the population is increasing.

If we impose the assumption in equation (19) upon the definition of the value of life in equation (14) and if we ignore the term $1/[(1 - D_0)(1 - D_t)]$, the shadow price of a reduction in the current mortality rate becomes

$$\frac{\partial C_0}{\partial D_0} = \frac{1}{\beta} \, YL \tag{24}$$

Rates of economic growth can now be computed in accordance with equation (22) from time series of $Y(t)$ and $D_j(t)$ for a range of values of the parameters β and r. The time series of $Y(t)$ can be obtained from the national accounts by deflating the current value of net national product by the implicit price deflator of consumption goods. Time series of $L(t)$ corresponding to each value of β and r can be constructed from available data on mortality rates.

The final step in the construction of the imputation is to choose reasonable values of r and β. We cannot estimate r and β separately, but we can use evidence on the value of life to impose a constraint on the two parameters together, and that constraint turns out to be sufficient for our purpose.

E. THE IMPUTATION FOR CANADA

For a wide range of the parameters r and β, the value of life and the corresponding growth rate of real income inclusive of an imputation for the increase in life expectancy have been computed in accordance with equations (23) with Canadian data for the years 1926 and 1974. The data required are time series of real net national expenditure per head to measure $Y(t)$, and age-specific mortality rates to measure $D_j(t)$. In each year the value of L for the population as a whole is taken to be a weighted average value of L in that year for all ages with weights reflecting the age distribution of the population in 1961. The rate of interest, r, is parameterized at 1, 3 and 5%, and β, which is the more critical variable, is given all values between 0.05 and 1.0 in steps of 0.05. For all combinations of r and β, the computed values of life and growth rates of net national product inclusive of the imputation for increased life expectancy are presented in Table 11.2. The growth rate of real net national expenditure per head over the years 1926 to 1974 was 2.83%. The effect of the imputation for increased life expectancy depends very much on the values chosen for the parameter β and r. For $r = 1\%$, the rate of economic growth inclusive of the imputation for increased life expectancy varies from 3.06% when $\beta = 1$ up to 7.27 when $\beta = 0.05$. For each combination of r and β we estimate the value of life according to equation (24), and our final estimate of the rate of economic growth is that corresponding to a value of life chosen to be more or less consistent with the 'observed' values recorded in Table 11.1.

Table 11.2 Growth rates 1926–1974 and the value of life

	r = 1%		r = 3%		r = 5%	
β	average value of life in 1961 $(1/\beta)Y(1961)L(1961)Y(t)[L(t)/L(1961)]^\beta(1/\beta)$	growth rate of income inclusive of an imputation for increased life expectancy —growth rate of $Y(1961)L(1961)Y(t)[L(t)/L(1961)]^\beta(1/\beta)$	average value of life in 1961 $Y(1961)L(1961)$	growth rate of income inclusive of an imputation for increased life expectancy —growth rate of $Y(t)[L(t)/L(1961)]^\beta$	average value of life in 1961 $(1/\beta)Y(1961)L(1961)$	growth rate of income inclusive of an imputation for increased life expectancy —growth rate of $Y(t)[L(t)/L(1961)]^\beta$
%	$ (000)	%	$ (000)	%	$ (000)	%
5	1360	7.27	930	6.13	686	5.39
10	680	5.05	464	4.48	343	4.11
15	453	4.31	310	3.93	229	3.69
20	340	3.94	232	3.66	171	3.47
25	272	3.72	186	3.49	137	3.35
30	227	3.57	155	3.38	114	3.26
35	194	3.47	133	3.30	98	3.20
40	170	3.39	116	3.25	86	3.15
45	151	3.33	103	3.20	76	3.12
50	136	3.28	93	3.16	69	3.09
55	124	3.24	85	3.13	62	3.07
60	113	3.20	77	3.11	57	3.05
65	105	3.18	72	3.09	53	3.03
70	97	3.15	66	3.07	49	3.02
75	91	3.13	62	3.05	46	3.00
80	85	3.11	58	3.04	43	3.00
85	80	3.09	55	3.03	40	2.99
90	76	3.08	52	3.02	38	2.98
95	72	3.07	49	3.01	36	2.98
100	68	3.06	46	3.00	34	2.97

The growth rate of income without the imputation for increased life-expectancy is 2.83%.
Notes to this table are in the appendix to this chapter.

Our imputation for changes in life expectancy is constructed on the assumption that the value of life in 1961 is \$150,000, that is, for each choice of r, the corresponding β is chosen to equate the expression $\partial C_0 / \partial D_0$ in equation (24) to \$150,000 when L and Y are as observed in 1961. Once this constraint is imposed on the values r and β, the effect of the imputation is almost independent of the choice of the interest rate. If $r = 1\%$, then, to the nearest 0.05, $\beta = 0.45$ and the growth rate is 3.33%; if $r = 3\%$ then $\beta = 0.30$ and the growth rate is 3.38%; if $r = 5\%$ then $\beta = 0.25$ and the growth rate is 3.35%. In all three cases, the effect of the imputation is to raise the rate of economic growth by about one-half of one per cent per year from 2.83% without the imputation to about 3.35%, give or take 0.03%.

The estimated increase of one-half of one per cent in the growth rate attributable to the improvement in life expectancy is by no means insignificant but seems to me to be rather low. The reason may be that I have underemphasized the importance of the fall in mortality rates in infants and children. The first hypothesis in the calculation is that each man is concerned with his own mortality rate exclusively, and since the great majority of people have passed infancy, the decline in the infant mortality rates cannot have a great effect on the final estimate. The decline in the infant mortality rate would have had a greater impact on the imputation if the interest of parents and prospective parents had been taken into account explicitly.

F. IMPUTATIONS FOR OTHER COUNTRIES

I have no direct intuition about the value of life in countries outside of North America, and no information with which to determine reasonable values of r and β. What can be done is to suppose that tastes are the same everywhere, so that combinations of r and β which are plausible for Canada are plausible for other countries as well. Calculations on these lines are set out in Table 11.3. The numbers in the table are derived in exactly the same way as the Canadian numbers were derived, and the table should be self-explanatory. The reader who is uncomfortable with the assumption that shapes of indifference curves and values of β and r are the same in Canada and elsewhere may interpret the statistics in Table 11.3 as indicating the growth of income of Sri Lanka, for instance, as it would be assessed by a Canadian in the circumstances of the Sri Lanka economy.

The interesting feature of Table 11.3 is the magnitude of some of the imputations for some of the underdeveloped countries. The growth rate of Sri Lanka is more than doubled, and the growth rate of Chile is almost

Table 11.3 Imputations for increased life expectancy in other countries

country	date	growth rate of GNP (%)	growth rate of GNP inclusive of an imputation for increased life expectancy			
			$r = 1\%, \beta = 0.45$	$r = 3\%, \beta = 0.31$	$r = 5\%, \beta = 0.23$
Chile	1931–1971	2.00	3.08	3.20	3.29
Costa Rica	1950–1973	3.13	4.34	4.38	4.41
France	1911–1972	1.97	2.78	2.87	2.95
Mauritius	1952–1971	−0.31	1.22	1.34	1.42
Japan	1930–1974	3.99	5.23	5.34	5.45
Singapore	1957–1974	6.27	7.16	7.17	7.19
Sri Lanka	1946–1968	1.43	3.23	3.51	3.70
Thailand	1956–1970	4.07	5.14	5.19	5.21
USA	1930–1974	3.88	4.53	4.59	4.63

Sources of data are listed in the appendix to this chapter.

doubled. If one may generalize from these scanty bits of information, it seems that in the period since the Second World War the under-developed countries, alleged by many authors to have prospered less on average than the rich countries, have in fact done very well. It was in this period that many poor countries enjoyed an improvement in life expectancy greater than that enjoyed by rich countries in this or any other period of time, an improvement that more than compensates for the difference between rich and poor countries in growth rates of GNP as conventionally measured.

G. MORTALITY RATES AND ENVIRONMENTAL CONDITIONS

The whole line of argument of this chapter and the imputation we derive might be objected to on the grounds that changes in mortality rates ought not to be thought of as benefits over and above ordinary goods and services because changes in mortality rates are purchased with income through the intermediary of ordinary goods and services. We have treated mortality rates as environmental conditions like pollution indexes. The essence of the objection is that mortality rates are more like breakfasts which are not purchased in themselves but need not be imputed for in the national accounts because the bread, butter, bacon and eggs of which breakfasts are composed are already counted as goods. We purchase reductions in mortality rates when we eat nutritious food, visit the doctor, or undertake expenditure on road safety; no imputation to economic growth is necessary because expenditure on food, medicine and road safety are included in income already.

It is undeniable that people determine their own mortality rates to some extent. There is abundant evidence that mortality rates vary with income, education and social class; the rich, the educated and the upper classes live longer than the poor, the uneducated and the lower classes.[14] Some evidence on mortality rates of adults classified by age, sex and educational attainment is presented in Table 11.4, and some evidence on infant mortality rates classified by family income of parents and by the educational attainment of father is presented in Table 11.5.

If we may take the evidence in Tables 11.4 and 11.5 as indicative of the broad pattern of mortality rates in Canada as well as in the United States—and there is no reason to doubt that this is the case—then we must recognize that mortality rates are not exclusively environmental

---

[14] Most of the evidence on this question available prior to 1967 has been collected in A. Antonovsky, 'Social Class, Life Expectancy and Overall Mortality', *The Milbank Memorial Fund Quarterly*, April 1967, pp. 31–73.

Table 11.4 Age-specific death rates for persons age 25 years and over, by education and sex: United States, 1962–63 (rate per 1000 population)

sex and age	total	education elementary or none	high school	college plus
both sexes				
25 years and over	16.1	28.7	9.0	9.1
25–44 years	2.3	3.6	2.1	1.6
45–54 years	7.6	9.8	6.5	5.9
55–64 years	17.4	20.0	15.0	13.6
65 years and over	62.6	66.8	53.8	55.1
male				
25 years and over	18.9	33.0	10.9	9.5
25–44 years	2.9	4.5	2.9	1.7
45–54 years	9.9	12.8	8.6	7.3
55–64 years	23.2	26.2	21.2	17.0
65 years and over	73.5	78.5	61.7	63.1
female				
25 years and over	13.5	24.4	7.5	8.6
25–44 years	1.7	2.6	1.5	1.5
44–54 years	5.3	6.5	4.8	4.3
55–64 years	11.9	13.9	9.8	10.3
65 years and over	53.8	56.7	48.6	48.3

Source: *Socioeconomic Characteristics of Deceased Persons*, Vital and Health Statistics, Series 22, Number 9, Table 3, p. 13, US Department of Health, Education and Welfare, 1969.

conditions. There remains, however, the possibility that mortality rates are in part environmental and that the environmental component is large enough to justify the imputation we have made in this chapter. What I am suggesting is that the mortality rate, $D_j(t, Y, E, S)$ of an individual of age j, whose income is Y, whose number of years of schooling is E, and whose social class is S in the year t may be looked upon as the sum of two parts, one dependent exclusively on the state of medical knowledge and industrial technology in the year t, and the other dependent on the financial, educational or social characteristics of the individual. The assumption is that

$$D_j(t, Y, E, S) = D_j^1(t) + D_j^2(Y, E, S) \qquad (25)$$

where D^1 is determined by environmental conditions and D^2 is determined within the household. Our problem is to decide whether income, education or other characteristics of individuals have a sufficiently large effect on mortality rates and whether the average values of these characteristics have varied sufficiently from 1926 to 1974 to explain observed changes in mortality rates without recourse to a term such as $D_j^1(t)$ which decreases in the course of time.

A comparison of Table 11.5 and Chart 11.1 at the beginning of this chapter shows that the observed decline in infant mortality cannot be explained by income, education or a combination of the two, for the historical decline in infant mortality is to one-tenth of its original level while the effect, as shown in Table 11.4, of a rise in personal income greater than the increase in Canadian income per head from 1926 to 1974 is to reduce infant mortality by no more than 30%. Similarly, the increase in educational attainment of fathers from '8 years or less' to '16 years or more', an increase significantly greater than the average rise in the educational attainments of Canadians, reduces infant mortality by less than 50%.

Table 11.5 Infant deaths per 1000 live births, by education of father and family income: United States, 1944–66

	education of father					
family income	all levels	8 years or less	9–11 years	12 years	13–15 years	16 years or more
All incomes	23.0	33.0	27.4	19.0	20.6	17.4
Under $3000	32.1	36.2	34.3	28.3	26.8	9.9
$3000—$4999	25.1	33.5	27.6	21.1	20.5	19.7
$5000–$6999	18.1	26.4	22.4	15.4	16.2	14.5
$7000–$9999	19.9	29.3	22.4	17.8	22.7	17.1
$10,000 and over	19.9	—	26.9	15.3	21.4	19.5

Source: *Infant Mortality Rates: Socioeconomic Factors*, Vital and Health Statistics Series 22, Number 14, Table 2, p. 13, US Department of Health, Education and Welfare, 1972.
Note: I suspect that the figure of 9.9 in the top right-hand corner of the table is for children of graduate students, children born in university hospitals to parents whose current expenditure and whose expected income over their lives is considerably in excess of $3000.

Some interesting suggestions about possible interactions among education, income and mortality rates have emerged from cross-section studies of State-wide averages of these variables in the United States.[15]

[15] See R. Auster, I. Leveson, and D. Sarachek, 'The Production of Health', in V. Fuchs (ed.), *Essays in the Economics of Health and Medical Care*, NBER, 1972, and M. Grossman, *The Demand for Health: A Theoretical and Empirical Investigation*, Occasional Paper 119, NBER, 1972.

Age-corrected mortality rates are regressed on education, income and other variables such as alcohol consumption, cigarette consumption and the price of medical services. The coefficient for education comes out negative as one would expect, but the coefficient for income comes out positive signifying that the life expectancy of the rich is less than the life expectancy of the poor when education and other relevant variables are held constant. The authors of these studies rationalize their results as follows. Almost everything we do has some impact on mortality rates, and the effect of an activity may be to reduce them as when we visit the doctor or to increase them as when we eat or drink too much. The positive correlation between income and mortality rates can be interpreted as signifying that the activities financed by increments of income, over and above some minimal amount, are on balance detrimental to health.[16]

If we accept these studies as signifying that, other things being equal, increases in income lead to increases rather than decreases in mortality rates and if we accept the explanation put forward above, then we would have to say that the derivative of the household component of mortality rates $D_j^2(Y, E, S)$, with respect to income, Y, is positive. This opens the interesting possibility that the effect of the increase in real income in Canada from 1926 to 1974 may have been to increase $D_j^2(Y, E, S)$; the effect might even have been strong enough to outweigh the opposite influence of other variables, in which case the environmental component of observed changes in mortality rates would be larger than the changes in mortality rates themselves.[17]

The increase in real income in Canada from 1926 to 1974 may have led to a decline in mortality rates indirectly, by enabling people to buy more education, but it is exceedingly unlikely that education could account for the whole of the decline, and the evidence suggests that the environmental contribution remains substantial. First, the strong negative association between education and mortality in the American data in Table 11.4 is insufficient to explain the full reduction in mortality rates in Canada. Second, differences among people in educational attainments might be a surrogate for occupational hazards and diseases that persist through time regardless of educational attainments. For instance, age-corrected mortality rates of transportation workers (other

[16] It is hard to rule out the possibility that the positive correlation between income and mortality rates is a statistical consequence of the high correlation between the dependent variables, income and education. Regression coefficients of multicollinear dependent variables tend to have opposite signs.

[17] Note that the influence upon mortality rates of expenditure on doctors and medicine is not overlooked in these calculations because medical expenditures are an increasing function of income.

than railroads) are three times those in the workforce as a whole, while age-corrected mortality rates of salesmen in retail trade are barely more than half.[18] Third, much of the decline in mortality rates is due to the eradication of certain diseases that affect rich and poor, educated and uneducated, alike. This is particularly noticeable in diseases of childhood such as diarrhoea, meningitis, and whooping cough, but adults have benefited from reductions in mortality rates from tuberculosis, maternal diseases, influenza, bronchitis and pneumonia. On the other hand, there has been an increase in recent years in mortality rates from heart disease, lung cancer, accidents and cirrhosis of the liver.[19] Fourth, differences among people in educational attainments may be a surrogate for social traits or attributes of social classes. Edward Banfield perceives of a lower class defined largely by its failure to prepare for the future, and Oscar Lewis speaks of a culture of poverty.[20] It is at least possible that people who educate themselves are also the people who look after their health and would do so whether they were educated or not. Fifth, the imputation for changes in life expectancy may be warranted even if the decline in mortality rates is due to expenditure on education because the full benefit of education is not recorded in the national accounts. As we have no measure of the output of education and for the want of a better procedure, the convention in the national accounts is to measure real output of education as a weighted average of numbers of teachers, numbers of school buildings, etc. There is no direct evaluation of education, and no allowance for the inculcation in students of the ability to reduce their mortality rates. For all of these reasons, I feel that the environmental component of observed mortality rates is a large enough portion of the total that the bias in treating mortality rates as though they were entirely environmental need not have a significant impact on our results.

There is, of course, another sense in which education may account for all of the observed declines in mortality rates. Education may well be a prerequisite for discoveries of cures of diseases and for improvements in the organization of our society. These very real benefits of education accrue as externalities conferred on everyone in the economy, and

[18] L. Guralnick, *Mortality by Occupation and Industry among Men 20 to 64 Years of Age, United States, 1950*, Vital Statistics—Special Reports, Vol. 53, No. 2, 1962, US Department of Health, Education and Welfare, Table 2.
[19] See *Life Expectancy Trends 1930–1932 to 1960–1962*, Statistics Canada, 84–518, and A. Joanklebba, *Leading Components of Upturn in Mortality for Men*, Vital and Health Statistics, Series 20, Number 11, US Department of Health, Education and Welfare.
[20] E. Banfield, *The Unheavenly City: The Nature and Future of Our Urban Crisis*, 1970, and O. Lewis, *The Children of Sanchez*, 1962.

indeed in the world as a whole. It is precisely benefits of this sort that we have in mind when we speak of mortality rates as environmental conditions. When one is measuring economic growth as an indicator of welfare, it does not matter whether changes in environmental conditions are man-made or God-given as long as everyone in the community is affected to the same extent.

Finally, I would like to emphasize that the imputation derived in this chapter is based on some very strong assumptions about the form of the utility function. All altruism is assumed away, even the concern of parents for children; the plausible conclusion that society places a high value on the lives of children is obtained from the implausible assumption that children put high values on their own lives because they expect to live a long time. Everyone of a given age is assumed to put the same value on a decline in mortality rates despite the fact that mortality rates are private commodities for which prices need not be the same for everyone, even in a perfectly competitive economy. The form of the utility function in equation (12) is inappropriate for someone whose consumption is close to the subsistence minimum, for the sharp distinction between consumption and mortality breaks down when consumption falls from just above to just below the subsistence level. In general, longevity, consumption and utility may be related in more complex ways than we have found it necessary to postulate to construct our imputation. Obviously, the numbers we have generated in this chapter must be taken with a pinch of salt. What stands, in my opinion, is the demonstration that the benefits of increased longevity are significant by comparison with economic growth as conventionally measured. Statistics of economic growth may be seriously misleading as indicators of whether people are becoming better off in the course of time if changes in longevity are not taken into account.

APPENDIX: NOTES TO TABLES 11.1, 11.2 AND 11.3

Notes to Table 11.1

1. *Hazard Pay*
Three collective bargaining agreements in the mining industry were observed to contain premiums for working underground for 14¢, 5¢ and 3¢ per hour. These were respectively: Opemiska Copper Mines (Quebec) Ltd and Le Syndicat des Travailleurs des Mines de Chibougamou–Chapais (1965), Lake Shore Mines Ltd and International Union of Mine, Mill and Smelter Workers Local 240 (1958), and Hollinger Consolidated Gold Mines Ltd and the United Steelworkers of America Local 4305 (1961). In the United States, the risk of a fatal

accident is 0.49 per million man hours in coal mining and is 0.05 in all industries combined (*Accident Facts 1970*, published by the National Safety Council, Chicago). Suppose that half of the premium for working underground is compensation for the risk of a fatal accident and the other half is compensation for the risk of non-fatal accidents and for inconvenience, and that, in the mines to which the agreements refer, the risk of a fatal accident above ground is 0.05 per million hours and the risk of an accident underground, in mining proper, is 0.49 per million hours, so that the extra risk of working underground is 0.44. The value of life implicit in the three agreements is therefore $159,000, $57,000 and $34,000 respectively. The questionable aspects of this calculation need neither emphasis nor elaboration. Note, however, that in principle hazard pay yields a true value of life in that, like all wage rates, it reflects valuations at the margin. If the hazard pay were set too low, the miners would be disinclined to work underground and if hazard pay were set too high they would be disinclined to work above ground. A United States airforce pilot whose basic salary was $12,012 was paid a premium of $2280 for engaging in especially dangerous test flights that raised his chance of losing his life from 0.1348% to 1.695% per year. The value of life implicit in that contract was [$2280/(0.01695 − 0.00348)] $167 thousand. See J. W. Carlson, *Valuation of Life-Saving*, a Harvard Ph.D., 1963.

2. *Medical Expenditure*

These figures are based on data from H. E. Klarman, J. O'S. Francis and G. D. Rosenthal, 'Cost Effectiveness Analysis Applied to the Treatment of Chronic Renal Disease', *Medical Care*, 1968, pp. 48–54. Discounting at 6%, they find the present values of the costs of hospital dialysis, home dialysis and transplantation to be $104 thousand, $38 thousand and $44.5 thousand, and that the years gained in the three treatments are 9, 9 and 17. The figures in our table are not the costs of the treatments but the implications of these numbers about the value of the life of an average man of 30 years of age whose life expectancy in 1961 is 45 years. The value of life of a 30-year old man that would make hospital dialysis, for instance, a marginal life saving expenditure is $104 × 18/7 thousand, where 18 and 7 are the approximate discounted life expectancies at 5% of 45 and 9 years of life.

In principle, all of these medical estimates may reflect intramarginal situations in that many people who have to pay their full share of the extra taxes required to finance these treatments would willingly vote to have these treatments made available for everyone even if the treatments were more expensive than they are now. Nevertheless, one gets the impression from the literature that the cost of hospital dialysis is, if anything, extramarginal in that the expenditure on hospital dialysis is often said to be more than society 'can afford'.

3. *Valuation of the Cost of Disease*

The source of this estimate is Dorothy P. Rice, *Estimating the Cost of Illness*, Health Economics Series, Number 6, US Department of Health, Education and Welfare, 1966, p. 93. The figure in Table 11.1 is an average of the discounted earnings of a man and a woman age 25–29 when the discount rate is 6%. For reasons discussed at the outset of this chapter, I believe that this type of calculation is inappropriate in principle for determining the value of life. I include it together with the valuation of loss of life in airplane accidents, because endorsement of this calculation by the US Government puts a certain weight on the estimate of the value of life independently of the validity of the method by which the estimate is arrived at, and signifies that the estimate itself is deemed reasonable.

4. *Valuation of the Cost of Airplane Accidents*

Gary Fromm has measured the cost of a fatality in an air crash as the present value of the lifetime earnings of the typical passenger ('Civil Aviation Expenditure' in R. Dorfman (ed.), *Measuring Benefits of Government Investments*, Brookings Institution, 1965). Assuming the average age of a passenger to be 40 years, and setting the discount rate at 6%, he estimates the cost per fatality in 1960 to be $373,000. We increase this number to $472,000 in Table 11.1 to approximate the present value of the earnings of an airline passenger whose income is typical of incomes of all airline passengers but who is only 30 years of age. Fromm thinks of his calculation as representing a lower limit to the true value of life. Leaving aside the question of the suitability of the present value of earnings calculation for evaluating the cost of loss of life, the contrast between Fromm's estimate of the value of life of an airline passenger who tends to be rich and Mrs Rice's estimate of the value of life of an average American, raises the interesting issue of whether a public decision-maker ought to accept private valuations in cost–benefit analysis where life saving is one of the benefits or costs. In accepting private valuation as a criterion for the public sector, the decision-maker is compelled to follow Fromm's procedure in placing a higher value on the saving of a life of a rich man than on the saving of the life of a poor man. And if this is the appropriate procedure in evaluating the cost of airplane accidents, ought it not also to be appropriate in deciding whether or not to undertake medical expenditure? The logic of this position would lead the national health service to supply dialysis to rich people but not to poor people because only the rich would have been prepared to bear the cost of insurance for dialysis or the cost of dialysis itself in the absence of the national health service. In general, the logic of this position would lead the national health to supply better medical care of all kinds to the rich than to the poor because the rich place a higher marginal valuation on any given standard of health care. Something is clearly wrong with this analysis. I think the source of the problem is that there is an inherent conflict in public sector decision-making between the principle that each dollar of benefit ought to be counted as equal to every other dollar of benefit 'to whomsoever the benefits may accrue' and the principle that all men should be treated equally in their dealings with the public sector. We tend to apply the former principle to road-building and the latter principle to civil rights and public provision of medical care. The principles conflict in the evaluation of the cost of loss of life in accidents. Fromm is inclined to draw the line between the two principles in such a way that accidents are covered by the 'to whomsoever the benefits may accrue' rule, while others, myself included, would be inclined to classify expenditures to prevent accidents together with medical expenditures.

5. *Traffic Safety*
A figure of $37,500 was recommended as the value of life for cost–benefit analysis of traffic safety by J. L. Recht, *How to Do a Cost/Benefit Analysis of Motor Vehicle Accidents*, National Safety Council, September 1966. This figure also seems to have been arrived at by discounting somebody's lifetime earnings. The figure of $100 thousand is presented, without justification or explanation other than that it is alleged to be customary, in a study conducted for the National Highway Safety Bureau of the US Department of Highways, No. FN-11-6495.

6. *Military Decision-Making*
The pilot of an F-86L jet fighter plane occasionally finds himself in a position where he might either eject himself from the plane allowing it to crash or attempt a landing. Instructions to a pilot as to when to eject himself from the airplane imply a value of life of *at least* $270 thousand, when consideration is given to his probability of survival if he abandons the plane, to his probability of survival if he tries to land the plane, to the cost of the plane, to probability of losing it in the event of an attempted landing, and to the damage that might be caused by a crashing plane. This figure is not very instructive because the cost of training a pilot for an F-87L jet is $300 thousand. J. W. Carlson, *Valuation of Life-Saving*, Harvard, Ph.D., 1963. Carlson also cited a case in which the air force

spent $9 million designing and producing an ejector seat which would save between 1 and 3 lives.

7. *Valuation of Risk in Occupational Choice*

The value of life can be computed from a cross-section of wages in many occupations. Wages are regressed on risk of losing one's life and many other job characteristics. The coefficient of risk in such a regression is the value of avoiding a small chance of losing one's life. The value of life was estimated this way in R. Thaler and S. Rosen, 'Value of Saving a Life: Evidence from the Labour Market', in N. E. Terleckyj (ed.), *Household Production and Consumption*, Studies in Income and Wealth, Volume 40, NBER, 1976, pp. 265–302.

Table 11.1 is a collection of numbers which are not obviously intramarginal. In my cursory examination of cost–benefit analysis in circumstances where the lengthening of lives is one of the benefits, I encountered many examples of projects which had to be intramarginal in the sense that no rational decision-maker could refuse to undertake such projects when the possibility of doing so is recognized. For instance, G. Torrance (*A Generalized Cost-Effectiveness Model for the Evaluation of Health Programs*, Faculty of Business, McMaster University, Research Series No. 101) found that the cost per newborn child saved in a programme of preventing haemolytic disease was $932.00. I would hope that this fact conveys no information about the value of life.

Notes to Table 11.2

The term $Y(t)$ is real national income defined, as discussed in Chapter 5, as the sum of personal consumption, government consumption and saving deflated by the price index for personal consumption and expressed in 1961 dollars.

Time series of age-specific mortality rates (for the first year of life, for the next four years, and for five-year intervals thereafter up to age 84, and with a final category of age 85 and above) were obtained from various issues of *Vital Statistics*, Statistics Canada, 84-001. Annual mortality rates were constructed on the assumptions that the rate for any grouping of ages applies equally to all ages within that group and that 90 years is the maximum length of life. These annual mortality rates do not correspond exactly to the terms D_j because of the special assumption that all deaths occurring in any year are concentrated on the first day. Consequently, the estimate of L differs slightly from the formula in equation (21). In the calculations leading to Table 11.2, the discounted life expectancy of a man who is now j years is measured as

$$L_j = \sum_{i=j}^{90-j} \frac{\prod_{k=j}^{i-1}(1-\bar{D}_k)(1-\bar{D}_i/2)}{(1+r)^{i-j}}$$

where the $\bar{D}_j$ are age-specific mortality rates obtained from vital statistics data. The numerator in the fraction is the sum of the probability of a man of age j completing at least $i - j$ man years of life $\prod_{k=j}^{i-1}(1 - \bar{D}_k)$ and half the probability of his dying $i - j$ years from now $\prod_{k=j}^{i-1}(1 - \bar{D}_k)\bar{D}_i/2$. The factor 2 is included in the expression above because a man who will die i years from now has an expectation of remaining alive for half of that year.

The term $L(t)$ in equation (22) is estimated as

$$L(t) = \frac{\sum_{j=0}^{89} P_j(61)L_j(t)}{\sum_{j=0}^{89} P_j(61)}$$

where $L_j(t)$ is the value of L_j in the year t and $P_j(61)$ is the Canadian population of age j in the year 1961.

Notes to Table 11.3

The principal sources of data were various issues of the UN *Yearbook of National Accounts Statistics*, the UN *Demographic Yearbook*, and *IMF Financial Statistics, 1976*. These sources were supplemented by: (a) for Chile, M. Mamalakis and C. W. Reynolds, *Essays on the Chilean Economy*, Irwin, 1965, statistical appendix; (b) for France, Annuaire Statistique de la France 1966, C. Kindelberger, *Economic Growth in France and Britain 1851–1950*, and *Long-Term Economic Growth 1860–1965*, US Department of Commerce, 1966; (c) for Japan, Kochi Emi, *Government Fiscal Activity and Economic Growth in Japan 1860–1960*, Kimokuniya (Tokyo 1963) and OECD, *Main Economic Indicators 1955–1971*; (d) for Singapore, H. T. Oshima, 'Growth and Unemployment in Singapore', *Malaysian Economic Review*, 1967, pp. 32–58; (e) for Sri Lanka, *Statistical Abstracts of Ceylon*, various issues; (f) for Thailand, J. C. Ingram, *Economic Change in Thailand 1850–1970*, Stanford University Press, 1971; and (g) for the United States, *Statistical Yearbook of the League of Nations*, 1938/39, and *Economic Report of the President*, 1974.

Gross national expenditure was used instead of net national expenditure to represent $C(t)$ because the information on the latter is frequently unavailable. As with the Canadian data, mortality rates in five-year intervals had to be attributed to each year separately, but in addition some even larger time intervals had to be dealt with, and the groupings of ages were not always consistent from year to year. The higher age groups were particularly troublesome. Two methods were used to derive mortality rates in five-year intervals from data on mortality rates in ten or fifteen-year intervals. If data were available for five-year intervals in another year, I would normally assume proportionality between mortality rates in the five-year intervals in the two years. Otherwise mortality rates in intervals longer than five years would be attributed to each year in the interval. The maximum age was assumed to be 90. Sometimes when the final open-ended time interval (intervals such as 'mortality rates for people over 70 years of age') began well short of age 85, mortality rates in five-year intervals were estimated by postulating that they rose in a systematic manner consistent with available data on population and mortality rates in the larger time intervals.

12

No Technical Change, No Growth

How important is technical change as a cause of economic growth?

This question has been central to the study of economic history, economic development, and growth theory *per se* ever since the revival of interest in economic growth at the end of the Second World War. For about ten years immediately after the war, the study of economic growth and the art of economic planning were dominated by Harrod–Domar models with constant capital–output ratios and no place for technical change at all.[1] Then in the mid-1950s the pendulum swung completely in the opposite direction as a number of studies, notably those of Abramovitz and Solow,[2] seemed to demonstrate that augmentation of factors of production could account for no more than a small part of observed economic growth, leaving a large unexplained residual—Solow put it at 9/10—that has to be attributed to something like technical change. The pendulum did not stay here long. It swung back toward factor augmentation and away from technical change as Denison adjusted the measure of the input of labour to account for the gradual improvement in the education of the labour force and added a large contribution for economies of scale,[3] and Jorgenson and Griliches revised the definition of capital and made more complete use of Divisia index formulae than had been done before.[4] Recently, the situation has become confused with some authors claiming that the whole problem is misconceived because capital cannot be measured in real

---

[1] A representative example of this type of analysis is 'Trends in Investment Policies in the Nineteen Fifties', *World Economic Report, 1959*, UN (E/3361), an attempt to explain differences in rates of growth among countries by shares of investment in GNP and marginal capital output ratios.

[2] M. Abramovitz, 'Resource and Output Trends in the United States since 1870', *American Economic Review*, 1956, Papers and Proceedings, pp. 5–23, and R. M. Solow, 'Technical Change and the Aggregate Production Function', *Review of Economics and Statistics*, 1957, pp. 312–20.

[3] E. F. Denison, *The Sources of Economic Growth and the Alternatives before Us*, 1962, *Why the Growth Rates Differ*, 1967, and *Accounting for United States Economic Growth*, 1974.

[4] D. W. Jorgenson and Z. Griliches, 'The Explanation of Productivity Change', *Review of Economic Studies*, 1967, pp. 249–83.

terms,[5] others claiming that the attribution of techical change as an explanation of economic growth is simply a failure on the part of economists to specify factors completely,[6] others revising the definition of technical change,[7] and with a large, and still unresolved, disagreement between the two main authorities in the field.[8] A new study incorporating the broadest definitions of income and capital to date has succeeded in explaining a large part of observed economic growth by capital formation, but the role of technical change has not been eliminated altogether.[9]

Though our main concern in this book is with the measurement of economic growth regardless of why it has occurred, our discussion of quality change in Chapter 8, our examination of the Divisia index in Chapter 9, and, especially, our insistence in Chapter 5 that real income has to be defined within the context of a general equilibrium model, however simple, have implications about the explanation of economic growth. It seems worth spelling out these implications because the matter is important for the formation of economic policy. Recommendations to promote economic growth are conditioned by views about the causes of growth. Someone who believes that growth is primarily the outcome of technical change tends to emphasize research, higher education, and the fostering of entrepreneurial talent as ways of stimulating growth. Someone who believes that growth is primarily the outcome of investment tends to emphasize the acquisition of capital goods.

In this chapter I shall try to uphold what would to most economists be considered an extreme view of the matter. I shall argue that with one important qualification economic growth is entirely technological in origin, that without technical change there would be no economic growth at all, and that—as an accounting identity—the rate of economic growth is equal in the long run to the rate of (labour-embodied) technical change. I shall argue that these propositions are obvious,

[5] T. K. Rymes, 'The Measurement of Capital and Total Factor Productivity in the Context of the Cambridge Theory of Capital', *Review of Income and Wealth*, 1972, pp. 69–109.

[6] S. Star, 'Accounting for the Growth of Output', *American Economic Review*, 1975, pp. 956–65.

[7] C. R. Hulton, 'Technical Change and the Reproducibility of Capital', *American Economic Review*, 1975, pp. 956–65.

[8] E. F. Denison, 'Some Major Issues in Productivity Analysis: An Examination of Estimates by Jorgenson and Griliches', *Survey of Current Business*, May 1969. Jorgenson and Griliches reply to Denison's critique, but their differences are not resolved.

[9] J. W. Kendrick, *The Formation and Stocks of Total Capital*, National Bureau of Economic Research, 1976.

almost trivial, and that the source of confusion on this issue—the reason why economists have been unable to agree about the role of technical change in economic growth—is not ultimately empirical, or even economic, but linguistic. We dispute about the answer because we have posed the question imprecisely. I shall try to show that when we do pose the question precisely and construct a model to reflect the question we have posed, the answer will come easily, almost without reference to the data.

We begin by examining three important studies of aggregate technical change in the United States. We consider certain statistical problems in these studies, notably that the use of the Divisia index can be a source of bias and that the nature of the inputs may be changing over time. Then we try to specify precisely the sense in which it can be said that technical change explains this or that percentage of observed economic growth, and we construct a model within which it is easily shown that technical change is a prerequisite to economic growth in the long run. Finally, we use the Canadian data to show that only a small portion of observed economic growth since 1926 could have taken place in the absence of technical change and that the rates of economic growth and technical change are approximately the same.

A. THREE STUDIES OF AGGREGATE TECHNICAL CHANGE

The three most innovative and influential studies of the role of technical change in economic growth—the studies by Solow, by Denison, and by Jorgenson and Griliches—have in common that they are, or may be looked upon as being, attempts to measure technical change as a property of a self-contained production function. They postulate a production function

$$y = f(x, t) \tag{1}$$

where y is output and x is a vector of inputs, and where the inclusion of the argument t signifies that the form of the production function is changing over time. The essence of the problem is to utilize the time series of x and y, together with assumptions about the general form of f, to infer how y would change if x did not. The rate of technical change λ between the year 0 and the year T may be defined indirectly in the equation

$$e^{\lambda T} = f(x^0, T)/f(x^0, 0) \tag{2}$$

where x^0 is the value of x in the year 0. The rate of technical change is the rate at which output would have increased between the year 0 and the year T if technology changed over the period as it was observed to do, but factor inputs remained the same. The three studies differ in the nature of the inputs accounted for and in the specification of the aggregate production function.

The earliest and simplest of these studies is that of Solow who estimated the rate of technical change year by year from the time series of real gross national product, man-hours and capital in accordance with the formula[10]

$$\mathrm{TC} = G_q - \nu_K G_k \tag{3}$$

where TC is the rate of technical change, the symbol G means 'the growth rate of' (so that for any x, G_x means $1/x \; dx/dt$), G_q is the growth rate of output per man-hour, G_k is the growth rate of capital per man-hour, ν_K is capital's share of income, and the instantaneous growth rates in equation (3) are estimated from incremental percentage differences in the time series. Solow's result was striking. Of the total increase in private non-farm real gross national product per man-hour between 1909 and 1949 of 104.6%, only 14.7% could be explained by capital formation, the remaining 85.3% being attributable by definition to technical change.

As it turned out, however, Solow's findings were not sustained by subsequent and more sophisticated analyses of the problem. Solow

---

[10] If the production function is $Q = f(K, L, t)$, then

$$\frac{\dot{Q}}{Q} = \left(\frac{f_K K}{Q}\right)\frac{\dot{K}}{K} + \frac{f_L L}{Q}\frac{\dot{L}}{L} + \frac{1}{Q}\frac{\partial Q}{\partial t}$$

from which it follows that

$$\frac{\dot{Q}}{Q} - \frac{\dot{L}}{L} = \frac{f_K K}{Q}\left(\frac{\dot{K}}{K} - \frac{\dot{L}}{L}\right) + \frac{1}{Q}\frac{\partial Q}{\partial t}$$

if there is constant returns to scale in L and K in the production function, that is, if $Q = f_K K + f_L L$. Equation (3) follows immediately when we define

$$\nu_K \equiv \frac{f_K K}{Q}, \quad G_q \equiv \frac{\dot{Q}}{Q} - \frac{\dot{L}}{L}, \quad G_k \equiv \frac{\dot{K}}{K} - \frac{\dot{L}}{L}, \quad \text{and} \quad \mathrm{TC} = \frac{1}{Q}\left(\frac{\partial Q}{\partial t}\right)$$

R. M. Solow, 'Technical Change and the Aggregate Production Function', *Review of Economics and Statistics*, 1957, pp. 312–20. In discussing Solow's data, I incorporate the correction by W. P. Hogan in the *Review of Economics and Statistics* (pp. 407–11) the following year.

himself considered his results to be rough and preliminary, and explicitly stated that they could be improved by replacing the labour and capital aggregates by 'many precisely defined inputs' and by adjusting for 'improvement in the quality of the labour input'. These modifications and others were incorporated into E. F. Denison's *The Sources of Economic Growth in the United States and the Alternatives before Us* (Committee for Economic Development, 1962). Denison's major adjustments to the data as utilized by Solow were for the effect of shorter hours on the quality of work per hour, for education, for improved utilization of women workers, and for changes in the age and sex composition of the labour force. Denison also subdivided the total capital stock into land and five separate categories of capital, aggregated growth rates of the different categories according to factor shares, and adjusted the weights every five years. Denison's main results are summarized in Table 12.1. As to the role of capital, Denison's findings are in broad agreement with those of Solow. Only 0.25% out of a total of 1.44% growth rate of real national income per person employed over the years 1909 to 1957 can be attributed to the growth of capital

Table 12.1 Sources of the growth rate of real national income per person employed

	percentage points in growth rate		
	1909–29	1926–57	1909–57
real national income per person employed	*1.22*	*1.60*	*1.44*
increase in total inputs per			
person employed	*0.75*	*0.78*	*0.77*
labour, adjusted for quality change	*0.49*	*0.66*	*0.59*
effect of shorter hours on			
quality of a man-year's work	0.02	−0.17	−0.09
annual hours	−0.23	−0.53	−0.41
effect of shorter hours on			
quality of a man-hour's work	0.25	0.36	0.32
education	0.39	0.72	0.58
increased experience and better			
utilization of women workers	0.07	0.12	0.10
changes in age–sex composition			
of the labour force	0.01	−0.01	0.00
land	*−0.11*	*−0.05*	*−0.07*
capital	*0.37*	*0.17*	*0.25*
non-farm residential structures	0.07	0.01	0.03
other structures and equipment	0.19	0.12	0.15
inventories	0.08	0.03	0.06
US-owned assets abroad	0.02	0.01	0.01
foreign assets in US	0.01	0.00	0.00
increase in output per unit of input	*0.47*	*0.82*	*0.67*

Source: E. F. Denison, *The Sources of Economic Growth in the United States and the Alternatives before Us*, Table 20, p. 149.

inclusive of land. But of the remaining 1.26%, only 0.67% is attributed to the increase in output per unit of input, with most of the balance attributed to an improvement in the quality of the labour force through education.

Denison incorporated education as a factor of production by augmenting the measure of the labour input in accordance with the increase in earnings attributable to the increase in educational attainment. If an educated person earns twice the wage of an uneducated person, if the labour force in the year 0 consists of four uneducated people and one educated person, and if the labour force in the year 1 consists of two uneducated people and two educated people then the labour force as assessed by Solow would decrease by $\frac{1}{5}$, $\{[(2 + 2)/(4 + 1)] - 1\}$, while the labour force as assessed by Denison would remain constant, $\{[(2 + (2 \times 2))/(4 + (1 \times 2))] - 1\}$. If output per head also remained constant, Solow would impute $\frac{1}{5}$ to technical change while Denison would observe no technical change at all. Actually, Denison would have scaled down the labour force slightly in this example by assuming that part of the difference in earnings between educated and uneducated people is due to the greater innate ability of those people society chooses to educate. Denison's method of accounting for education amounts in the end to treating workers with different educational attainments as separate factors of production. Growth rates of numbers of workers in the different educational categories were aggregated into an index of the growth rate of the labour input as a whole according to their shares of total labour income. Ideally, weights in the index should be adjusted annually, but Denison used weights based on the 1949 wage structure because 1949 was the only year for which the data were available.

The importance of technical change was reduced still further by the work of Jorgenson and Griliches[11] which advanced the study of the sources of economic growth in several respects: Jorgenson and Griliches took great care to define technical change as a parameter in a production function connecting observable data of inputs and outputs in the economy as a whole. Extending Solow's model of equation (3), they postulated a production possibility curve of the form

$$f(y_1, y_2, \ldots, y_m; x_1, x_2, \ldots, x_n; t) = 0 \qquad (4)$$

where $\partial f/\partial y_i \geq 0$ and $\partial f/\partial x_j \leq 0$ for all i and all j, y_i are outputs which may be consumption goods or new capital goods, x_j are inputs of capital

---

[11] D. W. Jorgenson and Z. Griliches, 'The Explanation of Productivity Change', *Review of Economic Studies*, 1967, pp. 249–83.

and labour, t is time, and f is homogeneous in degree 0, in all y_i and all x_j so that

$$\sum_{i=1}^{m} \left(\frac{\partial f}{\partial y_i}\right) y_i = \sum_{j=1}^{n} \left(-\frac{\partial f}{\partial x_j}\right) x_j \tag{5}$$

It is assumed that relative prices of goods reflect rates of transformation in production, that relative prices of factors reflect rates of substitution in use and that each factor in each use is paid the value of its marginal product:

$$-\frac{\partial y_i}{\partial y_k} = \frac{\partial f/\partial y_k}{\partial f/\partial y_i} = \frac{q_k}{q_i} \tag{6}$$

$$-\frac{\partial x_j}{\partial x_k} = \frac{\partial f/\partial x_k}{\partial f/\partial x_j} = \frac{p_k}{p_j} \tag{7}$$

$$\frac{\partial y_i}{\partial x_j} = \frac{-\partial f/\partial x_i}{\partial f/\partial y_j} = \frac{p_j}{q_i} \tag{8}$$

where q_i is the price of the output i and p_j is the price of the input j.

In the light of equations (6), (7) and (8), equation (5) becomes

$$\sum_{i=1}^{m} q_i y_i = \sum_{j=1}^{n} p_j x_j \equiv N \tag{5'}$$

which is simply that national expenditure is equal to national income; their common value is designated as N.

Technical change is now defined as the rate of growth of output per unit of input. Differentiating equation (4), we see that the rate of technical change turns out to be a Divisia index

$$TC \equiv \sum_{i=1}^{m} w_i \left(\frac{\dot{y}_i}{y_i}\right) - \sum_{j=1}^{n} v_j \left(\frac{\dot{x}_j}{x_j}\right) = \frac{1}{N}\left(\frac{\partial N}{\partial t}\right) \tag{9}$$

where $\partial N/\partial t$ is the rate of increase in national expenditure that would occur if all prices and all inputs remained constant, w_i is the share in national expenditure of the i output, v_j is the share in national income of the j input, and all terms in equation (9) are function of time.[12]

[12] From equations (6), (7) and (8), it follows that there is a parameter γ such that $\partial f/\partial y_i = \gamma q_i$ and $\partial f/\partial x_j = -\gamma p_j$. Differentiating f with respect to t, we get

$$\sum_i \frac{\partial f}{\partial y_i} y_i + \sum_j \frac{\partial f}{\partial x_j} x_j + \frac{\partial f}{\partial t} = 0 \tag{i}$$

All of the studies we have been considering agree in treating technical change as the growth of output per unit of input. The Jorgenson–Griliches formula of equation (9) makes this explicit and has the advantage over equation (3) that it would allow technical change to be measured as a function of growth rates of particular outputs and particular inputs without prior aggregation, if sufficiently disaggregated data were at hand.

In using equation (9) to measure aggregate technical change, it is necessary to maintain the distinctions between stocks and flows, and between stock prices and flow prices. The same variety of capital may enter twice into the equation, once as input and again as output. For instance, the number of tractors produced this year may be represented by the term y_k and the corresponding q_k would be the retail price of new tractors; the services rendered this year by the stock of new and old tractors combined may be represented by the term x_j and the corresponding p_j is not the market price of a tractor but the imputed rent per year of a unit of tractor services. A rule is derived that permits one to infer p_j from q_k, $\dot{q}_k$, the rate of interest, and the rate of depreciation of tractors. Special care is taken with price deflators for capital goods. Jorgenson and Griliches allege that the growth of the stock of highways, for instance, is underestimated because the value of investment in highways each year is deflated by a price index of inputs to highways—tar, gravel, labour—when it ought to be deflated by a price index of completed highways. The growth of the stock of highways is underestimated by this procedure if engineers are gradually learning to reduce the input of resources required per mile of a given quality of highway.

The calculations of Jorgenson and Griliches are summarized in Table 12.2. Their main result is the exact opposite of Solow's: of the 3.59% growth of output between 1945 and 1965, 3.47% can be explained by growth of input, and only 0.10% remains to be explained by technical change. They dramatize this result by commencing their calculation with

---

from which it follows that

$$\sum_i w_i \frac{\dot{y}_i}{y_i} - \sum_j v_j \frac{\dot{x}_j}{x_j} + \frac{1}{\gamma N} \frac{\partial f}{\partial t} = 0 \qquad \text{(ii)}$$

where $w_i = q_i y_i / N$ and $v_j = p_j x_j / N$. If t increases but all x_j remain constant, then

$$\frac{\partial f}{\partial t} = -\sum_i \frac{\partial f}{\partial y_i} \frac{dy_i}{dt} = \gamma \sum_i \frac{d}{dt}(q_i y_i) = \gamma \frac{dN}{dt} \qquad \text{(iii)}$$

for given values of q_i. Equation (9) follows immediately from equations (ii) and (iii).

Table 12.2   Total output, input and factor productivity in US private domestic economy 1945–1965: average annual rates of growth

	output	input	productivity
(1) initial estimates	3.49	1.83	1.60
estimates after correction for:			
(2) errors of aggregation	3.39	1.84	1.49
(3) errors in investment good prices	3.59	2.19	1.41
(4) errors in relative utilization	3.59	2.57	0.96
(5) errors in aggregation of capital services	3.59	2.97	0.58
(6) errors in aggregation of labour services	3.59	3.47	0.10

Table IX, D. Jorgenson and Z. Griliches, 'The Explanation of Productivity Change', *Review of Economic Studies*, 1967, pp. 249–83.

inappropriate time series of output, labour and capital, inappropriately combined to suggest that almost half of observed growth of output, 1.60%, must be attributed to technical change. Then by successively correcting for 'errors', they gradually reduce the residual until only 0.10% is left.

The meanings of the expressions in Table 12.2 are as follows:

(1) 'Initial estimates' of output, labour and capital are real US private domestic product, the number of workers employed and real capital stock estimated by the perpetual inventory method in which

$$K_{t+1} = K_t(1 - \delta_t) + I_t$$

where K, I and δ are real capital, real investment and the rate of depreciation.

(2) 'Errors of aggregation' refers to the effects on output, input and productivity of not weighting components of output, labour and capital by the Divisia Index.

(3) 'Errors in investment goods prices' arise from deflating investment by price indexes of inputs in the construction of capital goods rather than by price indexes of capital goods themselves.

(4) 'Errors in relative utilization' refers to the effects of ignoring changes over time in the intensity of usage of the existing stock of labour and capital as influenced by the decision to work fewer hours per week as real income increases, by involuntary unemployment of labour and capital, and by improvements in technique or organization enabling firms to use machines for more hours per year.

(5) 'Errors in aggregation of capital services' refers to the bias from weighting of capital goods in accordance with stock prices instead of service prices.

(6) 'Errors in aggregation of labour services' refers to the bias from

not weighting of numbers of men employed in accordance with their educational attainments in the manner described above in connection with Denison's calculations.

B. A CRITIQUE OF THE CONCEPT OF TECHNICAL CHANGE AS THE RATE OF GROWTH OF OUTPUT PER UNIT OF INPUT

The measure of technical change we are examining is that represented by the formula of Jorgenson and Griliches in equation (9),

$$\text{TC} = \sum_{i=1}^{m} w_i \left(\frac{\dot{y}_i}{y_i} \right) - \sum_{j=1}^{n} y_j \left(\frac{\dot{x}_j}{x_j} \right) = \frac{1}{N} \left(\frac{\partial N}{\partial t} \right) \tag{9}$$

where outputs y_i and inputs x_j are as disaggregated as the data allow and where rates of change $(\dot{y}_i/y_i)$ and $(\dot{x}_j/x_j)$ are approximated by percentage differences in time series. We discuss three aspects of this measure. First, we deal with the general question of whether the Divisia index is suitable for measuring technical change. Then, we question the assumption, implicit in all of these studies, that the nature of the inputs remains the same throughout the period spanned by the time series. And, finally, we consider problems arising from the fact that capital goods appear both as inputs and as outputs in equation (9).

(i) *The use of the Divisia Index*

The possibility of bias in this index can best be examined in a simple case. Suppose output is produced with two types of labour in accordance with the production function

$$y = f(x_1, x_2, t) \tag{10}$$

where y is output, x_1 is hours of uneducated labour, x_2 is hours of educated labour, and t is included as an argument in the production function to signify that f is a sequence of production functions which differ in form from year to year. In any year t, the production function is assumed to be homogeneous in degree 1 in x_1 and x_2, but technical change may alter the form of the production function from one year to the next. The production function may be illustrated on an isoquant diagram such as that in Figure 12.1 in which the vertical axis shows numbers of uneducated men, the horizontal axis shows numbers of educated men, the curved lines are isoquants for the year 0, and technical change consists of an inward shift of the unit isoquant.

As pointed out in Chapter 9 in connection with the index of real consumption, the Divisia index can be thought of as a means of correcting for the normal bias in the Laspeyres quantity index. Denison's method was to measure technical change as the increase in y/x where y is output, x is a Laspeyres index of inputs

$$x = x_1 + w^0 x_2 \qquad (11)$$

and w^0 is the relative wage of educated and uneducated labour in the base year. The bias in Denison's method is illustrated in Figure 12.1 for the example discussed above. Suppose that in the year 0, a unit of output is produced by the combined efforts of 4 uneducated men and 1 educated

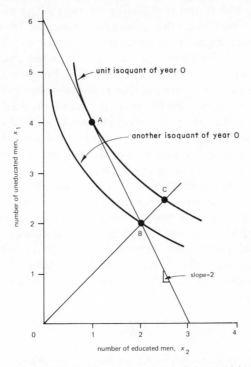

Figure 12.1 The bias in the Laspeyres measure of the total input of labour

man, and the relative wage of educated and uneducated labour is 2. This combination of x_1 and x_2 is indicated by the point A, the corresponding value of x according to equation (11) is 6 units of labour, and the locus of all combinations of educated and uneducated labour yielding 6 units of labour is the straight line through A of slope 2. In the year 1, a unit of output is produced by 2 uneducated men and 2 educated men as indicated by the point B. If we follow Denison's method, we are obliged to say that there has been no technical change, for the combination of 4 uneducated men and 1 educated man and the combination of 2 uneducated men and 2 educated men are both counted as 6 units of labour in equation (11) when the relative wage is 2, so that output per unit of aggregate input is the same in the two years.

On the other hand, it is evident that the mix of inputs available in the year 1 would not be sufficient to produce a unit of output in the year 0 because the isoquant through the point A lies above the point B. Some technical change must have occurred between the year 0 and the year 1 to enable inputs of labour in the year 1 to produce what they did. The rate of technical change can be assessed as a relation between the isoquants through A and B reflecting the technology of the year 0. As we have assumed that the production function in the year 0 is homogeneous in degree 1, the isoquants are necessarily homothetic and the measure of the reduction in real input from the year 0 to year 1 is CB/OB. As inputs of labour represented by the points A and B are requirements per unit of output, the measure of the increase in output per unit of input is CB/OB as well. These measures are entirely consistent with the rate of technical change as defined in equation (2) above. Only if C and B coincide, as would be the case if the elasticity of substitution between grades of labour were infinite, would the true measure of output per unit of input remain constant from year 0 to year 1. Otherwise, Denison's method of correcting the measure of labour input for the educational composition of the labour force overstates the increase in real input as assessed in relation to the set of base year isoquants, and understates the rate of technical change.

It is to avoid this bias that Jorgenson and Griliches insist on weighting inputs in accordance with the Divisia index of equation (9). In the simple case we are considering, the Divisia index of total labour input is defined by the equation

$$\frac{d}{dt}(\ln x(t)) = \sum_{i=1}^{2} v_i(t) \frac{d}{dt}(\ln x_i(t)) \tag{12}$$

where $v_i(t)$ is the factor share of the ith type of labour

$$v_i(t) \equiv \frac{w_1(t)x_i(t)}{\sum_{j=1}^{2} w_j(t)x_j(t)} \tag{13}$$

and $w_i(t)$ is the wage of the ith type of labour at time t. The rate of aggregate technical change, r, is defined as the growth rate of y/x

$$e^{rT} \equiv \frac{y(T)/x(T)}{y(0)/x(0)} \tag{14}$$

where x is now a Divisia index of total factor input. The Divisia index is correct in this context if and only if the rate of technical change r in equation (14) is equal to the rate λ, as defined in equation (2).

It is not difficult to construct a case in which these two rates are equal. Suppose technical change is Hicks neutral so that

$$y = f(x_1, x_2, t) = A(t)x(x_1, x_2) \tag{15}$$

and the function x, which may be thought of as the input of labour, is homogeneous in degree 1 and invariant over time. Suppose also that the wage of each type of labour in each year is equal to the value of the marginal product of labour

$$w_i(t) = p(t)\frac{\partial y(t)}{\partial x_i(t)} = p(t)A(t)\frac{\partial x(t)}{\partial x_i(t)} \tag{16}$$

where $p(t)$ is the price of output in the year t. In this case, the relative wage w_2/w_1 is dependent on the relative availability of the two types of labour x_2/x_1, and the form of the dependence is the same from year to year and regardless of how much output is produced. These are precisely the conditions, as stated in Chapter 9, under which the Divisia index is accurate. It follows, therefore, that the ideal measure λ of equation (2) and the measure r got when x_1 and x_2 are combined in a Divisia are necessarily the same.

In justifying their use of Divisia index, Jorgenson and Griliches state that 'if price ratios are identified with marginal rates of transformation of a production function with constant returns to scale, the index will remain constant if the shift in the production function is zero.'[13] This proposition is correct as we have shown, but it is not strong enough to guarantee that the Divisia index supplies an automatic correction for the bias in Denison's method. The impression that the Divisia index is in some sense ideal for productivity measurement is created by a confusion between necessary and sufficient conditions. While adherence of prices and quantities to an isoquant is sufficient to maintain a Divisia index constant, the constancy of the Divisia index is no guarantee that prices and quantities conform to an isoquant, and the Divisia index may perform very badly if the function it is intended to represent is changing its shape in the course of time.

In particular suppose technical change is not Hicks neutral. The function f in equation (10) is homogeneous in degree 1 in the inputs

[13] D. Jorgenson and Z. Griliches, 'The Explanation of Productivity Change', *Review of Economic Studies*, 1967, p. 253.

$x_1(t)$, $x_2(t)$ and would be correctly represented by a Divisia index if observed wages each year reflect first derivatives of the function f, that is, if

$$w_i(t) = \lambda(t)\frac{\partial}{\partial x_i(t)} f(x_1(t), x_2(t), 0) \tag{17}$$

But this equation is not satisfied. What actually happens is that relative wages reflect marginal products of labour in the production function of the *technology of the year t*ₒ

$$w_i(t) = \lambda(t)\frac{\partial}{\partial x_i(t)} f(x_1(t), x_2(t), t) \tag{18}$$

in which case none of the nice properties of the Divisia index can be expected to hold.[14]

This possibility of bias in the Divisia index of total labour input is illustrated with the aid of Figure 12.2 which reproduces the unit isoquant of the year 0 from Figure 12.1. It is convenient to think of the unit isoquant as gradually shifting from the unbroken curve at A to the broken curve at B in such a way as to remain tangent at all times to the chord AB, and we may suppose that the relative price of educated and uneducated labour remains constant throughout this process. The Divisia index shows no change from year 0 to year 1 because it does not 'know' that total labour input assessed with regard to the original set of isoquants has decreased, and it 'thinks' that the isoquant is the chord AB itself. This is an instance where the Divisia index is no better than the Laspeyres index Denison used. A further clockwise rotation of the isoquant at B could make the Divisia index worse. One might question the significance of this example on the ground that the passage from the isoquant through A to the isoquant through B could equally well be technical progress or retrogression depending on the starting point. Starting from A, it is progress but starting from B, it is retrogression. The cases are not symmetric with respect to time. If the proportion of educated labour is to be increased between year 0 and year 1, come what may, the shift in the isoquants is unambiguously beneficial in forestalling the decline that would otherwise have occurred in the marginal product of the factor of production that is becoming relatively more abundant.

[14] The bias that arises from using actual wages to construct weights in a Divisia index instead of wages as they would be if technical change had not occurred has been discussed by R. R. Nelson in 'Recent Exercises in Growth Accounting: New Understanding or Dead End', *American Economic Review*, June 1973.

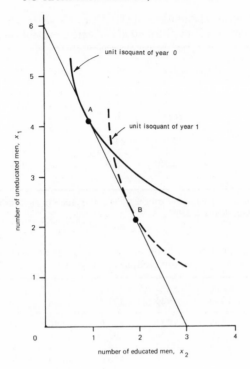

Figure 12.2 The bias in the Divisia index of the total input of labour

Though the method of Jorgenson and Griliches of measuring total labour input permits them to adjust their index to account for changes over time in the relative earnings of educated and uneducated men, their data display virtually no change in relative earnings, in which case their method and Denison's method turn out to be the same in practice. Their data on numbers and relative earnings of educated and uneducated workers are presented in Tables 12.3 and 12.4. From these data, one must conclude either that there is an infinite elasticity of substitution in use between the different educational classes of labour (that the isoquants at any moment of time are straight lines), or that real input of labour as a whole is substantially overestimated when technical change is measured in accordance with equation (9)—overestimated in the sense that the increase over time in the proportion of educated labour would have caused a substantial decline in the relative marginal product of educated labour and would have resulted in a slower growth of output per head but for technical change of the kind illustrated in Figure 12.2.

Two polar explanations of the data in Tables 12.3 and 12.4 are

Table 12.3 Civilian labour force, males 18 to 64 years old, by educational attainment (per cent distribution by years of school completed)

school year completed	1940	1948	1952	1957	1959	1962	1965
elementary 0–4	10.2	7.9	7.6	6.3	5.9	5.1	4.3
5–7	10.2	7.1	11.6	11.4	10.7	9.8	8.3
8	33.7	26.9	20.1	16.8	15.8	13.9	12.7
high school 1–3	18.3	20.7	19.4	20.1	19.8	19.2	18.9
4	16.6	23.6	24.6	27.2	27.5	29.1	32.3
college 1–3	5.7	7.1	8.3	8.5	9.4	10.6	10.6
4+ or 4	5.4	6.7	8.3	9.6	6.3	7.3	7.5
5+	—	—	—	—	4.7	5.0	5.4

Table XI, D. Jorgenson and Z. Griliches, 'The Explanation of Productivity Change', *Review of Economic Studies*, 1967.

Table 12.4 Mean annual earnings of males, 25 years and over by school years completed, selected years

school year completed	1939	1949	1956	1958	1959	1963
elementary 0–4	665	1724	2127	2046	2935	2465
5–7	900	2268	2927	2829	4058	3409
8	1188	2829	3732	3769	4725	4432
high school 1–3	1379	3226	4480	4618	5379	5370
4	1661	3784	5439	5567	6132	6588
college 1–3	1931	4423	6363	6966	7401	7693
4+ or 4	2607	6179	3490	9206	9255	9523
5+	—	—	—	—	11,136	10,487

Table XII, D. Jorgenson and Z. Griliches, 'The Explanation of Productivity Change', *Review of Economic Studies*, 1967.

illustrated in Figures 12.3(a) and 12.3(b). For the purpose of demonstrating a point, we suppose that an uneducated man may transform himself into an educated man instantly by studying part-time; an educated worker is one who acquires a complete education by studying for a few hours in the morning, who employs his knowledge in the afternoon and who forgets what he learned overnight. In a competitive economy, the relative wage of educated and uneducated labour depends on the number of hours of study required, and this may depend in turn on the number of educated workers supplied. We can imagine a production possibility curve of educated and uneducated labour. In both figures, production possibility curves in year 0 and year 1 are combined with sets of isoquants which may be thought of as derived indifference curves for the two types of labour. By assumption, the proportion of educated to uneducated labour is greater in year 1 than in year 0, but the relative wage is the same. The two figures differ in their explanations of the constancy of the relative wage. The explanation in Figure 12.3(a) is that the elasticity of substitution in production of educated and uneducated labour is infinite, that a carpenter can always transform himself into a brain surgeon by studying for seven out of eight hours in the working day. The alternative explanation in Figure 12.3(b) is that the elasticity of substitution in use of educated and uneducated labour is infinite, that eight carpenters working together can perform brain surgery.[15]

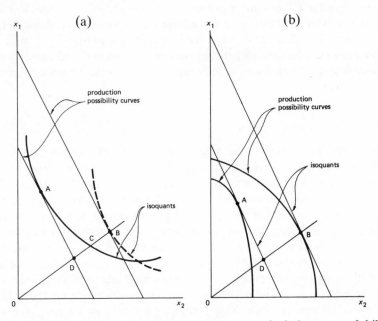

Figure 12.3 Alternative explanations of the constancy of relative wages of skilled and unskilled labour

The reason for emphasizing the contrast between the explanations of the constancy of the relative wage in Figures 12.3(a) and 12.3(b) is to draw attention to the fact that the input term in the definition of technical change, the term $\sum_{j=1}^{n} v_k(\dot{x}_j/x_j)$ in equation (9), is intended to measure the location of the vector x in a field of isoquants, not the outward shift over time in the production possibility curve. When input

[15] Of course, eight marginal carpenters can perform brain surgery in the sense that there is a chain of substitutions through different types of labour beginning with a brain surgeon and ending with eight carpenters. The question is whether marginal products of different types of labour are independent of the composition of the labour force.

is measured correctly, the set of value shares v ought to reflect the relative usefulness of carpenters and brain surgeons at the base year technology, not the cost of converting one into the other. In the circumstances of Figure 12.3(a), the true measure of the growth of labour input is BC/OC, which is less than that indicated by the Divisia index; in the circumstances of Figure 12.3(b), the true measure is BD/OB which is correctly reflected in the Divisia index. The Divisia index reflects the growth of labour input correctly if there is an infinite elasticity of substitution in use between educated and uneducated labour, and the Divisia index overestimates the growth of labour input if the elasticity of substitution in use within the technology available in the base year is less than infinite but the isoquants are twisting over time so as to preserve the spread between wages of educated and uneducated labour despite the increase in the proportion of educated workers in the labour force.

(ii) *The nature of the inputs*

One's suspicion that the observed consistency of relative wages is not a demand phenomenon but is instead an aspect of technical change, so that equation (9) leads to an overestimate of the growth of the labour input and an underestimate of the rate of technical change, is reinforced when one considers the composition of the labour force within any educational category. In applying equation (9) to time series of factor inputs for the years 1940 to 1965, the number of college graduates is treated as one of the inputs, x_j, as though each college graduate were a perfect substitute for every other college graduate and as though the typical college graduate in 1965 were a perfect substitute for the typical college graduate in 1940. This assumption may well be true of some fields of study; the 1940 vintage of Doctor of Divinity or Ph.D. in Medieval Literature may be a perfect substitute for the 1965 vintage. This assumption is obviously not true of the sciences; the 1940 vintage physicist or chemist is a very different person from the 1965 vintage, and the computer specialist and biophysicist of 1965 have no counterparts in 1940. The difference between the 1965 college graduate and the 1940 college graduate is not merely that the 1965 graduate is more productive in the sense that he can do some given multiple of the work of his 1940 counterpart. The 1965 graduate is equally productive in some occupations, more productive in others, and he possesses skills that were unknown in 1940 because they depend upon technology developed in the intervening period. The point I am making is that the relative wage of college graduates has been preserved because, and only because, technical advance has brought forth new skills and has made it profitable for people to acquire these skills, so that what we measure as labour input contains a very large component of technical change.

To determine the true measure of labour input with respect to base year isoquants, we would have to know what the economy would be like today if there had been no technical change since the base year. The 1965 vintage college graduate trades his skill for the skill of a 1940 vintage college graduate, and all industrial processes learned since 1940 are abandoned. Then we observe how the market responds to the altered skill-composition of the labour force and use the new observed wage structure in computing the terms v_j for equation (9). I think it very unlikely that the premium on educated labour would be preserved in the face of changes in the composition of the labour force as large as those observed from 1940 to 1965. Indeed, it is doubtful whether there would be any premium at all, for many college graduates would have to work at jobs for which their skills are not required.

A similar point can be made about capital. The capital–labour ratio has increased substantially since 1940 and it is doubtful whether the marginal product of capital would be as high as it is today if existing machines had to be traded in for machines of the 1940 vintage counted as equivalent according to the price indexes used to deflate the value of machinery and other capital goods in the national accounts.

(iii) *The role of capital as an input and as an output*

Suppose that output consists of grain C and new machines $\dot{K}$, and that input consists of labour L and machines K. Equation (9) reduces to

$$\text{TC} = sG_{\dot{K}} + (1-s)G_C - \alpha G_L - (1-\alpha)G_K \qquad (19)$$

where s is the rate of saving, α is labour's share of output, G_K is the growth rate of the capital stock, $G_{\dot{K}}$ is the growth rate of investment, and so on. Note particularly that K appears twice in equation (19), once positively in G_K with the coefficient s and again negatively in G_K with the coefficient $(1 - \alpha)$, where $(1 - \alpha)$ is usually though not necessarily greater than s. Now recall the section in Chapter 5 where it was argued that K is really an intermediate product from a dynamic point of view in that it is created by the sacrifice of consumption and is gradually used up or worn away in the process of creating extra consumption later on, a sequence $C \to K \to C$. One can easily imagine a technical change which simultaneously makes capital cheaper but less efficient, so that more of it is created for a given sacrifice of consumption but more of it is needed to augment future consumption by any given amount, leaving the consumer exactly as well off as he was before. In particular, a given percentage increase in the output of new capital goods coupled with the same percentage increase in capital requirements, resulting in identical increases in G_K and G_k in equation (19), would have no effect in the long run on output per head, but the overall measure of technical change in equation (19) would be affected whenever $s \neq 1 - \alpha$. This is a disturbing implication of the equation, for the measure of technical change ought not to increase or decrease without any actual or potential change in the welfare of consumers in the long run. We shall return to this problem after introducing an alternative notion of technical change in the next section.

C. A REFORMULATION OF THE PROBLEM

Let us step back for a moment, put the statistical details aside, and ask ourselves afresh what it is we expect to learn about the economy when we set about to measure the rate of aggregate technical change. In studying technical change we are playing the role of economic historian; we are trying to find out what forces have created the economy as it is, or we are seeking hints about how to promote growth tomorrow. We are asking questions of the form 'what would have happened if . . .'. How large would income per head be today and what rate of growth of income per head would we have experienced if technical change had stopped abruptly in 1926? Alternatively, what rate of technical change is required to transform the economy of 1926 into that of 1974? If that is our problem—and I cannot imagine what else it might be—then it follows at once that it is inappropriate to contrast technical change and capital formation as sources of economic growth because the rate of capital formation in any year t is itself dependent on technical change in the capital goods industry in all years prior to t. If technical change has been rapid, then income is large, and so too is investment corresponding to any given rate of saving. The question asked in the three studies reviewed above—what part of observed economic growth cannot be explained by growth of inputs of all kinds—begins to disintegrate when we recognize that the nature and magnitude of the inputs would not have changed as they have done since 1926 if technology had not changed as well.

Nor can the history of income per head, with or without technical change, be inferred from an isolated production function. We cannot begin to compare the progress of the economy under alternative technologies until we have a model of the development of an economy over time. We need a growth model with one or more parameters to represent the rate of technical change. The model may be simple but it must be complete in the sense that the history of the economy can be traced out from the history of exogenous variables that are in some sense independent of changes in the technology of production.

The simplest model I can think of to meet these requirements is the one-sector model in which real income was defined in Chapter 5. It consists of a production function

$$Y(t) = f(K(t), e^{\lambda t}L(t)) \tag{20}$$

a factor augmentation equation

$$\dot{K}(t) = s(t)\,Y(t) \tag{21}$$

and a disposition of income equation

$$Y(t) = C(t) + \dot{K}(t) \tag{22}$$

where K, L, C, Y, s and λ are capital, labour, consumption, income, the rate of saving and the rate of technical change, where $L(t)$ and $K(0)$ are exogenous and $s(t)$ could either be exogenous or determined through the maximization of an intertemporal welfare function such as

$$U = \int_0^\infty e^{-\rho t} u\!\left(\frac{Y(t)(1-s(t))}{L(t)}\right) dt \tag{23}$$

in which u is the static utility function and ρ is the discount factor on annual utilities. Note that the capital stock is only exogenous on the first day of the model and that the rate of technical change is assumed to be embodied in labour. The reason for the latter is to enable the economy to evolve into steady state growth (a condition where all variables grow at constant rates forever); no other specification of technical change will lead to that result. Nor need a distinction be made between instantaneous productive capacity and long-run productive capacity in the definitions of $\dot{K}$ and K if capital does not depreciate or if it depreciates by exponential decay. It is a well known property of this model that if the rate of saving is constant

$$s(t) = s \tag{24}$$

and the labour force grows at a constant rate

$$L(t) = e^{nt}L(0) \tag{25}$$

then the rate of growth of consumption per head in the long run is exactly equal to the rate of technical change[16]

$$G_{C/L} = \lambda \tag{26}$$

Thus, in the long run there can be no alternative to technical change as a source of economic growth. Without technical change (if $\lambda = 0$), the economy settles down to a state in which no permanent growth of consumption per head is possible. Even in the short run, the alternative to technical change as a source of increase in consumption per head is not capital formation (for capital formation increases with λ) but saving. The rate of saving is exogenous to the model and could be increased or decreased independently of λ as long as the rate of interest exceeds the sum of the rate of technical change and the rate of population growth.[17] These results are familiar to every undergraduate who has studied the neoclassical theory of economic growth but their implications for growth accounting seem to have been overlooked.

At this point there may occur to the reader an objection which will take us to the heart of the problem. Surely there is something wrong with the treatment of capital in the model, for we seem to have two independent time series of capital with no reason whatsoever for supposing them to be the same. We have the time series of capital in the national accounts and a second time series of $K(t)$ which is endogenous

---

[16] The production function in equation (20) can be transformed into an equation connecting growth rates of Y, K and L.

$$G_Y = (1 - \alpha)G_k + \alpha(G_L + \lambda)$$

where α is labour's share of income. From equation (21), it follows that $G_{\dot{K}} = G_Y$ as long as s is constant. If the economy is in steady state growth then $\dot{K}(t) = Ae^{vt}$ for some unknown values of A and v so that

$$K(t) = \int_0^t Ae^{vt}\,dt = \frac{A}{v}e^{vt}$$

implying that $G_{\dot{K}} = G_K$. From equations (23) and (24) it follows that $G_C = G_Y$ and $G_L = n$. Equation (26) follows at once from these statements about growth rates and from the fact that $G_{C/L} \equiv G_C - G_L$. This result was first proved in H. Uzawa, 'Neutral Inventions and the Stability of Growth Equilibrium', *Review of Economic Studies*, February, 1961, pp. 105–18.

[17] This qualification is necessary to ensure that an increase in s causes a permanent increase in C/L. It is easily shown that if this condition fails to hold, the extra income resulting from an increase in the rate of saving is less than the extra capital required to preserve the new, higher capital–output ratio.

to the model. And the nonsense is compounded by the implication of equation (22) that the relative price of capital goods and consumption goods is constant when, in fact, we know it to be variable over time.

There are two, more or less equivalent, ways of dealing with this objection. The first is to impose the model onto the data by redefining investment and capital stock in units of consumption forgone. Investment would become the difference between $Y(t)$ and $C(t)$ expressed as an amount of grain. The base year capital stock would be the value in grain of the actual capital stock in the base year, and $K(t)$ would be built up recursively from equation (21). We would ignore the time series of capital stock in the national accounts on grounds that any value of capital in the national accounts in excess of our measure of the capital stock in units of consumption forgone is indicative of a kind of technical change in the industry producing capital goods; the capital stock in the national accounts would be deemed unacceptable as an explanatory variable for the growth of output per head in circumstances where the object of the exercise is to measure technical change as a residual.

The other way of dealing with the observed time series of capital stock is to modify equation (21) to account for the connection between saving, $s(t)Y(t)$, measured in units of grain, and capital formation, $\dot{K}(t)$, expressed in units of machines. Equation (21) would then become

$$p(t)\dot{K}(t) = s(t)Y(t) \qquad (27)$$

where $p(t)$ can change over time. But here we must be careful, for a fall in the price of capital goods is itself a kind of technical change which must somehow be added to λ in equation (20) to get the total technical change in the economy as a whole. It is reasonable to consider λ alone to be a measure of the rate of technical change when λ is the only source of progress in the economy. It is unreasonable now that progress can arise from a fall in $p(t)$. In fact, it can be shown[18] that if the fall in the price of capital goods is exponential, that is, if

$$p(t) = p(0)\,e^{-\beta t} \qquad (28)$$

for some positive parameter β, then

$$G_{C/L} = \lambda + \frac{1-\alpha}{\alpha}\beta \qquad (29)$$

[18] The proof is simple. Equation (29) follows immediately from the equations in footnote 16 when we replace the growth equivalent of equation (19), $G_{\dot{K}}=G_Y$, by the growth equivalent of equations (27) and (28), $G_{\dot{K}}=G_Y+\beta$.

Since the growth of consumption per man is what counts, the consumer is completely indifferent as to the size of λ or β individually as long as their weighted sum in equation (29) is the same. In general, in a large model with many possible sources of technical change, an aggregation rule is required to measure 'the' rate of technical change for the economy as a whole. The model might contain many commodities, many production functions, and both intermediate and primary factors of production. There might be a separate rate of technical change for each production function, or technical change might be such as to augment one or more of the inputs. Thus the model might contain n technical change parameters, λ_1 to λ_n, that need to be aggregated to an overall rate of technical change λ^* for the system as a whole. For each model, we need a function

$$\lambda^* = g(\lambda_1, \ldots, \lambda_n) \tag{30}$$

and we need a criterion for deciding what that function must be. I suggest that the appropriate criterion for choosing a function g is that λ^* should equal the rate of growth of consumption per head when the economy is in steady state, so that λ^* can play the role of λ in equation (26).

There is one other difficulty to consider. If we do measure technical change as the rate of growth of output per unit of input within an isolated production function, and if we measure output not in units of consumption forgone but as an aggregate of consumption goods and investment goods, then a decline in the price of capital goods will buoy up the measure of output per unit of input because more investment goods will be produced. Real income defined as $C(t) + p(0)\dot{K}(t)$ will grow more rapidly than the variable $Y(t)$ in equation (20) and the estimate of λ got by regressing real income on L, K and t will exceed the value of λ in equation (26). This is a significant step in the direction of equation (29), but the rates of technical change as the growth rate of output per unit of input and as the steady state growth rate of consumption per head still differ to some extent. Consider an economy represented by the equations (20), (24), (25) and (27). Suppose the economy really were in a steady state growth so that the actual growth of consumption per head was $\lambda + \beta(1 - \alpha)/\alpha$ in accordance with equation (29). As mentioned at the end of the last section, the growth rate of consumption per head is not reflected in the measure of technical change as the growth rate of output per unit of input in equation (19) except in the special case where the rate of saving is equal to capital's share of output. Actually, since the rate of technical change in equation (19) is disembodied while that in equation (29) is embodied in labour, one would expect the latter to be uniformly higher, and would count the rates as being 'the same' if one were the appropriate multiple of the other at all for any given body of data. But it is a consequence of the weighting of outputs by s and $1 - s$ and inputs of α and $1 - \alpha$ in equation (19) that, of two economies, one may have the greater growth rate of output per unit of input while the other has the greater growth rate of steady state consumption per head.

To appreciate the magnitude of the discrepancy, consider two economies, A and B, with parameters λ, β, s and α as shown in Table 12.5. In economy A technical change is concentrated in the production function. In economy B technical change takes the form of a cheapening of new capital goods. Since labour's share is set at 0.5 in both economies, it follows from equation (29) that λ and β have the same impact per unit on $G_{C/L}$ and that technical change defined as the value of $G_{C/L}$ in steady state growth is greater for economy B than for economy A. But equation (19), where technical change is defined as the growth rate of output per unit of input, seems to tell an entirely different story. Since λ is technical change embodied in labour, it is a substitute for G_L in equation (19), and T.C. $= \lambda\alpha$ when λ changes and β does not. Similarly T.C. $= \beta s$ when β changes and λ does not. Technical change assessed according to equation (19) is substantially lower for economy B than for economy A.

Table 12.5   the rates of growth of output per unit of input and of consumption per head

	λ	β	s	α	TC equation (19)	$G_{C/L}$ equation (29)
economy A	4%	0	0.1	0.5	2%	4%
economy B	0	5%	0.1	0.5	0.5%	5%

Note. From equations (20) and (27), it follows that T.C. $= \lambda\alpha + \beta s$.

D. A DEMONSTRATION THAT THE RATE OF TECHNICAL CHANGE IS
APPROXIMATELY EQUAL TO THE RATE OF GROWTH OF CONSUMPTION PER HEAD

Equation (26) tells us that the rate of growth of consumption per head is exactly equal to the rate of technical change embodied in labour when that is the only sort of technical change in the model and when the economy is in steady state growth. For an economy that is not in steady state growth, we can use the time series of the exogenous variables to investigate: (i) what portion of observed economic growth between any pair of years would have taken place in the absence of technical change:

(ii) what rate of technical change embodied in labour is required to generate the observed change in output per head; and (iii) how closely the estimated rate of technical change approximates the rate of growth of consumption per head.

We shall attempt to answer these questions for the Canadian economy from 1926 to 1974. For this computation the model developed in the last section is modified as follows to account for depreciation, to allow for the possibility that part of the capital stock is unemployed from time to time, to specify the form of the production function, and to convert the model from continuous time to a sequence of years:

(a) The production function has a constant elasticity of substitution between labour and capital, and technical change is labour-augmenting,

$$Y^t = f(\hat{K}^t, L^t e^{\lambda t}) \tag{31}$$

where Y^t is output in the year t, and $\hat{K}^t$ and L^t are amounts of capital and labour employed. The elasticity of substitution, σ is parameterized in the calculations described below at $\sigma = 4, 2, 1, \frac{1}{2}$ and $\frac{1}{4}$, and labour's share in the base year is parameterized at $\frac{1}{2}, \frac{2}{3}$ and $\frac{3}{4}$.

(b) The labour force, measured in man-hours, and the rate of unemployment are exogenous time series, independent of the rate of technical change.

(c) The rate of unemployment of capital is the same as the rate of unemployment of labour,

$$\hat{K}^t = K^t(1 - u^t) \tag{32}$$

where $\hat{K}^t$ is the amount of capital employed; K^t is the amount of capital available and u^t is the rate of unemployment of labour.

(d) Income may be either consumed or invested, and the relative price of consumption goods and investment goods is 1.0:

$$Y^t = C^t + I^t \tag{33}$$

where C^t is consumption and I^t is investment. The amount of investment depends on the rate of saving

$$I^t = s^t Y^t \tag{34}$$

where s^t is the observed rate of saving in the year t.

(e) Capital depreciates at the same rate each year

$$K^{t+1} = K^t(1 - D) + I^t \tag{35}$$

where the rate of depreciation is parameterized at $D = 2\%$ and 5%.

The data requirement for estimating technical change in this model is small because income and capital are endogenous. We need the initial and final values of income, Y^{26} and Y^{74}, the initial capital stock K^{26}, the full time series of the rate of saving, the rate of unemployment and the labour force—s^t, u^t and L^t. Note particularly that K in this model is not the capital stock as measured by, for instance, the perpetual inventory method. It is the capital stock as it would be if the relative price of capital goods and consumption goods remained constant over the period while the exogenous variables s^t and L^t remained as they were observed to be.

We do, however, attempt to extend the concept of investment to cover the acquisition of human as well as non-human capital. As educational investment and educational capital are difficult to quantify, and because we cannot rely on such measures as can be obtained, it is thought best to present two estimates of technical change with expenditure on secondary and higher education included as part of investment in one and excluded from the other. When expenditure on education is excluded, the rate of saving each year is the ratio to gross national product of the sum of 'gross fixed capital formation' and 'value of the physical change in inventories' (the expressions in quotations are categories in the national accounts), and the capital stock in 1926 is inclusive of residential buildings. When education is included as part of investment, the rate of saving is augmented for the direct cost of schooling as well as forgone earnings of students.

Educational investment is estimated from time series of numbers of students in secondary school and university and cost per student assessed in units of consumption goods. With some interpolation, we can obtain complete time series of numbers of students from 1926 to 1974. The cost per student in each year t is constructed from an estimate of the sum of direct cost and earnings forgone in 1961 scaled up or down by the proportion between labour income per man hour in the year t and the year 1961, the assumption being that the wages of teachers and forgone earnings of students increase together with productivity in the economy as a whole. In principle, we could construct a measure of the initial stock of human capital in 1926 in the manner that Statistics Canada constructed its initial stock of non-human capital, namely, by cumulating and discounting investment for many years prior to 1926. We do not adopt that procedure for want of data. Instead we resort, quite arbitrarily, to the assumption that the ratio of human capital to human capital formation in 1926 was equal to the ratio of non-human capital to non-human capital formation.

Tables 12.6 and 12.7 summarize the results of an attempt to determine how large Canadian income per head would be in 1974 if

Table 12.6 Estimates of the ratio of Canadian gross national expenditure per man-hour of labour in 1974 and 1926 as it would have been if technical change had ceased in 1926

		$D = 2\%$					$D = 5\%$				
		$\sigma = 4$	$\sigma = 2$	$\sigma = 1$	$\sigma = \frac{1}{2}$	$\sigma = \frac{1}{4}$	$\sigma = 4$	$\sigma = 2$	$\sigma = 1$	$\sigma = \frac{1}{2}$	$\sigma = \frac{1}{4}$
no account taken of educational capital	$\alpha = \frac{1}{2}$	1.82	1.74	1.60	1.41	1.22	1.11	1.11	1.10	1.10	1.08
	$\alpha = \frac{2}{3}$	1.43	1.39	1.32	1.22	1.13	1.06	1.06	1.06	1.06	1.05
	$\alpha = \frac{1}{4}$	1.28	1.25	1.21	1.15	1.09	1.04	1.04	1.04	1.04	1.03
investment includes acquisition of educational capital	$\alpha = \frac{1}{2}$	2.04	1.92	1.72	1.46	1.23	1.23	1.22	1.21	1.18	1.14
	$\alpha = \frac{2}{3}$	1.54	1.48	1.38	1.25	1.13	1.13	1.13	1.12	1.10	1.08
	$\alpha = \frac{1}{4}$	1.34	1.30	1.24	1.16	1.09	1.09	1.09	1.08	1.07	1.05

The ratio of real income per man-hour in 1974 and 1926 is 5.49 if forgone earnings of students are excluded from income, or 5.74 if forgone earnings are included.

Table 12.7 Estimates of the rate of labour-augmenting technical change in the Canadian economy from 1926 to 1974

		$D = 2\%$					$D = 5\%$				
		$\sigma = 4$	$\sigma = 2$	$\sigma = 1$	$\sigma = \frac{1}{2}$	$\sigma = \frac{1}{4}$	$\sigma = 4$	$\sigma = 2$	$\sigma = 1$	$\sigma = \frac{1}{2}$	$\sigma = \frac{1}{4}$
no account taken of educational capital	$\alpha = \frac{1}{2}$	3.48	3.49	3.49	3.49	3.50	4.09	4.13	4.24	4.67	*
	$\alpha = \frac{2}{3}$	3.50	3.50	3.50	3.51	3.51	3.82	3.84	3.88	4.00	5.16
	$\alpha = \frac{3}{4}$	3.52	3.52	3.52	3.52	3.52	3.72	3.73	3.75	3.81	4.10
investment includes acquisition of educational capital	$\alpha = \frac{1}{2}$	3.34	3.35	3.37	3.40	3.44	4.00	4.02	4.08	4.27	*
	$\alpha = \frac{2}{3}$	3.48	3.48	3.49	3.50	3.52	3.81	3.82	3.83	3.88	4.16
	$\alpha = \frac{3}{4}$	3.52	3.53	3.53	3.54	3.56	3.74	3.75	3.75	3.78	3.86

* No rate of technical change would be sufficient to raise income per head to its 1974 value if $\alpha = \frac{1}{2}$ and $\sigma = \frac{1}{4}$.
The rate of growth of real gross national expenditure per man hour from 1926 was 3.55% if forgone earnings of students are excluded from income, 3.64% if forgone earnings are included.

technical change had stopped in 1926, and to estimate the rate of technical change required between 1926 and 1974 to generate the observed income per head in 1974. The general procedure in constructing these estimates is: (a) to postulate values of the elasticity of substitution σ, the rate of depreciation D, and labour's share of output in the year 1926; (b) to determine the remaining parameters of the production function from the given values of Y^{26}, L^{26} and $\hat{K}^{26}$; (c) to combine the time series L^t, u^t and s^t in accordance with equations (31) to (35) to determine a time series Y^t corresponding to any given rate of technical change λ; (d) to set $\lambda = 0$ in computing Table 12.6; and (e) to determine by an iterative procedure the value of λ sufficient to equate the computed Y^{74} to the actual value of Y^{74}. This procedure yields a time series of the capital stock (K^t) which is conceptually different from the number of machines available in the year t; the stock K^t relevant to Table 12.6 measures the number of machines there would be if our assumptions about depreciation were correct and if technical change had ceased in 1926. All measures of income and capital are in constant (1961) dollars, but, to maintain consistency with equation (33), we treat consumption goods as the numeraire and deflate money income by the national accounts implicit price deflator of consumption goods only, not of income as a whole. Specifically, we set Y^{26} and Y^{74}, the only data on income that we need, equal to the current values of gross national expenditure in 1926 and 1974 deflated by the implicit price deflator of 'personal consumption'. We then set K^{26} to be the product of Y^{26} and the capital–output ratio in 1926, where capital and output are both measured in current (1926) dollars.

In interpreting the numbers in Tables 12.6 and 12.7, several points should be borne in mind. First, since the whole supply side of the economy is compressed into one aggregate production function, the estimated rate of technical change depends very much on the elasticity of substitution that is assumed. The higher the elasticity of substitution, the more scope there is for capital formation to raise income per head and the lower is the estimate of the rate of aggregate technical change. Furthermore, it is a peculiar property of our production function that there is an upper limit to output per unit of labour regardless of the size of the capital stock whenever the elasticity of substitution is less than 1. The blanks in some of the boxes in the case where $\sigma = \frac{1}{4}$ and $\alpha = \frac{1}{2}$ indicate that no rate of technical change however high could enable an economy represented by the postulated production function to generate the income per head observed in 1974. Second, except for the increase in the technical change parameter, λ, the production function is assumed to remain unchanged throughout the whole of the period from 1926 to 1974. Third, the production function is assumed to have constant returns to scale in labour and capital. This assumption is an important one and it is probably contrary to fact. If technical change really stopped in 1926, if the rate of growth of population were unaffected, and if savings were maintained at a rate sufficient to preserve the capital–labour ratio, the output per head would nonetheless decline, in all probability, because of the limited supply of farm land and other natural and environmental resources. Technical change has two tasks to perform. It increases output per head for a given capital–output ratio and it compensates for population growth. Only its work in the former task is reflected in Tables 12.6 and 12.7, and the impact of technical change is underestimated as a result. Fourth, our assumption that the rates of saving and population growth are exogenous and independent of the rate of technical change is probably contrary to fact, but it is difficult to say by how much or in what direction the rate of population growth, in particular, would change if technical change ceased. Fifth, our estimate of educational investment is particularly crude. It is included to underline the fact that expenditure on human capital formation ought to enter this calculation as an increase in capital and not as an increase in labour.

Little need be said of the results themselves. The rates of technical change in Table 12.7 are substantially higher than those estimated by Denison or by Jorgenson and Griliches but are broadly consistent with those estimated by Solow when due allowance is made for the fact that rates in Table 12.7 are labour-augmenting while Solow's rates are Hicks neutral. Table 12.6 illustrates that only a few percentage points of the 549% increase in income per man-hour could be accounted for by investment, and Table 12.7 illustrates that the rate of technical change is approximately equal to the rate of growth of output per head. Thus, we have illustrated what should have been obvious from the beginning, but was obscured by the manner in which technical change was studied, that economic growth depends predominantly on technical change and cannot occur to any significant extent in its absence.

APPENDIX: THE SOURCES OF DATA AND COMPUTATIONAL PROCEDURES IN TABLES 12.6 AND 12.7

The primary data for Table 12.6 were as follows:

(i) L^t: a time series of hours of labour per year computed by multiplying hours of work per man by the number of workers employed as shown in Table 7.3.

(ii) U^t: a time series of the rate of unemployment of labour from 1926 to 1974. See notes to Table 7.3.

(iii) s^t: a time series of the rate of saving from 1926 to 1974.

(*National Income and Expenditure Accounts*, Volume 1, 1926–74, Statistics Canada, 13-531, Table 10).

(iv) K^{26}: the 1926 capital stock in 1961 dollars. In 1926, the value in current dollars of the capital stock in manufacturing industries, non-manufacturing industries and the public sector was $9701 million and the value of the capital stock in housing was $4497 million. The sum of these numbers is converted to 1961 dollars by the national accounts deflator for personal consumption. The values of the capital stock are from an unpublished estimate by Statistics Canada.

(v) Y^{26} and Y^{74}: real income in consumption units. For each year, gross national expenditure in current dollars is deflated, not by the deflator for gross national expenditure as a whole, but by the deflator for personal consumption. (*National Income and Expenditure Accounts*, Volume 1, 1926–1974, Statistics Canada, 13-531, Tables 2 and 7.)

The capital stock each year is estimated recursively by the formula

$$K^t = K^{t-1}(1-D) + s^{t-1}Y^{t-1}$$

where D, the rate of depreciation, is parameterized as indicated in Table 12.6, and the time series of Y^t is determined from a production function

$$Y^t = f(L^t e^{\lambda t}, (1-U^t)K^t)$$

with elasticity of substitution and labour's share in 1926 as indicated in Table 12.6 and a constant term chosen to balance the equation when $\lambda = 0$ for 1926.

Table 12.7 presents a similar calculation with income and capital expanded to account for the creation and use of educational capital. In addition to the information cited above, this calculation requires:

(vi) F^t: an imputation to real income for earnings forgone of students. This is defined as

$$F^t = f_s N_s^t + f_u N_u^t + f_g N_g^t$$

where the subscripts s, u and g refer to secondary, undergraduate and graduate schooling, N_i^t is the number of students of type i in the year t, and f_i is the forgone earnings of the i type of student. Statistics of N_s^t, N_u^t and N_g^t are from the quantity data in Chapter 10, statistics of f_s, f_u and f_g are from Table 12.8 and the time series of real wages is from the data used to compile Table 7.3.

(vii) e^t: the rate of educational investment. This is defined as the ratio of expenditure on education inclusive of forgone earnings of students to gross national expenditure inclusive of the imputation for forgone

Table 12.8   Cost per student in 1961 ($ per student)

	secondary $i = s$	undergraduate $i = u$	graduate $i = g$
direct cost	600	1600	3000
forgone earnings f_i	1000	2000	5000
total e_i	1600	3600	8000

Source: Rough estimates supplied by Barry Lacombe and David Dodge based on studies done under the auspices of the Economic Council of Canada.

earnings of students defined in (vi). All of the expressions in the numerator and the denominator of the definition of e^t are deflated by the price index for personal consumption. Educational expenditure is estimated as

$$e^t = (e_s N_s^t + e_u N_u^t + e_g N_g^t) \left(\frac{\text{real wage in } t}{\text{real wage in 1961}} \right)$$

(vii) m^t: the rate of population growth in the year t attributable to migration. Statistics of net migration per decade are obtained from various issues of the *Canada Yearbook*. Rates for each year were estimated as the average rate over the decade—one-fifth of the ratio of total migration to the sum of the population in the first year and the population in the final year of the decade.

(ix) J^{26}: the stock of educational capital in 1926. For want of a better measure, we estimate the stock of educational capital in 1926 by assuming that the ratio of the stock of educational capital to the investment in educational capital is equal to the ratio of the stock of ordinary capital to the investment in ordinary capital, i.e.

$$J^{26} = K^{26} \frac{e^{26}}{s^{26}}$$

We now define time series of ordinary capital K^t and educational capital J^t according to the equations

$$K^t = K^{t-1}(1 - D) + s^{t-1} Y^{t-1}$$

and

$$J^t = J^{t-1}(1 - D)(1 + m^{t-1}) + e^{t-1} Y^{t-1}$$

where Y^{26} and Y^{74} are now redefined to include forgone earnings of students deflated by the national accounts deflator for personal consumption and where the sum $(J' + K')$ is the new measure of total capital in the estimation of the constant term in the production function from evidence of Y^{26}, L^{26} and $(J^{26} + K^{26})$, the postulated values of labour's share in 1926, and the elasticity of substitution.

13

Alternative Measures of the Rate of Economic Growth in Canada, 1926 to 1974

We began this book with the statement that the rate of economic growth in Canada from 1926 to 1974 has been 2.45% per year. That is the rate when we define economic growth in the usual way as the rate of appreciation of real gross national expenditure per head. In the course of the book, we have considered how the statistics might be modified or different measures constructed to correspond more closely to the meaning of economic growth in common speech and in models of economic development. In this chapter, we shall try to pull together the statistical implications of our analysis. We shall consider the joint effect on the measure of economic growth of the reinterpretation of investment as real saving rather than real capital formation, the broadening of the concept of depreciation to account for the effect of population growth on the capital–labour ratio, the measurement of real consumption from quantity data, the reinterpretation of public consumption as cost of production rather than final product, and the imputations for leisure and life expectancy. Other possible modifications of real income, notably the imputations for changes in the distribution of income and for the depreciation equivalent of the extraction of minerals from the ground, will not be considered because we cannot account for these phenomena in long time series. The core of the chapter is a sequence of almost self-explanatory tables reviewing the history of gross national expenditure per head, showing alternative measures of the growth rate of real consumption, comparing rates of investment under alternative definitions of investment and income, tracing the history of the relative sizes of personal consumption, government consumption and saving, and, finally, showing how the rate of economic growth is affected by various combinations of changes in the definition of income. To avoid excessive detail, we shall not present complete time series of real income and other variables but shall show only the years 1926, 1974, 1961, and every fifth year from 1930 to 1970 except for 1960.

The first table (Table 13.1) is a review of the history of real gross

Table 13.1   Indexes of real per capita gross national expenditure and its components 1926–1974

	gross national expenditure	personal consumption	government consumption	investment
1926	100	100	100	100
1930	106	115	120	121
1935	88	102	108	51
1940	120	117	219	87
1945	162	147	542	79
1950	165	169	192	179
1955	188	192	273	201
1961	201	211	283	206
1965	239	241	306	282
1970	278	276	407	279
1974	325	330	465	381
growth rate 1926–1974	2.45%	2.49%	3.20%	2.79%

Source: *National Income and Expenditure Accounts*, 1926–74, Volume 1, Statistics Canada, 13-531. Investment is the sum of the national accounts categories 'gross fixed capital formation' and 'value of physical change in inventories'. The base year is 1971.

national expenditure per head and its main components from 1926 to 1974. We see that real gross national expenditure per head in 1974 was a full three and a quarter times what it had been in 1926, falling in the first decade and rising rapidly thereafter. The major components grew even faster, personal consumption only marginally so, investment more so and government consumption by almost three quarters of a per cent. The apparent anomaly that the total grew less rapidly than any of its components is explained by the fact that the list of components is incomplete. The missing element is the difference between exports and imports which was positive in 1926 and negative in 1974.

Six variants of real personal consumption per head are presented in Table 13.2. To emphasize growth, the data are presented as indexes rather than as dollar values, and the growth rates for the periods 1926–1974 and 1935–1974 are presented at the bottom of each column. The variants themselves are personal consumption as assessed in the national accounts, the same with an imputation for leisure, the same with imputations for leisure and life expectancy, personal consumption assessed directly from quantity data, the same with an imputation for leisure, and the same with imputations for leisure and life expectancy. The recomputation from quantity data is taken directly from Chapter 10 and the imputations for leisure and life expectancy are constructed as

Table 13.2 Alternative measures of the size and growth rate of personal consumption per head in Canada, 1926–1974

	personal consumption assessed in the official national accounts	with imputation for leisure	with additional imputation for life expectancy	personal consumption as assessed from quantity data	with imputation for leisure	with additional imputation for life expectancy
1926	100	100	100	—	—	—
1930	115	123	126	—	—	—
1935	102	112	120	100	100	100
1940	117	121	132	110	103	105
1945	147	173	197	127	136	144
1950	170	217	257	131	153	169
1955	192	254	312	146	175	201
1961	211	291	366	156	196	230
1965	241	341	432	173	222	262
1970	276	410	530	195	264	318
1974	330	503	654	228	315	384
growth rates						
1926–1974	2.49%	3.36%	3.91%	—	—	—
1935–1974	3.02%	3.85%	4.35%	2.12%	2.95%	3.45%

Note: The current value of real consumption in 1961, as assessed in the official national accounts, was $1851 per head.
Source: Column 1 is taken over from Table 13.1. Column 2 is the sum of consumption in constant 1961 dollars and the imputation for leisure as computed in Chapter 7. Column 3 is the product of column 2 and the expression $(DLE(t)/DLE(61))^{1/\beta}$ where DLE is discounted life expectancy, t is the current year, 1961 is the base year, and values of DLE are as defined and computed in Chapter 11. The fourth, fifth and sixth columns are the same as the first, second and third columns except that they are additionally deflated by the quality index of total consumption from Chapter 10.

discussed in Chapter 7 and 11. The imputation for leisure is additive. It is set at zero for the base year (1961), it is positive for any year when more leisure was enjoyed than was the case in the base year, and it is negative for any year when less leisure was enjoyed. The quantity of leisure over and above that enjoyed in the base year is evaluated each year at the real wage of labour. The imputation for life expectancy on the other hand is multiplicative according to the formula developed in Chapter 11, with the multiplier set at 1.0 in the base year, at something in excess of 1.0 for any year when people tend to live longer than they do in the base year, and at less than 1.0 otherwise. These imputations are easily carried over from the time series of real consumption in the national accounts to the time series constructed from quantity data.

Notice how large are the effects of these changes in the definition of real consumption. Real consumption per head as measured in the accounts increases 3.3-fold over our entire period. The imputation for leisure raises that to 5.0-fold. The additional imputation for changes in life expectancy raises that to over 6.5-fold, almost twice the original figure. The recomputation from quantity data reduces the growth rate by about 1% per year, but it is increased again when the imputations are added back. Clearly, we are dealing with changes large enough to affect our perception of economic history in Canada. Even the timing of growth is affected somewhat. The growth rates in the years 1935 to 1950 appear considerably lower (as compared with subsequent periods) in the series constructed from quantity data than in the series in the official national accounts. On the other hand the years from 1926 to 1939, which show virtually no growth of real consumption per head in the official accounts, did contain a decrease in hours of work (among the employed population) and a marked increase in life expectancy.

To pass from the growth rate of real personal consumption to the growth rate of real income as a whole, we have to account for investment (defined here as in Chapter 5 as a generic term referring collectively to all concepts of the difference between income and consumption) and for government consumption. The measure of investment in gross national expenditure is the sum of gross capital formation and value of physical change in inventories. Though a measure of income as the sum of consumption and net investment would be preferable as a basis for assessing the rate of economic growth, a measure consisting of consumption and gross investment is used instead because it is believed inappropriate or excessively difficult to express capital consumption allowances in real terms. The output of new capital goods can be measured in real terms. Capital consumption allowance, being a decline in value of a mix of capital goods produced at various times in the past, can only be expressed in money terms. I am not convinced that the distinction is as sharp as it is often believed to be, for the nature of new capital goods may change as much in the course of time as the nature of depreciation. But, the whole problem can be circumvented if we follow the procedure suggested in Chapter 5 of treating real income as the sum of real consumption and real saving, the latter defined as the value of investment deflated by the price index of consumption goods.

The shift in the definition of investment from real capital formation to real saving has several partly conflicting, partly reinforcing effects on the measure of economic growth. The share of investment in real income falls by about 10% on average. The time series, as may be seen in Table 13.3, becomes more variable, not only because of the fixed deduction of capital consumption allowance, but because the other difference between saving and capital formation—exports minus imports on current account—is one of the most volatile elements in the national accounts.

Table 13.3 Shares in total income of personal consumption, government consumption, saving, and capital formation

| | shares in net national income of | | | gross capital formation and value of physical change in inventories as a percentage of gross national expenditure |
	personal consumption (%)	government consumption (%)	saving (%)	
1926	75	8	17	18
1930	87	10	2	21
1935	91	12	−3	11
1940	76	18	6	6
1945	66	33	1	8
1950	75	12	13	24
1955	75	16	11	24
1961	75	18	7	21
1965	70	17	13	26
1970	67	22	11	21
1974	64	22	14	25

Source: Same as Table 13.1. Saving is the national accounts category defined as investment less capital consumption allowance and Canada's deficit on current account with non-residents (essentially imports–exports). Net national income is defined here as the sum of personal consumption, government consumption, and saving.

The ratio of capital formation to gross national product seems to rise over the period, but there is no clear trend, either up or down, in real saving. On the other hand, much of this difference is accounted for by the increase, shown in Table 13.4, in the relative price of capital goods

Table 13.4 Relative prices of government consumption and gross capital formation with personal consumption as the numeraire, 1926–1974, (1926 = 100)

	1926	1930	1935	1940	1945	1950	1955	1961	1965	1970	1974
government consumption	100	99	113	113	120	122	138	160	174	201	219
gross capital formation	100	100	110	113	119	122	130	126	135	132	145

Source: Same as Table 13.1. The relative prices are ratios of the deflators in the national accounts.

which may be genuine but could very well be due to the difficulties, discussed in Chapter 8, in accounting for quality change.

The share of government consumption in real income has increased markedly. Government's share grew from just over 8% in 1926 to 21% in 1974, though about half of this change is offset by changes in relative price of public consumption, shown in Table 13.4 to have doubled over the period. The combined effect of changes in the value and price of government consumption upon the measure of economic growth depends on how government consumption is accounted for. It could be excluded altogether, as Kuznets would recommend, on the ground that government consumption is for the most part a cost of production, intermediate product, or prerequisite to the goods and services we enjoy, but does not itself contribute to economic welfare today. Alternatively, one could argue that much of government expenditure—notably expenditure on health and education—is really a form of investment and ought to be treated as part of real saving. In that case, the change in the relative price of government consumption would be ignored, for the value of government consumption would be deflated by the price index for personal consumption. An additional complication arises from the virtual impossibility of accounting for changes over time in the productivity of labour in the public services. The price index for government consumption in Table 13.4 is essentially a wage index that may not reflect the cost of services of the public sector.

There is also some question as to what investment ought to contain. Indeed, the more one thinks about the concept of investment, the less solid does it become. Some alternative measures of the rate of investment are presented in Table 13.5. In 1973, the ratio of gross investment (defined in the usual way as the sum of gross fixed capital formation and value of physical change in inventories) to gross national product was 24%, and the ratio of saving to net income was about 15%. The rate of saving is increased by reclassifying education as investment, but we cannot include all expenditure on education as part of net saving because most of it, particularly expenditure on primary and secondary schooling, is required to preserve the capital stock per head by insuring that new entrants to the labour stock are as well educated as people already there. The figure for educational saving in the fifth row of the table is an estimate of the sum of direct current expenditure and earnings forgone in university education alone. The combined effect of reclassifying education, research and development as saving is to raise the rate of saving from 15% to 20%. It is difficult to quantify the dissaving equivalent of population growth, especially as the effect of population growth on future income per head depends to some extent on whether growth is through natural increase or through immigration.

Table 13.5   Alternative measure of the rate of investment in 1973

	millions of current dollars (%)	rates	
(1) gross national expenditure (GNE)	122,582	—	
(2) net national income (NNI)	109,679	—	
(3) investment in tangible capital	28,791	23.5	% of GNE
(4) saving in tangible capital	15,975	14.6	% of NNI
(5) saving in education	4732	4.3	% of NNI
(6) saving in research and development	515	0.5	% of NNI
(7) depreciation equivalent of population growth	−4605	−4.2	% of NNI
(8) depreciation equivalent of oil production	−6950	−6.3	% of NNI

Note to Table 13.5

Source: The data in this table are from *National Income and Expenditure Accounts*, Volume 1, 1926–1974, Statistics Canada, 13-531 (NIEA); *Financial Statistics of Education*, 1971–1972 to 1973–1974, Statistics Canada, 81-208 (FS), *Industrial Research and Development Expenditure in Canada*, 1973–1975, Statistics Canada, 13-203, (IR); *Fixed Capital Flows and Stocks*, 1971–1975, Statistics Canada, 13-211, (FCF): an unpublished time series of residential capital stock supplied by Statistics Canada (H); and the rough estimate of the depreciation equivalent of oil production from Chapter 6. Item (1) is the sum of gross fixed capital formation and value of physical change in inventories from the national accounts. Item (2) is national income defined here as the sum of personal consumption, government consumption (NIEA, Table 2) and saving (NIEA, Table 10). Item (3), investment in tangible capital, is the sum of gross fixed capital formation and value of physical change in inventories (NIEA, Table 2). Item (4) is saving as defined in the national accounts. Item (5) is the sum of the operating cost of universities (FS, Table 39) and imputed earnings forgone, the latter being the product of total enrolment in universities from Chapter 10 and imputed average real wage in Canada defined as labour income (NIEA, Table 2) per man employed (NIEA, Table B). Item (6) is current expenditure only (IR, Table I). Item (7) is the product of the increase in population over the year and the capital stock per head, where capital stock is mid-year net stock in current dollars, both residential and non-residential (NIEA, Table A, FCF and H). Item (8) is as estimated in Chapter 6.

Population growth through natural increase requires extra expenditure on education and a sharing out of the privately owned capital stock that is avoided when population growth is through migration, but there remains a dissaving equivalent of migration from the acquisition by migrants of a *pro rata* share of property in the public domain. Our measure of the dissaving equivalent of population growth is not based on a detailed sorting out of the different effects of population growth on income per head, but is just the product of number of extra people and the capital stock per head. The effect of this imputation to the rate of saving is to reduce the rate by 4%. The depreciation equivalent of oil production is an even more contentious concept. The figure in dollars worth in Table 13.5 is the amount of petroleum extracted valued at the shadow price of petroleum in the ground, where the shadow price is the difference between the wellhead price and the cost of extraction. It is arguable that this measure is an overestimate because the discovery of new oil reserves is not accounted for (a case, though by no means a conclusive one, for ignoring increases over the year in proven reserves is presented in Chapter 6), or that the dissaving equivalent of the using up of raw materials should be increased to account for minerals of all kinds and not just petroleum. All that I hope to convey by these rough estimates of the depreciation equivalents of population growth and mineral production is that their magnitudes, though difficult if not impossible to measure accurately, may well be large, perhaps even large enough to wipe out net saving altogether, reinforcing the proposition put forward at the beginning of this book, and again in Chapter 12, that technical change is the *sine qua non* of economic growth.

The final and summary table (Table 13.6) shows the combined effect of variations in the definition of personal consumption in the columns and variations in the relation between personal consumption and income along the rows. The former are the shift from real consumption assessed by deflation in the national accounts to real consumption assessed directly from quantity data, and the imputations for leisure and life expectancy. The latter are the change from gross national product to net income as the sum of consumption and saving, the treatment of government consumption as an intermediate product, and the reduction of the rate of saving to account for the depreciation equivalent of population growth. All rates are shown for the period 1935 to 1974 for which we have time series of real consumption based on quantity data. Rates based on definitions of real income that do not depend on the series of quantity data are also shown for the period 1926 to 1974.

The usual measure of economic growth—the rate of appreciation of real gross national product per head—appears in the top left corner. All

Table 13.6 Alternative measures of economic growth in Canada (percentage increase in real income per head per year)

definitions of income	1926–1974			1935–1974			1935–1974		
	assessed in the official national accounts	with imputation for leisure	with imputation for life expectancy	assessed in the official national accounts	with imputation for leisure	with imputation for life expectancy	assessed from quantity data	with imputation for leisure	with imputation for life expectancy
(1) real gross national expenditure	2.45	2.99	3.33	3.34	3.88	4.38	2.81	3.32	3.83
(2) real consumption plus real net saving									
(a) saving not reduced by depreciation per head	2.83	3.45	4.00	3.95	4.63	5.14	3.05	3.73	4.23
(b) saving reduced by depreciation per head	2.87	3.52	4.07	3.93	4.64	5.14	3.02	3.74	4.24
(3) real consumption plus net real saving with government consumption treated as an intermediate product									
(a) saving not reduced by depreciation per head	2.50	3.20	3.75	3.65	4.46	4.96	2.75	3.56	4.06
(b) saving reduced by depreciation per head	2.52	3.27	3.82	3.61	4.46	4.96	2.71	3.56	4.06

Sources explained in the text.

other rates in the top row are computed by replacing the measure of real personal expenditure in the national accounts with the appropriate series from Table 13.2. The growth rates in the other rows are of measures of real income of the general form

$$\frac{C+I}{P} M$$

where C is the current value of consumption, I is the current value of the rest of income (however defined), P is the price index, and M takes a value of 1 if there is no imputation for life expectancy but is different otherwise. The imputations for leisure and life expectancy are carried over directly from Table 13.2, except that the imputation for life expectancy is now applied to income as a whole. The variable M takes the value $(DLE(t)/DLE(61))^{1/\beta}$ where DLE is discounted life expectancy as defined and estimated in Chapter 11. The term C includes government consumption in rows 2(a) and 2(b) but not in rows 3(a) and 3(b). The term I is measured by the national accounts category of saving in rows 2(a) and 3(a), and is reduced by the product of the net change in population and the capital stock per head in rows 2(b) and 3(b). In the first six columns, the price index P is the national accounts deflator for consumption goods, and, in the last three columns, it is the product of that index and the index of quality change in total consumption as defined and computed in Chapter 10. All entries are annual growth rates of real income per head. Looking over the table we see that changes in the definition of consumption affect the measure of economic growth by more than changes in other components of real income. In the last row, for instance, growth rates vary by a factor of almost two, from a low of 2.52% per year to a high of 4.96%, while in the last column they vary by only 10%, from a low of 3.83% to a high of 4.24%.

The reader, considering these alternative measures of economic growth in the light of the theory developed in the course of this book, must decide for himself which concept of real income—one of these or some other—corresponds best to his sense of the meaning of economic growth and he must decide which growth rate is the most appropriate summary statistic of the progress of the economy as a whole.

Index